Bernard C. Dietrich
Tradition in Greek Religion

Bernard C. Dietrich

Tradition
in Greek Religion

Walter de Gruyter · Berlin · New York
1986

BL
782
.D53
1986

Printed on acid free paper
(ageing-resistant – pH 7, neutral)

Library of Congress Cataloging-in-Publication Data

Dietrich, Bernard C. (Bernard Clive), 1928–
Tradition in Greek religion.

Bibliography: p.
Includes index.
1. Greece--Religion.   I. Title.
BL 782.D53   1986   292'.08   86-1463
ISBN 0-89925-174-9 (U.S.)

CIP-Kurztitelaufnahme der Deutschen Bibliothek

Dietrich, Bernard C.:
Tradition in Greek religion / Bernard C. Dietrich. –
Berlin; New York: de Gruyter, 1986.
   ISBN 3-11-010695-7

© 1986 by Walter de Gruyter & Co., Berlin 30
Printed in Germany
Alle Rechte, insbesondere das der Übersetzung in fremde Sprachen, vorbehalten.
Ohne ausdrückliche Genehmigung des Verlages ist es auch nicht gestattet, dieses Buch oder Teile
daraus auf photomechanischem Wege (Photokopie, Mikrokopie) zu vervielfältigen.
Satz: Dörlemann-Satz, Lemförde · Druck: Hildebrand, Berlin
Bindearbeiten: Verlagsbuchbinderei Dieter Mikolai, Berlin

For A. C. D.

Preface

The present book in some respects complements my *Origins of Greek Religion* and will, I hope, also be received not unkindly. The central theme is still continuity but a continuity of ideas. The subject is deeply controversial and will never be fully resolved for all those who demand chapter and verse for every theory, every assumption, however reasonably based on the available evidence. Nevertheless a certain element of risk, a mild spirit of adventure, do seem necessary, if there is to be progress in the study of Greek religion. I gladly admit to using both but always within the realm of the legitimate according to the sources. A discussion of sites and particular artefacts without illustrations is rather less than ideal. I apologise for not having pictures which would have added to the time and cost of production.

A grant by the British Academy in 1983 made it possible to visit Cyprus in order to study important sanctuaries south of the Attila Line. I am most grateful for their generosity and to Dr. Diana Buitron for inviting me to stay at the grand Museum in Episkopi and join her 'dig' at Kourion. I also thank my wife for her patient support and advice and Miss M. Delargy for helping so efficiently with the technical preparation of the text and bibliography. The incredible despatch and efficiency of the de Gruyter Press are beyond praise: *utinam ita essent omnes*.

Aberystwyth September 1985

Contents

Preface VII

Introduction XI

The Religious Unity of the
    Minoans and Mycenaeans 1

Tradition in the History of
    Greek Religion 41

Divine Concepts and Forms 87

An Archaic Sanctuary of
    Apollo in Cyprus 121

    Appendix on the tholos 176

Conclusion 179

Abbreviations 184

Bibliography 187

Index 197

πατρίους παραδοχὰς, ἅς θ' ὁμήλικας χρόνῳ
κεκτήμεθ', οὐδεὶς αὐτὰ καταβαλεῖ λόγος,
οὐδ' εἰ δι' ἄκρων τὸ σοφὸν ηὕρηται φρενῶν
Eur. *Bacchae* 201–3

Introduction

Greek religion is one of the most significant aspects of the classical tradition in European thought. The family of gods provided the model for Etruscans and Romans and lived on to be turned into symbolic figures by Neoplatonist philosophers. Every Grammar School child knows the names of the Olympians, every student of Classical Civilisation is familiar with the spheres of their functions and rampant intervention in human affairs from Homer to 5th century drama. Enough temples survive in Greece and Italy, enough sculptures, originals and later copies, to remind us constantly of the splendour and beauty of the gods. The finest manifestations of classical Greek culture ultimately sprang from its religion. And yet, as we know it, it is in the main a literary religion. One scholar quite rightly complains that too often historians confuse Greek religion with myth or with the poetic image of the gods[1]. The reason lies in the nature of the source material which, apart from the archaeological remains and inscriptions, is almost exclusively literary. Despite their close connection with cultic performances or religious festivals, epic and lyric poets and dramatists are unreliable reporters of cult procedure. There is no *hieros logos* to record prescribed form of ritual or prayer. In fact there are no trustworthy accounts of contemporary ritual before Strabo, Pausanias and Plutarch. Much of our information about cults comes from minor local historians of the 4th century whom later authorities copied unless, like Apollodorus, they borrowed their information from Hesiod and other poets.

Given such inadequate sources, it is difficult if not impossible to write a comprehensive history of Greek religion. Modern scholars over the last two hundred years or so have tried to tackle the problem through different points of view in order to give the subject a sem-

---

[1] *Cf.* F. Robert, *La Religion Greque*, Paris 1981, 3. Nilsson still intended his monumental history of Greek religion to replace O. Gruppe's *Griechische Mythologie und Religionsgeschichte*, see the preface to *GGR³*.

blance of coherence. Such views generally reflected the prejudices of the times regarding the meaning and function of myth for instance or simplistic theories of evolution which were popular in the late 19th and early 20th century. Methods varied from the study of comparative myth to vegetation cult and the annual rebirth of nature deities. The latter led to comparisons with the practices of other modern 'primitive' societies. Anthropology and Sociology came into vogue over the last hundred years. Mannhardt, Usener, Dieterich in Germany, Frazer, J. Harrison amongst others in this country, were leading lights of the 'Ethnologische Schule'[2]. Subsequent studies, even the most wayward Marxist, Psychoanalyst, Structuralist theories of Greek religion, to a large extent evolved from the work of these pioneers. Nilsson was no exception. His *Griechische Feste*, which first appeared in 1906, has recently been reissued. It is a detailed study of rites and practices and consequently followed the same route as S. Wide (*Lakonische Kulte* 1893), Dieterich and Wilamowitz. The model is basically the same for Deubner and still for H. W. Parke's latest study of Greek festivals (L. Deubner, *Attische Feste*, 1932; H. W. Parke, *Festivals of the Athenians*, London 1977)[3].

The methodology is very sound of course and remains fundamental to the study of the subject. But the venturesome might want to look for a somewhat wider picture in the context of the whole society at the time, consider its origins, its traditions which explain their religious beliefs and practices. Greek religion had a long history. The impressive gods and cults of the classical *polis* began in the prehistoric past. Their origins, their continuous development are important indicators of the Greek conception of divine form and divine power in classical times. The historical view is necessary therefore. It need not dim one's feeling of admiration, even wonder and awe at the splendid manifestations of classical Greek religion. But to consider gods and ritual as 'Urphänomene' which lack rational explanation, as did W. F. Otto and K. Kerenyi, though understandable, misses a vital part which adds to the understanding of these phenomena[4]. Yet how

---

[2] For accounts of modern research see Nilsson, *GGR*[3] I, 3–13; Burkert, *Gesch.* 21–27.

[3] *E. g.* Nilsson, *GGR*[3] I, 10, 'Seitdem (Dieterich) ist keine . . . grundsätzliche Änderung der Methode und der Richtung der Forschung eingetreten'.

[4] For refs. see Burkert, *Gesch.* 26–7, who aptly speaks of Otto's 'sublime Privatreligion'.

far is an historical view of the past reliable or even possible when virtually all the extant evidence is archaeological? In any case monumental remains on their own do not reveal the beliefs of the people who built the sanctuaries. Recently someone complained that Minoan/Mycenaean religion has hitherto only been studied to establish the nature of the gods and the mechanics of cult rather than the social and political aspects of their religious ideology[5]. The 'new' archaeology is trying to fill the gap by reconstructing social systems from a kind of holistic study of human and monumental archaeological remains together with that of geography, geology, geomorphy, soils, vegetational history and the like[6]. It is a greatly expanded 'ecological', 'processual' or 'systems' archaeology which ultimately purports to become an 'archaeology of ideas' looking into the thought processes of the members of bygone societies. As a purely theoretical construct the new science has obvious weaknesses but no more so than other treatments of the subject which, in the absence of documentary evidence, are also based on theoretical methods. Archaeology becomes misleading only if its theories are mistaken for factual data, although the actual evidence often consists of fairly unrepresentative ceramic and other manufactured remains and a probable pattern of their distribution[7]. Assumptions produce inferences which lead to established dogma regarding entire social systems and their religious customs. However, the primary sources, which gave rise to the assumption in the first place, could conceivably have been misread or be altogether insignificant. For example votives, which used to be deposited in tombs in Greece, from the 8th century B.C. were dedicated in temples and shrines. The process seems to herald new attitudes of worship and could be connected with contemporary political changes[8]. But very much the same thing had occurred centuries before at the end of the prepalatial period in Crete and

---

[5] J. F. Cherry, 'The emergence of the state in the prehistoric Aegean', *Procs. Cambr. Philol. Soc.* 210, NS 30 (1984) 34.

[6] *E.g. Mycenaean Geography*, J. Bintliff (ed.), *Procs. Cambridge Colloquium Sept. 1976*, Cambridge 1977; *cf.* C. Renfrew, 'Phylakopi and Questions of Cult in the Aegean Late Bronze Age', *Minutes Mycenaean Seminar 21 March 1979*, Inst. Class. Studs. London.

[7] For an excellent review of these developments in archaeology, together with bibliography, see I. Hodder, 'Archaeology in 1984', *Antiquity* 58 (1984) 25–32.

[8] F. de Polignac, *La naissance de la cité grecque*, Paris 1984, 24–6.

probably elsewhere for practical reasons alone[9]. Others have drawn conclusions about 'polity and religion' in Crete from the introduction of fixed sanctuary areas in postpalatial Crete and Mycenaean Greece[10]. However, purpose-built 'bench' shrines had been in use within settlements in all periods[11].

If we accept, as now seems inevitable, that prehistoric religious practices survived and had an impact on archaic and classical Greek religion, then we must explore these inherited practices with all available means. All of these are theoretical when it comes to reconstructing ideas and cultural and social systems from relatively few physical remains. The archaeology of sites, structures and artefacts of course continues as the most important source of information about prehistoric societies. But it is not the only, and occasionally not even the most useful, tool because its limitations are so often overlooked. Vincent Desborough, who knew more than most about the Aegean Late Bronze Age, once criticised my unbounded faith in archaeological evidence in an earlier study of the origins of Greek religion. There is no doubt that archaeological continuity, or for that matter discontinuity, is inconclusive evidence regarding the nature of a cult that occurred in one place. More trustworthy information about the survival of old, or reemergence of neglected ideas, is provided by tradition, traditional beliefs and practices which continued into historic times from the past. What these traditions were can only be securely established from written texts of later periods, so that we are obliged to work backward in time in a reverse process. This becomes legitimate, I believe, if the conclusions are constantly controlled by comparison with the whole of the Greek world and the eastern Aegean with which Greece remained in close cultural contact throughout most of its history from the Late Stone Age.

This modest volume then is no history of Greek religion but another step in my exploration of its beginnings and development. My 'Origins' worked almost exclusively with archaeological data, 'Tradition' tries to widen the perspective in order to reinforce the picture of comparative architectural forms of sanctuaries in the Aege-

---

[9] G. C. Gesell, *The Archaeological Evidence for the Minoan House Cult and its Survival in Iron Age Crete,* thesis Chapel Hill 1972, 33.
[10] Renfrew, see n. 6.
[11] Gesell. *opcit* 3 *etc.*

an, continuing types of votives and the like. The book looks beyond the physical continuity of sanctuary to continuity of concept or the substance of a cult even in a new location. The first two chapters consider traditions from the Stone and Bronze Ages in Greece, the form in which they survived, and their significance in later Greek religion. Despite the impressive evidence of continuity from the Bronze Age into historical times, a few but important divine figures, cults and festivals of archaic and classical Greece seem to link up more closely with pre-Bronze Age Neolithic cultures. In other words, some vital religious traditions appear to have lain dormant during the brilliant urban cultures of the Middle and Late Bronze Age in the western Aegean until they reemerged in the Iron Age. From the point of view of gods and cult the Minoan and Mycenaean civilisations are more closely related to one another than to what preceded them in the Greek world, and they give the impression almost of being intrusive elements. This conclusion, although it is primarily arrived at through a study of cults, should nevertheless reopen the controversy regarding the unity or diversity of Minoan and Mycenaean civilisation in the Late Bronze Age. In any event continuity in Greek religion was more complex than a straight-forward transference of Bronze Age values into later times. The third chapter deals with the Greek concept of divinity and to what extent archaic and classical attitudes to divine power could be said to have changed from the past. In fact there is no evidence of what might be called evolution from primitive to sophisticated forms regarding the gods. So the first three chapters might be regarded as a sort of *prolegomena* to a fuller history which ultimately must be more concerned with the classical than the Bronze or Stone Age. The last chapter looks in some detail at the history of a particular cult in the island of Cyprus where tradition through the ages has been more visible than elsewhere and always meaningful. The outcrop of rock in the Telesterion at Eleusis is overlooked and scuffed by countless boots of tourists. It is no longer part of the site though once central to the mysteries in tradition. Conversely Hylates' Cave near Paphos, which had been founded over 2000 years ago as a mark of respect to ancient Bronze Age tradition, is still surrounded by an aura of numinous power.

A number of colleagues and friends have contributed to, and occasionally amended or altered, my views in this book. At least the substance of all the discussions has at one time or another been the subject of seminars or public lectures with their attendant critical debates. From all of these I have learnt much and also from private communications with scholars whose advice I have sought. All these I thank most sincerely but do not hold them to account for any errors which remain.

The Religious Unity of the Minoans and Mycenaeans

Two questions, which are important to religious historians, concern the relationship between Minoan and Mycenaean religion and their individual or joint impact on historic Greek religion. In the absence of literary evidence the actual nature of religious belief will always remain conjectural, but the substantial archaeological documentation provides a fair impression of the date, types and distribution of cults in Crete and on the mainland during the Bronze Age. Such evidence is, however, notoriously difficult to interpret: do common archaeological features indicate shared practices? Does the material evidence for continued occupation also signify enduring beliefs? Conversely, should novel fashions of divine representation be read as proving the arrival of new gods? Or does a missing link in the sequence of archaeological levels invariably mean a break in worship at a cult site which for a time may have seen nothing more than simple libations and other perishable offerings? There is obviously little merit in answering either pair of questions too positively. The doctrinaire archaeologist, who refuses to consider the possibility that not every historical event left a clearly decipherable trace, would seem to be as liable to error as the romantic historian given to unfounded hypothesis. Within these extreme limits the available evidence does offer guide lines to the interpretation of shared and individually evolved cultures particularly in the light of what is known from surviving religious institutions in historical times.

However, the question whether Minoans and Mycenaeans observed similar or quite different gods and cults throughout their history is far from settled, although after generations of debate the orthodox view appears to favour the latter, especially for the later periods of both cultures. By the time Nilsson wrote the second edition of his book on Minoan/Mycenaean religion[1], he had abandoned his earlier idea of a common religion and ultimately become convinced that Minoan and Mycenaean religious beliefs

---

[1] *Minoan/Mycenaean Religion and its Survival in Greek Religion*[2], Lund 1950, 30f.

could be shown to differ[2]. This view seems reasonable if, beginning with the early Minoan period, one compares the mass of Cretan evidence of cult sites, structures and implements with the paucity of equivalent finds on the mainland. But can the monumental remains, or their absence, offer adequate evidence, especially in the case of the mainland whose stormier history exposed it to more destructive changes?

It used to be thought for example that Minoan and Mycenaean art not only reflected national temperament but could be told apart by the differing choice of subject: the free and undisciplined forms of the one and the warlike, disciplined, heraldic, 'square' features of the latter. But all these criteria proved to be poor guides in the light of new discoveries, like the Theran frescoes, which depict scenes which were once thought to belong to the repertoire of the Mycenaean artists. In fact Minoan/Mycenaean art appears not to have been 'mutually exclusive' by any means[3]. In art as in religion it is misleading to express dogmatic views regarding what could and could not be Mycenaean traditional forms, because there is no evidence of either in, let alone prior to, Middle Helladic[4]. Therefore judgements that

---

[2] *Geschichte der griechischen Religion*[3], Munich 1967, I, 256 ff.; 329 ff.; 336. Most archaeologists agree. But the debate continues, sometimes introducing novel criteria of assessment without, however, any more definitive results, e. g. C. Renfrew, 'Questions of Minoan and Mycenaean cult', *Sanctuaries and Cults in the Aegean Bronze Age* (Procs. 1st Inter. Sympos., Swedish Inst. in Athens, 12–13 May, 1980), Stockholm 1981 *(SCABA)*, 27–33, with discussion highlighting the difficulties of the topic. See also the summary and conclusions of the general discussion, pp. 210–11 which reflect the many differing views of modern scholars.

[3] "Iconographically, can we surely distinguish what is Minoan and what is Mycenaean?", S. A. Immerwahr, "Mycenaeans at Thera", in *Studs Schach,* 178; J. Hurwitt, "The Dendra Octopus Cup", *AJA* 83 (1979) 416 n.23. See also F. L. Crowley on common designs on ships in the Theran frescoes, and on the inlaid daggers from Mycenae, *AJA* 87 (1983) 83–5. On the artistic *koine* of the Theran frescoes see the discussion of P. Betancourt, S. Immerwahr, S. Hiller on R. Laffineur, "Mycenaeans at Thera: Further Evidence?", *Thalassocracy,* 138–9. Cycladic, Theran and Minoan religion at the beginning of LBA "functioned in the same way", N. Marinatos, "Minoan Threskeiocracy on Thera", *Thalassocracy* 167.

[4] Hurwitt, op. cit. 415; O.T.P.K. Dickinson, *The Origins of Mycenaean Civilization (SIMA),* Göteborg 1977, 84.

Mycenaean art can be distinguished by its 'Ritterlichkeit'[5], or that Mycenaean religion imposed male divinities on an exclusively female Aegean pantheon in Crete and mainland Greece are highly subjective and presuppose that Mycenaean culture may have been unique or isolated and intrusive sometime during or after the Middle Bronze Age. Neither thesis is subject to proof.

Little or nothing of the mainland finds, since the earlier Shaft Grave Circle at Mycenae, shows independence in matters of religious cult or ceremony from Minoan custom. This is true at least until the final Mycenaean period when peculiarly Mycenaean types of clay figurines appear to suggest a mainland conception of an older goddess[6]. In the Late Neolithic period Crete and Greece shared a common culture[7] mainly under outside Aegean influence from east and north[8]. Subsequently, however, during the Early Bronze Age mainland contacts with Crete were sporadic and indirect[9]. Minoan influence became more noticeable in Middle Helladic at Lerna and the Laconian site of Ayios Stephanos. The connection worked both ways notably through the nearby Minoan settlement at Kastri on Kythera[10]. Minoan/Mycenaean cultural sharing began to become evident in different areas apart from Mycenae, notably in the Messenian *tholoi* which probably descended from Cretan types[11], in

---

[5] F. Schachermeyr, *Die Ägäische Frühzeit*, vol. 2, *(Die Mykenische Zeit und die Gesittung von Thera)*, Vienna 1976, 307 *cf. Griechische Frühgeschichte,* Vienna 1984, 73.

[6] For a succinct chronological survey of Mycenaean *vis à vis* Minoan cult features see J. T. Hooker, *Mycenaean Greece*, London 1976, 190–212. The author unambiguously expresses his view that Mycenaean religion could be defined and described separately from that of Minoan Crete, p. 191.

[7] *E. g.* S. Weinberg, "The Stone Age in the Aegean", *CAH³*, Cambridge 1970, 618.

[8] F. Schachermeyr, *Die Ägäische Frühzeit*, vol. 1 *(die vormykenischen Perioden des griechischen Festlandes und der Kykladen)*, Vienna 1976, 174 ff.; 290.

[9] J. B. Rutter & C. W. Zerner, "Early Helladic-Minoan Contacts", *Thalassocracy* 75–82 with modern literature.

[10] *Op. cit.* 77; J. N. Coldstream & G. L. Huxley, "The Minoans of Kythera", *Thalassocracy* 107–8.

[11] M. S. F. Hood, "Tholos tombs of the Aegean", *Antiquity* 34 (1960) 166, 76; I. Pini, *Beiträge zur Minoischen Gräberkunde*, Wiesbaden 1968, 49; K. Branigan, *The Tombs of Mesara*, London 1970, 152–8. Hooker, *Mycen. Greece*, 36; J. B. Rutter, "Stone Vases and Minoan Ware: A Facet of Minoan Influence on Middle Laconia", *AJA* 83 (1979) 464–9. K. Branigan, J. Sakellarakis, S. Hood in the discussion of O. T. P. K. Dickinson, "Cretan Contacts with the Mainland during the Period of the

special vase forms in Southern Laconia as at Ayios Stephanos[12], and most significantly in the Mycenaean Shaft Graves.

The wealth of the graves, after a prolonged period of seeming poverty on the mainland, has been interpreted by some as due to the arrival of new princes from outside[13]. But the archaeological evidence does not bear out this view[14], and the occupants of both Grave Circles at Mycenae would appear to be native mainlanders[15]. The question what religious traditions they were heir to is important to the history of Greek religion[16], because it is likely to throw light on the nature and form of what historians call the Mycenaean empire or world. For the moment it is enough to recognize that the Shaft Graves were a feature of continuing culture with its origins in the distant past.

Apart from a few isolated instances, like the altar and remains of burnt offerings on an island off the Messenian coast at Methone[17], the finds from both Circles constitute our earliest identifiable reference to Mycenaean religious concepts and cult. These are predominantly Minoan in character containing some of the best known Minoan religious elements like the *rhyta*, double axe, horns of consecration, cultic knots, five examples in gold of the tripartite shrine (Graves III & IV), altar, and two examples of a Dove Goddess (Grave III). These

---

Shaft Graves, *Thalassocracy*, 118. For the view that many *tholoi* were an independent development see O. Pelon, "Sur deux tholoi de Messenie", *BCH* 98 (1974) 37–50. Dickinson, *The Origins of Mycenaean Civilization*, 61; 91; G. S. Korres, "The Relations between Crete and Messenia", *Thalassocracy* 148–9.

[12] Rutter, *ibid.*.

[13] Sp. Marinatos-M. Hirmer, *Kreta, Thera und das Mykenische Hellas³*, Munich 1976, 70; 79; 82. *Cf.* the discussion of foreign origins in Hooker, *Mycen. Gr.* 45 ff.

[14] E. g. Schachermeyr, *Ägäische Frühzeit*, vol. 1, 243; most recently R. A. van Royen – B. H. Isaac, *The Arrival of the Greeks, The Evidence of The Settlements*, Amsterdam 1979, 46 f.

[15] Hooker, *Myc. Gr.* 54; Dickinson, *Orig. Mycen. Civ.* 107 ff.; "Mycenaean Geography: an archaeological viewpoint" in *Mycenaean Geography* (ed. J. Bintliff) *(Proc. Cambr. Colloqu., Sept. 1976)*, Cambridge 1977, 19. The grave type and burial customs of the Shaft Graves have been described as un-Minoan, R. Hägg, "Degrees and Character of the Minoan Influence on the Mainland", *Thalassocracy* 120.

[16] Schachermeyr, for example, in *Äg. Frühz.*, vol. 1, 243, considers the possibility that the kings in Grave Circle B were foreign warlords who brought the chariot with them and became Graecised after conquering the Mycenaean world.

[17] A. K. Choremis, "MHaltar on Nissakouli" (in Greek), *AAA* 2 (1969) 10–14.

objects belonged to cult although they were not found on a demonstrable cult site but had been buried with the dead with secular items of use and adornment. No contemporary shrines of any sort have yet been found. Again no argument, which hopes to separate mainland from Cretan styles in techniques and subject matter of painting and seal or ring engraving, can be convincing because so relatively little survives. There is no point in producing artificial 'internal' criteria or subjective judgments of 'free', 'dynamic' Cretan art *versus* the 'ponderous', heraldic mainland style[18]. Though possibly valid from the purely artistic view, such distinctions carry no information regarding differences in religious beliefs or practices[19].

Seal stones were few and far between on the mainland during EBA and virtually absent in MBA[20]. Their number increased dramatically at the beginning of the Mycenaean period. Many examples have been found of Cretan imports, locally cut stones, Minoizing products and the like. However, in technique and style they are extremely similar, if not identical[21]. The same applies to the theme of individual scenes[22]. Seal stones from the Shaft Graves, and the *stelae* generally, show scenes of hunting and fighting[23]. Recognizable cult scenes appear somewhat later on gold rings from graves on the Mycenaean acropolis and elsewhere in Greece. Perhaps the best known is the Great Goddess ring found south of Circle A on the Mycenaean acropolis and slightly later than the Shaft Grave period[24]. However, like the

---

[18] H. Biesantz, *Kretisch-mykenische Siegelbilder*, Marburg 1954, ch. III; V.E.G. Kenna, *Cretan Seals*, Oxford 1960, 79–81; A Sakellariou, *Mycenaean Glyptic* (in Greek), Athens 1966, 91 ff.; "A propos de la chronologie des gemmes myceniennes", *Die Kretisch-mykenische Glyptik und ihre gegenwärtige Probleme*, Boppard 1974; *cf.* E. Vermeule, *Götterkult (Archaeologia Homerica)*, Göttingen 1974, 28 f.; Hooker, *Myc. Gr.* 44 f.

[19] Vermeule, *Götterk..* 29, concludes that the artefacts of Minoan cult in the Shaft Graves had lost their religious meaning and served for decorative purposes only. *Cf.* Hooker, *Myc. Gr.* 194.

[20] I. Pini, "Minoische Siegel ausserhalb Kretas", *Thalassocracy* 123–4.

[21] For discussion with modern literature, see R. Hägg. "On the nature of the Minoan influence in early Mycenaean Messenia", *OpAth* 14 (1982) 27 n. 23–7.

[22] There is a distinction in themes according to E. Vermeule, *The Art of the Shaft Graves* (Lectures in memory of Louise Taft Semple, Third Series), Cincinnati 1975, 47. But see Pini, *Thalassocracy 128 and n. 39* for examples.

[23] E. g. Graves III & IV, Marinatos-Hirmer, *Kreta* No. 230.

[24] Marinatos-Hirmer, *op. cit.* 229.

famous large ring from Tiryns[25], it had been taken from an earlier
grave and then reburied before the end of the Mycenaean age[26]. Its
religious 'vocabulary' is Minoan and cannot be convincingly
distinguished from scenes on contemporary rings which were found
in various Cretan graves in Isopata and Phaistos[27]. The same is true of
numerous other examples from Mycenae, Tiryns, Pylos and so on[28].
Dress, figures, implements, altars, shrines are all Minoan regardless
of the import of each particular scene depicted[29]. Accordingly the
finds from the Shaft and subsequent Mycenaean graves suggest to the
unbiased observer the familiarity, not to say community, of concept
of divinity as well as cult in Greece and Crete at the end of the Middle
and beginning of the Late Bronze Age. There are furthermore no *a
priori* grounds for supposing either that the Mycenaeans considered
objects with Minoan imagery as devoid of religious significance or
that they worshipped other forms of gods which vanished without a
trace.

The contents of the Shaft Graves are varied and show that the
Mycenaeans were in contact with other cultures like that of Egypt,
although its influence is not too easy to define[30]. A point of great
interest is that the finds from Grave Circle A and the earlier Circle B
reveal a link with Cycladic forms on Thera, Melos, Keos and
Kythera[31]. On Thera for example the figures on a recently discovered
miniature fresco[32] recall those on the so-called Siege Rhyton from

---

[25] Marinatos-Hirmer, *op. cit.* 229.

[26] Marinatos-Hirmer, *op. cit.* 178.

[27] Marinatos-Hirmer, *op. cit.* 115.

[28] Marinatos-Hirmer, *op. cit.* 228 (Mycenae Treasure); 229 (Top: Tiryns); 232,
sealstone from *tholos* in Pylos showing Minoan altar, horns with two boughs in
centre and female worshipper.

[29] Marinatos' suggestions, *ad. loc.*, are imaginative rather than verifiable. Nor would
it be possible to read mainland features of cult into the Greek scenes, Hooker, *Myc.
Gr.* 197 f.

[30] See *e. g.* the discussion in Hooker, *Myc. Gr.* 50 ff.

[31] Hooker, *Myc. Gr.* 47; on Minoan/Mycenaean/Cycladic mutual influence during
the Shaft Grave Period see S. Immerwahr, "Mycenaeans at Thera", 186; 190.

[32] Room 5, West House, Akrotiri, Sp. Iakovides, "Thera and Mycenaean Greece",
AJA 83 (1979) 101 f. The significance of the Theran frescoes, particularly in the
West House, has been much discussed and most recently by G. Säflund, "Cretan
and Theran questions", *SCABA* 195–208, and N. Marinatos, "The West House at
Akrotiri as a Cult Center", *AM* 98 (1983) 1–19. Other relevant literature is cited in
the latter study on p. 2 n. 2.

Grave IV. The warriors depicted on both are Mycenaeans who accordingly must have made their presence felt in the Aegean at least as early as the fifteenth century B. C. Minoan art, however, provided the common denominator for styles and form on Thera, Keos, Kythera, at Phylakopi on Melos and no doubt on other Cycladic islands, as well as on the mainland of course, a point which hints at partnership rather than absolute Mycenaean and Cycladic dependence on Crete[33].

It is not unreasonable to suppose the same community to have obtained in religion. Once more some of the Cycladic and other Aegean islands turn out to be the most useful guides in this context of Minoan and Mycenaean interdependence. The famous temple at Ayia Irini on Keos for example saw Helladic before Minoan cult which was not felt to be alien to Cycladic beliefs because both had links with, or indeed were based on, a tradition which began in the Middle Bronze Age if not earlier[34]. Local differences notwithstanding, the inference seems to be that in matters of religious belief Minoan, Helladic and Cycladic cults shared part or whole of the same tradition, which would mean that the Minoan religious figures and scenes on artefacts from mainland graves of the Middle Bronze Age were far from being alien intruders in Mycenaean cult. The Mycenaean culture or presence, which suddenly manifested itself in Greece at the beginning of the Late Bronze Age, did not practise its own peculiar brand of religion distinct from that in contemporary Crete. Both, so to speak, were part of one unit. It is worth remembering on the one hand that not a few of those features, which are often cited as typically Minoan, had been introduced from other mainly eastern regions of the Aegean, and on the other that some of these very features reappeared as characteristically Mycenaean in the temples which the settlers from the mainland built or took over in their new eastern homes in the fourteenth and thirteenth centuries B. C.

---

[33] *Cf.* n. 3 and 31 above. On Minoan/Mycenaean elements in Shaft Grave art see E. Vermeule, "The Art of the Shaft Graves at Mycenae". On Phylakopi, see also R.L.N. Barber, "The Status of Phylakopi in Creto-Cycladic Relations", *Thalassocracy* 179–82.

[34] See J. C. van Leuven, "Aspects of Mycenaean Religion" *(Mycenaean Seminar)* 15 th Jan. 1975, Inst. Class Studs., London, 10. J. L. Davis, "Cultural Transaction and the Minoan Thalassocracy at Ayia Irini", *Thalassocracy* 164–5 and discussion on 166.

Thus beside the obviously oriental hybrid demons and creatures like sphinx and griffin, the Minoans borrowed and passed on to Greece an eastern goddess type. The two miniature figures in gold leaf of a nude goddess, with birds on her head and in one case on her arms, which Schliemann found in Grave III[35], are commonly identified as the "Dove Goddess" and an early form of Aphrodite. Although the context of the find may suggest that these particular examples served primarily decorative purposes[36], the type was clearly that of a Minoan goddess who was frequently represented in Cretan art from MMIII in Knossos to Subminoan at Karphi[37]. Yet the Mycenaeans did not really take over this goddess from the Minoans, as has been supposed[38], but shared in the worship of a figure with distinct eastern ancestry. This eastern Aphrodite was generally shown in the nude unlike other Minoan divinities[39] in a convention which was so strictly observed that until the end of the Geometric period in Cyprus, when the two types were eventually fused, the draped Cretan goddess remained clearly distinct from the nude eastern figure[40].

Again the type of sitting goddess was popular in both Cretan and Mycenaean cult. She appears on rings from Knossos, Phaistos, Thebes, Mycenae, Tiryns[41]. The scene on the great ring from Mycenae showing the goddess, sitting under a tree and attended by worshippers[42] vividly portrays shared religious concepts which may ultimately have begun with the figure of the sitting goddess in Neolithic Anatolia[43]. Cultic tree, pillar, baetyl and aniconic divine representations in general, the Mycenaeans and Minoans had also borrowed from the east where they continued in use contemporaneously with the west at the end of the Middle, and in the Late, Bronze

---

[35] H. Schliemann, *Mycenae*, new ed. Darmstadt 1963, figs. 267/8.
[36] M. P. Nilsson, *MMR²*, 397; Vermeule, *Götterkult*, 28.
[37] Vermeule, *ibid.*
[38] Vermeule, *op. cit.* 58f.
[39] Nilsson, *MMR²*, 397; *Gesch.³* I, 291; 350f.; W. Burkert, *Griechische Religion der archaischen und klassischen Epoche*, Stuttgart 1977, 81.
[40] V. Karageorghis, "The goddess with uplifted arms in Cyprus", *Scripta Minora 1977–78, in hon. E. Gjerstad (Kungl. Hum. Vetenskaps Lund)*, Lund 1977, 24f.
[41] Vermeule, *Götterkult* 16ff.; 59.
[42] Note 24 above.
[43] B. C. Dietrich, *The Origins of Greek Religion*, Berlin 1974, 102f.

Age from Mikal's pillar or *stele* at Beth Shan[44] to Troy VI[45] and Kition in Cyprus where Phoenician settlers reused Mycenaean temples[46]. Thus much of the religion in the western Aegean had common links with the Near East, as at Byblos[47], and in its earlies stages with Çatal Hüyük and elsewhere in Anatolia[48].

It is certainly quite possible that the Minoans transmitted ideas to their neighbours on the mainland and other Aegean islands, ranging from the more superficial, like the custom of divine processions[49], to fundamental concepts including a theocratic community centred on the palace[50]. But these ideas had not infrequently been foreshadowed elsewhere[51], that is to say they had not been conceived by the Minoans but were equally at home in the Mycenaean world once they had travelled to the west. In other words, some Minoan/Mycenaean religious practices were not only derived but indistinguishably shared among the two cultures at the beginning and end of the Late Bronze Age.

Nowhere in the Aegean was this integration of religious institutions more visibly complete than in Cyprus at the end of the Bronze Age.

---

[44] Dedicated by Thuthmosis III, L. H. Vincent, *Rev. Bibl.* 37 (1928) 524–8; A. Rowe, *The Topography and History of Beth Shan*, Philadelphia 1930, 14 f.; W. A. Ward, "The Egyptian Inscriptions of Level VI", in E. W. James, *The Iron Age at Beth Shan*, Philadelphia Univ. Mus. 1966, 171; D. Conrad, "Der Gott Reschef", *Ztsschrft. f. d. altestam.-Wiss.* 83 (1971) 164.

[45] "Late Bronze Age Troy: Religious Contacts with the West", *Historia* 29 (1980) 498–503.

[46] Achaean Temples I & IV, BCH 93 (1969) 520–7; 94 (1970) 251–8; 95 (1971) 377 ff.; 388; 96 (1972) 1064.

[47] See the discussion of the paper by F. G. Mayer, "The Paphian Shrine of Aphrodite and Crete", in *Cyprus and Crete* 317.

[48] Dietrich, *Origins* 106; 111.

[49] Vermeule, *Götterk.* 58.

[50] Dietrich, *Origins* 24; 25; 35; 40 etc. For the chronology of Mycenaean dependence on Minoan palace forms – in the second Palace Period – and bureaucracy, see P. Warren, "The Emergence of Mycenaean Palace Civilization" (*Mycen. Geography*, 1977) 68–75. The Mycenaean "take-over" of the palace at Knossos has most recently been described by E. Hallager, *The Mycenaean Palace at Knossos*, Stockholm 1977, cf. the review in *Ét. Class.* 47 (1979) 386. In his most recent book Schachermeyr describes Mycenaean culture as 'eine Art von satellitenhaftem Ableger der minoischen Entwicklung', *Griech. Frühgesch.*, 1984, 74.

[51] Compare the procession of the goddess Shauskaya in the Yazilikaya rock-relief, K. Bittel, "The Great Temple of Hattusha – Bogazköy", *AJA* 80 (1976) 67 f.

The impact of western concepts on native Cypriot and eastern religion produced a curious amalgam which persisted on the island until well into historic times. But the Minoan/Mycenaean contribution to this mixture was homogeneous: in fact some features, which are generally described as Minoan, came to be introduced to Cyprus not from Crete but from the Greek mainland and by Mycenaean settlers in the midst of the quite abundant Cypriot archaeological evidence two or three important characteristics will illustrate this community of cult. Three of the apparently most distinctly Minoan features that come to mind are the so-called tripartite shrine, the horns of consecration, and the figure of the goddess. The latter was portrayed in innumerable figurines, from the Middle Minoan Snake Goddess to her image in Late Minoan times, with upraised arms.

Tripartite shrines are well known ever since the discovery of the five small golden plaques in the Shaft Graves III and IV at Mycenae[52]. The horns of consecration, pillars, and the doves on the two flanking "niches" of the shrine are manifestly Minoan. In fact the subsequent find of the "Grandstand Fresco" at Knossos[53] and certain architectural features at the western end of the Central Court of the Palace of Knossos[54] suggested that this particular façade was the common form of Middle Minoan palace shrines. Since then discoveries of the foundations of a tripartite shrine at the villa at Vathypetro (LM I, c.1600 B.C.)[55], and of others depicted on rings (Arkhanes)[56] and vases, like the *rhyton* fragment from Knossos (Gypsades)[57], and the restored *rhyton* from Kato Zakro[58], show that this type of sanctuary was in vogue elsewhere in Crete. It was found in peak and open air

---

[52] Schliemann, *Mykenae*, 307f. and fig. 423.

[53] A. Evans, *The Palace of Minos at Knossos*, London 1925–36, II, fig. 371.

[54] Evans, *P.M.* II, fig. 526.

[55] F. Matz, *Crete and Early Greece*, London 1962, 111; M. S. F. Hood, *The Minoans*, London 1971, 136; Marinatos-Hirmer, *Kreta* 41; 135f., Pl. XXII. For a different view see B. Rutkowski, *Cult Places in the Aegean World*, Warsaw 1972, 53f.

[56] G. A. Christopoulos – J. C. Bastias (eds.), *Prehistory and Protohistory*, Athens 1974, 214.

[57] Rutkowski, *Cult Places*, fig. 61.

[58] Rutkowski, *Cult Places* 163ff. fig. 58–60.

cult areas, as well as in "private" houses (during Middle and Late Minoan times)[59].

This kind of cult façade did reappear later in some Mycenaean frescoes and as purely decorative motive on secular buildings. But there is no real evidence of similar shrines having been in cultic use on the mainland, so that the Shaft Grave plaques, which were cut in the same tripartite shape, could have been devoid of religious significance for their Mycenaean owners[60]. That this was not so, appears from more recent finds. The Mycenaean settlers in Cyprus in fact used this form for their new temples at the end of the Bronze Age[61]. It is also significant that the tripartite design was no Minoan invention but derived from eastern models[62], which might have been as early as Sumerian culture[63], or possibly originated in Egypt[64].

Schliemann had already pointed to the similarity of the tripartite sanctuaries from the Shaft Graves to the temple of Paphian Aphrodite on coins[65]. These are late, of course, and no physical remains of any tripartite structure actually survived in the area of the Bronze Age Sanctuary I at Paphos[66]. But the coins unmistakably preserved a tradition from the past[67] which endured more clearly in the Mycenaean temples in Cyprus of the same period notably at Kition and Enkomi[68].

Like the mixture of styles in the statuette of the Horned God,

---

[59] The form and significance of tripartite shrines are discussed by Rutkowski, *Cult Places* 166 f. and n. 26 (with reference to other modern views), and most recently by J. W. Shaw, "Evidence for the Minoan Tripartite Shrine", *AJA* 82 (1978) 329–448.

[60] Vermeule, *Götterk.* 28; 29; 58; Hooker, *Myc. Gr.* 194.

[61] H. W. Catling, "Cyprus in the Neolithic and Bronze Age Periods", *CAH²*, Cambridge 1966, 69; V. Karageorghis, *The Ancient Civilization of Cyprus*, London 1969, 141; *BCH* 95 (1971) 379 ff.

[62] E. g. Kamil-ek-Lodz in Syrian Bega, F. G. Maier, *Acts* (Nicosia 1979); 233; see álso the discussion (V. Karageorghis) on p. 317.

[63] Burkert, *Griech. Rel.* 65 and n. 70.

[64] A. Altherr-Charon, "Origine des temples à trois cellae du bassin méditerranéen est: état de la question", *Ant. Class.* (Belg.) 46 (1977) 387–440.

[65] Schliemann, *Mykenae* 308.

[66] Maier, *Acts* (Nicosia 1979) 233.

[67] Maier, *op. cit.* 234, suggests that the tripartite *cella* structure at Paphos may have been temporary.

[68] Karageorghis, *Anc. Civ. Cyprus*, 136–144; 144–149; *BCH* 95 (1971) 379 ff.; 98 (1975) 871 ff.; 100 (1976) 884; *AR* 1975/76, 41–43.

which the Mycenaean settlers deposited in the central *cella* of the tripartite sanctuary in Enkomi sometime in the twelfth century B.C.[69], the distinctive architecture was an amalgam of eastern and western styles in which, however, the Minoan/Mycenaean part again appears to have provided one indistinguishable element. The Minoans had engaged in trade with Cyprus perhaps from as early as Middle Bronze Age times[70], but certainly at the end of the age. Yet there is no evidence of any kind of extensive Minoan settlement on Cyprus at the time[71], while the Mycenaeans arrived in considerable force in the thirteenth and twelfth centuries B.C.[72], bringing with them what must be regarded as their own style of religious architecture[73]. Thus the tripartite form of sanctuary at the end of the Bronze Age equally expressed Minoan and Mycenaean religious feeling. What particular cultic significance underlay such an arrangement of three *cellae* in Crete and Greece is another matter. The very recent discovery at Arkhanes of a free-standing tripartite "temple" of the late Middle Minoan period may yet throw light on this question[74]. This find if correctly interpreted, together with the Cypriot evidence, certainly contradicts the commonly held belief that the sets of three niches with horns and pillars were outward looking façades, and cult ceremonial occurred in front of these and not within[75]. Nor is the triple form of the sanctuary a guarantee that the cult involved multiple aspects of a deity[76]. All that can be said with any degree of assurance is

---

[69] On the date of the temple and on the Horned God, see Karageorghis *op. cit.* 142; Schachermeyr, *AAlt* 25 (1972) 156; P. Dikaios, "The Bronze Statue of a Horned God from Enkomi", *AA* (1962) 29f.; C.F.A. Schaeffer, *AfO* 21 (1965) 68.

[70] E.g. G. Cadogan, *Cyprus and Crete* 63–68.

[71] V. Karageorghis, "Some Reflections on the Relations between Cyprus and Crete during the Late Minoan IIIB Period" in *Acts* (Nicosia 1979) 199–203. Minoans and Mycenaeans probably co-existed on other island sites in the Eastern Aegean during the last stages of the Bronze Age, as at Trianda on Rhodes and on Kos, *cf.* C.B. Mee, "The First Mycenaeans in the Eastern Aegean", Summary of paper read before the Mycenaean Seminar at the London Institute of Class. Studs., 19th March 1980.

[72] Karageorghis, *Anc. Civ. Cyprus* 141.

[73] Catling, "Cyprus in the Neolithic and Bronze Age Periods", 69.

[74] Discovered by G. Sakellarakis and announced in "Macedonie" 17/8/79; "Pantheon" 1980, 58ff.; *The Times* 15/2/1980. See now *BCH* 104 (1980) 673. The excavation of the sactuary is still incomplete.

[75] Rutkowski, *Cult Places* 167; 307; Shaw, *AJA* 82 (1978) 448. *Cf.* above n.61.

[76] See *e.g.* Altherr-Charon, *Ant Class* (Belg.) 46 (1977) 389–440.

that in Cyprus these temples were the home of an Astarte/Aphrodite figure in historic times; and this agrees with the tradition that the Arcadian king Agapenor on his return from Troy founded the Paphian shrine of Aphrodite[77]. But while the tripartite temple survived and indeed became almost universal in the religious architecture of conservative Cyprus in the beginning of the Iron Age[78], the form disappeared in the west.

Open-air altars were common on Minoan and Mycenaean cult sites[79]. But size and shape differed on the mainland and in Crete suggesting different cult practices[80]. Cretan altars, particularly from peak sites like Jouktas, had horns of consecration, while Mycenaean types were comparatively rare and unusual as at Tiryns and Mycenae[81]. Also the grouping of temple and altars within a *temenos* at Mycenae has been described as un-Minoan[82]: the arrangement seems more closely related to the later Greek "Normal-Heiligtum" consisting of altar, temple and cult image[83]. One wonders, however, how real such distinctions were in terms of cult practice, since the implements of cult were the same[84]. Still more significant is that the Mycenaean settlers in Cyprus erected horns of consecration in their sacred precincts, near or actually on their altars in Kition, Myrtou Pigadhes and in Aphrodite's temple at Paphos[85]. These horns were relatively rare in Greece and not clearly associated with religious contexts[86], so that the Cypriot evidence proves extremely valuable for a comparison of Minoan and Mycenaean religious forms. It is possible of course to attribute the Cyprus horns of consecration to a

---

[77] *Il.* 2, 609ff.; Hyg., *Fab.* 97; Apoll., *Bibl.* III,10,8; 7.6f.; *Ep.* VI, 15 (ed. Frazer, p.259); III, 11; Paus. 8,5,2 etc., *cf. BCH* 98 (1974) 871ff.

[78] J. Karageorghis, *La Grande Déesse de Chypre et son Culte*, Lyon 1977, 171.

[79] On Min./Mycen. altars see Nilsson, *MMR²* 117ff.0, C.G. Yavis, *Greek Altars. Origins and Typology. Including the Minoan/Mycenaean Offertory Apparatus*, St. Louis Univ. Studs. 1949, *passim*; Vermeule, *Götterkult* 12 and n.7 with further modern literature; 38f.

[80] Vermeule, *Götterk.* 12; 38; 59.

[81] Vermeule, *Götterk.* 38f., "portable" and the like.

[82] Rutkowski, "Religious Architecture in Cyprus and Crete in the Late Bronze Age", *Acts* (Nicosia 1979) 224. See ch. IV, 14–16.

[83] Burkert, *Gr. Rel.* 94.

[84] *MMR²* 123.

[85] V. Karageorghis, *Acts* (Nicosia 1979) 199f.

[86] Vermeule, *Götterkult* 59.

few Minoan settlers[87], but the several and successive altars at Kition of different shapes and sizes, as well as the altar at Myrtou Pighades were linked with contemporary Mycenaean models[88].

One other feature of considerable importance emerging from the Cypriot remains concerns the practice of making burnt offerings on or near some of the altars. Before the remarkable finds at Mycenae within the last fifteen years there was virtually no evidence of "Brandopfer" in Greece and Crete in the Bronze Age. Now in various areas about the five different temples at Kition, which extended in use over some two to three hundred years, such burnt sacrifice was a common ceremonial feature. The practice seems strikingly un-Mycenaean and more at home in historical Greece[89]. It may be that the custom had originally been a Semitic import which first impinged on Greek culture in the religious melting pot of Cyprus[90]. However, the round altar in Temple II at Kition with its remains of ash and burnt animal bones was contemporary with (IIIB, 13th cent.) and modelled on, the large round altar in the processional way on the west slope of the Mycenaean acropolis south of the so-called House of Tsountas[91]. The Mycenaeans evidently sacrificed and burnt animals in Cyprus and in Greece and no doubt in Minoan Crete as well, at sites like Kato Symi Viannou where Minoan/Mycenaean cult continued into historical times. An altar of stone stood on the latter site in the open and on the compacted ashes of burnt sacrificial animal offerings and libations ever since protopalatial times[92]. The habit of making "Brandopfer" to the gods the Minoans and Mycenaeans incidentally shared with the earlier pre-

---

[87] Cf. n. 85 above.

[88] BCH 95 (1971) 384; 386; 388; 97 (1973) 651; 653; 660; 98 (1974) 867; 99 (1975) 831; AJA 77 (1973) 53; 1975/76, 41–43; G. Mylonas, "Contribution to the Religion of the Achaeans", East Meol 101–104.

[89] Burkert, Gr. Rel. 71.

[90] Burkert, Gr. Rel. 95; cf. "Opfertypen und antike Gesellschaftsstruktur", in Der Religionswandel unserer Zeit im Spiegel der Religionswissenschaft, Wissensch. Buchgesellschaft. Darmstadt 1976, 178 ff.

[91] BCH 97 (1973) 651; Arch. Rep. 1975/76, 41 f.; Mylonas, East Meol 101 ff.; cf. Temple V., BCH 100 (1976) 877.

[92] On the peak cult at Kato Symi Viannou on the western slopes of the Lasithi mountains in Crete see below and D. Levi, "Caratteri e Continuità del Culto sulle Vette Montane", PdP 181 (1978) 302.

Bronze Age world on the Greek mainland no less than with the historical Greeks.

The arrival of settlers in Cyprus at the end of the Bronze Age introduced to the island a novel western fashion of depicting the Great Goddess with arms lifted up above her head. The new was superimposed on earlier Cypriot forms[93] and became common in sanctuaries at Enkomi, Kition, Paphos and other settlement sites[94]. The consensus of opinion seems to be that the type was a Cretan import, even though, as was seen above, the bulk of the immigrants came from the mainland of Greece[95]. The many examples had distinctively Minoan facial and other features[96]. The gesture of upraised arms, however, more closely suggests the typical somewhat earlier Mycenaean "Psi" type goddess figurine[97]. The earliest known goddess figurine with upraised arms was recently found in Limassol. Its date is the eleventh century B.C. and therefore later than comparable examples from Tiryns[98]. Accordingly, whatever its original home may have been, Minoan/Mycenaean traditions were inextricably mixed. So it is not surprising that the mainland shrine at Tiryns, where the oldest examples of these idols were found, is the earliest known instance of a free standing sanctuary outside Crete[99].

The goddess was essentially the same in Crete, Greece and in Cyprus, where the migrants identified her with the Aprodite/Astarte figure as at ancient Paphos[100]. She was a nature goddess concerned with fertility and vegetation, but more particularly she was revered as a community figure who protected each settlement separately. For this reason she could be associated with the products of the com-

---

[93] V. Karageorghis, *Scripta Minora*, London 1977, 13.

[94] V. Karageorghis, *Scripta Minora* 7 ff.; J. Karageorghis, *La Grande Déesse*, 123 f.; K. Nicolaou, "Ninoan Survivals in Geometric and Archaic Cyprus", *Acts* (Nicosia 1979), 249–56.

[95] J. Karageorghis, *La Gr. D.* 127; Maier, *Acts* (Nicosia 1979) 233: from Aegean and Crete.

[96] M. Yon, "Chypre et la Crete au XI S." *Acts* (Nicosia 1979) 246.

[97] T. Dothan, in the discussion of Nicolaou's paper, *Acts* (Nicosia 1979) 318. But see J. Karageorghis, *La Gr. D.* 127.

[98] LH IIIC V. Karageorghis, *Scripta Min.* 28 f., and see the discussion of Nicolaou's paper in *Acts* (Nicosia 1979) 318; *BCH* 102 (1978) 666; 103 (1979) 559; *AR* 1977/78, 26 f.; 1978/79, 16.

[99] *AR* 1977/78, 27; *BCH* 102 (1978) 668.

[100] J. Karageorghis, *La Gr. D.* 225.

munity like copper at Kition and elsewhere in Cyprus[101] and generally she was known under her special or localised community title. At Paphos for example the old Mycenaean title of "Queen", *Wanassa*[102] became Paphia and, probably under Phoenician influence, finally Aphrodite/Astarte[103]. At Amathus the goddess was addressed as "The Cypriot", or "The Golgian" at Golgoi, and so on[104]. To the Minoans and Mycenaeans, who brought their goddess with them in the twelfth and eleventh centuries B.C., she appeared with upraised arms. In archaeological terms the sudden appearance of the style is brilliant evidence of the timing of the Mycenaean arrival in Cyprus and their religious conformity with Crete. The figurine was deposited in the new sanctuaries breaking with the former Cypriot practice of placing idols of the goddess in the tombs[105]. The people of Cyprus conservatively continued the style and fashion of portraying their goddess in this way at least until archaic times, that is for half a millennium unlike Crete and Greece where the form became rare after the Geometric period[106]. The actual religious significance of the gesture is quite another question which should not, however, materially affect the continuity of the divine figure or her nature that was in essence shared by other communities. Hence the easy syncretism in Cyprus of the Greek *Wanassa* with the Cypriot nature goddess and the eastern Astarte[107]. The gesture of raising both arms beside the head was not infrequently represented in prehistoric art[108]. In Crete and Greece the fashion was temporary at the end of the Bronze Age and merely one mode of showing the goddess[109].

---

[101] *RM* 121 (1978) 15f. and further references.

[102] *RM* (1978) 6.

[103] O. Masson, "Remarques sur les Cultes Chypriotes à l'Epoque du Bronze Recent", *East Meol* 116; *cf. Les Inscript. Chypriotes Syllabiques*, 1961, 103f.; 112–115; 206 n.1; 245; 259–62 *etc.*

[104] See the previous note.

[105] J. Karageorghis, *La Gr. D.* 123f.; V. Karageorghis, *Scripta Minora* 7ff.

[106] J. Karageorghis, *La Gr. D.* 135ff.; V. Karageorghis, *Scr. Min.* 24.

[107] *Cf.* V. Karageorghis, *Scr. Min.* 5.

[108] There are many examples. They are mainly of adorants, however, and not of divinities, J. Matinger, "Adorants in Prehistoric Art", *Numen* (1979) 215–230.

[109] S. Alexiou, *The Minoan Goddess with Upraised Hands* (in Greek), Herakleion 1958; R.V. Nicholls, in *ACE* 4ff. See now also M.S.F. Hood, *The Arts in Prehistoric Greece* (Pelican Hist. of Art), 1978, 108f. The idols often habe holes

No doubt Minoans and Mycenaeans lived side by side in Cyprus, as in other parts of the eastern Aegean like Kos and Rhodes, at Trianda[110] but the former appear to have been in the minority, so that religious practices, including the sanctuaries and sacred precincts, were those of the Mycenaean settlements. On the other hand, as the Mycenaeans evidently brought with them customs of divine representation and worship, which were indistinguishable from those obtaining in Crete, their religion at the time may be said to have reflected Minoan belief. There is little doubt that by the Late Bronze Age both cultures with their palace systems and theocratic societies shared common divine concepts and worship[111]. A few aspects of this common religion began before the Bronze Age, notably some divine names, cult sites and cult practices including methods of making offerings. At the other end of the period, as is now generally accepted, significant features of Minoan/Mycenaean religion survived into historical times. The overall impression, however, is that Minoan/Mycenaean cult in the main presented a picture of a unified self-contained phase in the history of "Greek" religion despite its clearly evolving antecedents in the Stone Age past and of course its important bequest to archaic and classical Greek religion.

Indeed shrines and cult sites were not the same in Crete and Greece. Nevertheless superficial differences in the shape and form of altars, design of dress on idols, or styles and techniques of vase and fresco painting are poor criteria in a religious history. Local architectural and stylistic divergencies do not on their own signal different beliefs. Purely physical, geographical features of certain Minoan cults, like the site of the cave for example, may have only survived in tradition, myth or even ritual in Greek religion. Thus the transfer of a cult to a new specially constructed sanctuary is liable to obscure the history of continuity of this cult which the archaeological evidence, or rather its absence, argues to have ended with the abandonment of the original site. But the case for religious innovation has to be proved on other grounds as well. It is not enough to say that

---

    pierced in their ears, presumably to hear the worshippers' prayer, confirming their "divine" status.

[110] Above n. 71.

[111] Contrast Rutkowski, *Cult Places* 315 and n.6, "social, political and economic development (on the mainland) was manifestly different from that on Crete."

some typically Minoan cult sites like caves, peaks and "domestic" shrines were uncommon on the mainland[112], not least perhaps because a few still await discovery by the excavator.

Our picture of Minoan and Mycenaean religious administration changes almost constantly. Until recently Nilsson's view prevailed unopposed that Minoan worship within settlements was predominantly "domestic", being confined to private houses, villas, and, in larger communities, to the palace. Accordingly, the two examples, which had been indentified on the mainland at Berbati and Asine, tended to be classified as Cretan imports in the closing phases of the Bronze Age[113]. In other words, separate temple structures were a later Greek phenomenon without precedent in the Bronze Age. This story now turns out to be wrong. Nothing remains, of course, of open-air sanctuaries, although they were common to both the Minoan and Mycenaean worlds, to judge from the many scenes on gold rings from Crete and Greece, as at Mycenae and Pylos. More rewarding evidence, however, has come to light of independent shrines within, or associated with, towns. In Crete such structures were in use since the Early Bronze Age, as witness the "town shrine" at Myrtos with its delightful figure of the Lady of Myrtos[114], while Mycenaean examples have turned up at Mycenae, Tiryns and on the island of Melos at Phylakopi[115]. Nothing certain is known of mainland cult sites before the end of Middle Helladic: the "temples" there of course belonged to the Late Bronze Age, while Cretan examples of independent shrines have also been identified in Middle Minoan namely at Mallia[116] and Gournia[117]. However, the temple at Ayia Irini on Keos, with its contonous history of use by Minoans and

---

[112] *E. g.* Rutkowski, *Cult Places* 67 ff.; 271.

[113] LH IIIB & C; especially Nilsson, *MMR²* 110 ff.

[114] P. Warren, *Myrtos*, Oxford 1972, 81 ff. Sinclair Hood identifies and discusses nine examples of "temples" in Crete, dating from Early, Middle and Late Minoan times, in "Minoan Town-Shrines?", *Greece and the Eastern Mediterranean in Ancient History and Prehistory* (1977); 158–172.

[115] J.C. van Leuven, "The mainland tradition of sanctuaries in prehistoric Greece", *World Archaeology* 10 (1978) 139–148. For a possible five separate Minoan sanctuaries at Akrotiri on Thera see N. Marinatos in *Thalassocracy* 167–76.

[116] MM II, J.C. Poursat, *BCH* 90 (1966) 514–551; Hood, *op. cit.* 164 f.

[117] Hood, *op. cit.* 160 ff.; Rutkowski, "Religious Archit. in Cyprus and Crete in the L.B.A.", *Acts* (Nicosia 1979) 224.

Mycenaeans from EH II until LH (LM) III[118] illustrates the interdependence, if not identity, of cults on both sides of the Cretan Sea.

The three mainland "temples" are of great interest to a better understanding of Mycenaean religion. With the probable exception of Tiryns, they were not so much individual "temples" as two or more connected shrines in a general religious area: a kind of sacred *temenos* containing one or more altars, although the altar/hearth could also be within a cult room (Mycenae). The general concept and arrangement had much in common with the roughly contemporary Mycenaean temples in Cyprus. At Mycenae Taylour excavated two sets of cult rooms on the steep terrain between the Citadel House and the great ring wall[119]. They were basements and the most important set consisted of a group of oblong rooms reminiscent of the *megaron* form. The main room had a low central platform, shelves for idols and offerings like the typical shelf in a Minoan sanctuary, pillars and stairs leading up to a kind of deposit room where other idols were found. To the left of it was a triangular alcove enclosing the outcrop of the natural rock. This *megaron* was probably considered the equivalent of a subterranean chamber. The other complex of rooms, to the west of the *megaron*, centred on a large cultic room with an oval hearth/altar in the middle, a clay bath tub against the wall, and a bench with various articles including a wonderfully wrought ivory lion and the head of a youth with a Minoan-type band, or cap, about his forehead[120].

Important frescoes in the room depicted a goddess in Mycenaean dress[121] and a series of horns of consecration, as well as another image

---

[118] The eight prehistoric chronological periods were established in 1978, see *BCH* 103 (1979) 601. Recently large structures, which may turn out to be temples in the Late Bronze Age, have been discovered in Crete at Zakro, Arkhanes and in Kommos in southern Crete. The remarkable Building T at Kommos lies beneath later Greek temples in a sanctuary area although its precise function has yet to be established, J. W. Shaw in *Hesperia* 53 (1984), 251–87; *BCH* 108 (1984) 831; 833–5. Another large structure (MM III – LM I) from Symi may belong in this category, too, although its function has not yet been explained, *Ergon* 1983 (1984) 86–89; *BCH* 108 (1984) 829.

[119] W. Taylour, *Antiquity* 43 (1969) 91 ff.; 44 (1970) 270 ff.; *AJA* 75 (1971) 266 ff.

[120] *Cf.* Schachermeyr, *D. Äg. Frühz.*, vol. 2, 113.

[121] Buttoned on one shoulder.

of the goddess holding a pointed implement in one hand and faced by two worshippers. The mixture of Minoan/Mycenaean motifs is completed with a painted idol, with upraised arms and in Minoan dress, (which turned up in a neighbouring chamber). Subsequent work in the area of the House of Tsountas, west of, but connected with, Taylour's shrine, uncovered other sacred structures notably a two-roomed sanctuary with evidence of hearth and sacrifices[122]. The entire complex, which was connected with the Mycenaean citadel by a processional or ceremonial route, saw the celebration of cult during LH IIIB and until the end of IIIC. One quite remarkable feature is the apparent intermingling of Minoan and Mycenaean type idols throughout. Architectural changes during the two phases of use evidently did not significantly affect the nature of the cult. For example, the double shrine east of Tsountas' House had begun as a single sanctuary in IIIB, while a large circular open-air altar, which must have been a focal point of cult during the same period, was abandoned in IIIC[123]. The Mycenaean sanctuaries stood above Middle Helladic remains which may or may not have belonged to earlier structures[124].

At Phylakopi, too, we are dealing not so much with a single "temple" as a religious complex including an earlier West Sanctuary (LH IIIA) to which was later joined the East Sanctuary (LH IIIB). To the east and south of this pair respectively, which remained in joint use until LH IIIC, there was an open area with a round stone altar or baetyl[125]. At the end of the period both shrines collapsed through earth-quakes, so that the inhabitants decided to move a few miles westward to the site of Ancient Melos[126]. The Melian complex, although on a considerably smaller scale, conveys the same impression as the Mycenaean sacral area: a kind of agglutinative set of

---

[122] Reports by Mylonas and Iakovides in *Ergon* from 1970. See also *AR* 1968/69, 11–13; 69/70, 11–13; 70/71, 10 f.; 71/72, 9 f.; 72/73, 13 f.; and an overall view by G.E. Mylonas, "The Cult Centre of Mycenae", *Proc. Brit. Acad.* 67 (1981) 307–20. A good description (with references) of the campaigns from 1970–75 can be found in Schachermeyr, *Äg. Frühz.* vol. 2, 106 ff.

[123] Schachermeyr, *op. cit.* 109.

[124] Some of the remains came from a destroyed MH tomb, Schachermeyr, *ibid.*

[125] Reports in *AR* 1975/6, 25 f.; 1977/78, 52–54; C. Renfrew, "The Mycenaean Sanctuary at Phylakopi", *Antiquity* 52 (1978) 7–15.

[126] *Antiquity* (1978) 12.

rooms devoted to different aspects of cult and sheltering altars/ hearths and platforms with dedicatory figurines, as well as further altars in the open *temenos*. The West Shrine at Phylakopi had as many as three altars or platform shelves in three of its corners. This sanctuary area produced remarkable features and finds. Outstanding among these are in particular a narrow room west of the West Shrine, with a niche in the connecting wall with the shrine, concealing offerings of terracotta bulls and a grotesque head[127]. Two bronze figures of a 'Smiting God', which were discovered near the sanctuary wearing a conical hat and with a club in the raised right hand, recall a type of Reshef figure and suggest eastern influence[128].

The arrangement of the cultic structures had contemporary Mycenaean parallells but ultimately derived from the east[129]. The several 'Psi' type figures from the West Shrine and, from the narrow west room, the grand figure of the 'Lady of Phylakopi' with arms upraised[130], as well as the numerous wheel-made terracotta bull *rhyta* from both shrines show that the substance of the cult would have been equally at home in Crete at the time[131]. The five male figures in the West Shrine have been described as unique in the Aegean world[132]. But the bisexual characteristics of one of them and even the beard of the not so feminine Lady of Phylakopi herself were oriental and Cypriot features which, like the 'Smiting God', produced a mixture of eastern and Cretan as well as Mycenaean cult elements at the sanctuary[133].

The third known free-standing Mycenaean shrine at Tiryns easily fits the same picture of religious affinity which exceeded strict regional boundaries. An earlier sanctuary from LHIIIB was destroyed by earthquake and superseded in IIIC by another shrine on the same

---

[127] *Antiquity* (1978) 10.
[128] *Antiquity* (1978) fis. 2 & 3. See below ch. IV, 160–1; 166–7.
[129] See ch. IV, 135–6.
[130] Now broken off.
[131] Denied by the excavator, *Antiquity* (1978) 8; 14; *cf.* Renfrew, in the summary of his paper "Phylakopi and Questions of Cult in the Aegean Late Bronze Age", *Mycenaean Siminar*, London Inst. Class. Studs. 21 March 1979. It is interesting that no double axes or horns of consecration have turned up at Phylakopi. Possibly they figured in frescoe paintings which are now lost. *Cf.* ch. IV, 142–3.
[132] *Antiquity* (1978) 13.
[133] See below ch. IV, 166.

site, but different orientation[134]. Neither sanctuary appears to have been a part of a larger religious complex like Mycenae and Melian Phylakopi. The dedications are familiar, however: they include three large idols (fragmentary), thirty 'Psi' figurines and the fragments of two bull rhytons, one of which had been decorated with the painting of an upright zoomorphic daemon or god[135]. Thus architecturally the sanctuary was more closely related to Minoan Crete[136], but in cult offerings, and hence cult type, does not fall outside the pattern which we have tried to establish. It is not surprising therefore that the most recent work in the area showed the earlier sanctuary to have been built within an older open sacred area containing idols and the large (1/2 metre) figure of a goddess with upraised arms. This last indeed represents the earliest example of this type anywhere in Crete or Greece[137].

How important then was the actual form of the "temple" to a cult? Is it true to assume that variations of the one entail differences in the other? Surely the available evidence is inadequate to answer either question satisfactorily. A recent study detects a Mycenaean preference for a southeasterly orientation of its sacred structures[138]. The practice seems significant until it is remembered that the Mycenaean sacred area could be changed around during its period of usage without noticeable effect on cultic practice. The point is dramatically illustrated in Tiryns where the earlier building complex, after natural damage, was replaced by a new sanctuary which was, however, aligned along a different axis[139]. Superficially the arrangement at Mycenae and Phylakopi with one or more "temples" and altars could be described as un-Minoan[140], but the Cretans most likely had also been familiar with this kind of set-up earlier on in their history.

Open courts with an altar in front of sacred buildings and/or tombs

---

[134] *AR* 1977/78, 26f.; 1978/79 16; *BCH* 101 (1977) 548; 102 (1978) 666–8; 103 (1979) 559.

[135] *BCH* (1978) 668, fig. 2.

[136] *BCH* (1978) 668; *AR* 1977/78, 27.

[137] See above p. 15 and n. 98; *BCH* 103 (1979) 559.

[138] Van Leuven, *World Arch.* (1978) 139–148. Hood contrasts the fixed orientation of the Mycenaean shrines with the more random arrangement which prevailed in Crete, *Greece and the East. Medit.* 172.

[139] *AR* 1977/78, 27.

[140] Rutkowski, *Acts* (Nicosia 1979), 224.

were nor uncommon in Mesara in the Early and Middle Bronze Age as at Platanos and Apesokari[141]. Even more closely comparable is the large sanctuary complex of some eleven rooms or more associated with a paved open court and probably an altar at Kato Syme[142]. Perhaps the recently discovered Middle Minoan: "temple" at Arkhanes on the western slopes of Mt. Jouktas also fits this pattern of "compound" sanctuary areas[143]. Again the presumably unimpeachably Mycenaean cult at Tiryns occurred in a "Minoan" type shrine, and yet its position near the city wall calls to mind that of the Late Bronze Age Temples 4 and 5 at Kition and others, as at Enkomi in Cyprus[144]. The temples in Kition were, of course, the home of Mycenaean cult before being converted by Phoenician settlers in Geometric times.

At the end of the Bronze Age Minoan and Mycenaean "temples" like peak sanctuaries followed more than one pattern and could have evolved quite naturally into the well-known archaic Greek arrangement of temple, (fire) altar and cultic image[145]. Regional differences in cult must be established by means of other criteria in particular through different cult symbols, implements and votive offerings. This is extremely difficult, not to say impossible, on the available evidence which shows that very often cultic vessels, appurtenances and symbols were the same in places of Minoan and Mycenaean influence. In so far as it is possible to judge, the surviving paraphernalia seem to point to a common basic nucleus of cult revolving about the central figure of a goddess and the bull. These two elements most visibly link most cult sites in east and west, in Crete and mainland Greece. Regional differences were generally confined to the special localised names of the deity without touching

---

[141] C.R. Long, "Shrines in Sepulchres?", *AJA* 63 (1959) 59, with further references; Hood, *The Minoans*, 142f.; K. Branigan, *The Tombs of Mesara*, London 1970, 132ff.

[142] *AR* 1978/79, 38. The Mycenaean altar may have been at, or on the spot of, the later Hellenic one.

[143] See n.74 above.

[144] *BCH* 102 (1978) 916; *AJA* 84 (1980) 66. The temples in Kition flank the city gates like other eastern examples.

[145] For a somewhat different view see Burkert, *Gr. Rel.* 94. For the evolution of Greek temple architecture from Minoan and Mycenaean forms see N. Coldstream, *Geometric Greece*, London 1977, ch. 13.

her fundamental nature. Aphrodite in Paphos possessed essentially the same prerogatives as city goddesses as did Hera at Argos and Athena in Cretan Gortyn or in Athens. It is noteworthy therefore that the conservative descendants of the Mycenaean settlers at Paphos still preserved the figure of the "Goddess with Upraised Arms" among the many other votives to Aphrodite at the time when her sacred precinct was first mentioned by Homer[146].

In the light of the preceding discussion it is now possible to consider and account for one of the major discrepancies in the physical distribution of Minoan and Mycenaean cult sites. Mountain peaks and caves were peculiarly Minoan cult sites. This certainly seems to be true of caves few of which on the mainland can be shown to have witnessed cult in Mycenaean times[147]. To some extent no doubt this was due to the poor Greek evidence, for there are signs that caves were inhabited and saw cult over long periods in the Stone Age. The Franchthi Cave near Hermione in the Argolid, the Alepotrypa Cave in Laconia, and the Kitsos Cave in Laurium, are good examples of this point[148]. What cult there was in the mainland caves probably differed little in substance from that in contemporary Cretan and much earlier Anatolian caves[149]. So much seems clear from the finds like the head of a stalagmite type marble idol from the Alepotrypa Cave[150] and some similarly shaped figurines which were found mixed together with other Middle Helladic remains in the Sarakinos Cave at Orchomenos[151]. However, no unambiguous example of actual *Mycenaean* cult in Late Helladic has as yet been identified.

---

[146] K. Nicolaou, "Archaeological News from Cyprus 1977–78", *AJA* 84 (1980) 68.

[147] Faure holds that at least in the Peloponnese and Cyclades caves continued to be used until historical times as burial and cult sites, P. Faure, "Chronique des Cavernes Cretoises (1972–77)", *BCH* 102 (1978) 639. See also the bibliography and full description of caves in the annual catalogue (from 1971) by Miss Giammoulidou in *Platon* under the title *Historika Spelaia tes Archaiotetes*.

[148] Detailed reports in *BCH* from 96 (1972). Further caves in Thessaly are discussed in *BCH* 104 (1980) 634.

[149] Dietrich, *The Origins of Greek Religion*, 93 ff.

[150] G. A. Papathanassopoulos, "Excavation of the Cave at Dirou – 1970/71" (in Greek), *AAA* 4 (1971) 12–26, fig. 18; 19; *cf. BCH* 95 (1971) 888.

[151] *BCH* 102 (1978) II, 696, fig. 118–20. For the Neolithic Deros Caves at Mani in Laconia and Skotini Cave and twenty others on Euboea, see *AR* 1977/78, 18; 33.

Peak sites continued to be frequented in Crete until historic times. By then there is clear evidence of cult on the summits of hills and mountains in Greece as well. In both countries the two divine names most commonly associated with these sites were Zeus and Apollo, the latter quite often as Hyacinthus. In fact the epithet of Hyacinthus linked peak cults in Greece and Crete. For example Apollo Hyacinthus was honoured in a peak sanctuary at Pyrgos near Tylissos, and special coins were minted bearing his name during the Hyacinthia festival in town[152]. On the mainland, in Laconian Amyclae, the god also enjoyed a similar cult which quite probably began in the Late Bronze Age[153]. Hence the link may antedate the end of that age, although this must remain unproved until it can be established whether the Laconian cult of Hyacinthus had travelled south or originally been imported to Greece from Crete[154].

Apollo, with the local name of Aktios, had a peak cult in historic times at Anactorion on the Ambracian Gulf, and another one nearby at Leucas[155]. At the former site Augustus still paid homage to the god after the battle of Actium[156]. Zeus was associated with numerous peaks in Greece, the best known of which is Mt. Hymettus in Attica. His sanctuary there was in use not before the end of Proto-geometric[157]. In fact, with one or two exceptions, peak cults in Greece cannot be attested before Geometric times and most of them flourished in the eighth and seventh pre-Christian centuries[158]. Mycenaean remains have turned up at a few sites, like Hymettus, Oros, and Ayios Elias at Mycenae[159], but in uncertain contexts.

---

[152] D. Levi, *PdP* (1978) 301.

[153] Dietrich, "The Dorian Hyacinthia A Survival from the Bronze Age", *Kadmos* 14 (1975) 133–42.

[154] See the article cited in the previous note.

[155] Strabo 325; Plut., *Pomp.* 24; Ael., *Nat. An.* 2,8.

[156] Suet., *Aug.* 18; Dio Cass. 51, 1.

[157] There may have been an altar on the summit as early as the twelfth century B.C. However, the sparse remains from Early, Middle and Late Helladic can not obviously be connected with Zeus' sanctuary which probably began its "life" in the second half of the tenth century B.C., *AJA* 44 (1940) 1 ff.; M.K. Langdon, *A Sanctuary of Zeus on Mount Hymettos (Hesperia Suppl. XVI)*, Princeton 1976, 7; 74 f. Other Greek peak sites of Zeus are discussed in Append. B, *op. cit.* 112.

[158] Langdon, *op. cit.* 112.

[159] *Op. cit.* 87.

There were really two types of peak cult which ought to be told apart. The first and un-Mycenaean type, according to present-day knowledge, occurred in a sacred *temenos* with, or without, sanctuary buildings on an isolated peak or mountain summit. Its form and nature have been discussed elsewhere. As far as it is possible to see, they were concerned with the worship of an apotropaeic, protective deity of nature[160]. The second type was also celebrated on the top of a mountain, but in association with a human settlement. The latter was represented in Crete throughout the Bronze Age: from the Early Minoan Fournou Korifi, in the south of the island, with shrine and bell-shaped goddess figurine[161], to the Middle Minoan "peak site" at Pyrgos[162], and finally to the famous settlement of Karphi at the very end of the Bronze Age. Karphi, like Pyrgos, though more than one and a half millennia later, may have been used as a natural defensive position[163].

Architecturally both types differed considerably from one another, as the shrine in the latter often formed an integral part of the living quarters and therefore was indistinguishable from a domestic shrine in house or palace. The shrine in Pyrgos IV, for example, had been built on the first floor of a large "country house" of the New Palace period[164]. But offerings in these "settlement" or "domestic" shrines did not differ substantially from those in pure peak sanctuaries with their horns, goddess with upraised arms[165], and even terracotta models of animals and beetles[166]. Thus scholars generally discussed both types under one heading[167] which implies, however, that every

---

[160] This view was put forward in *Historia* 18 (1969) 257–275; 20 (1971) 513–23. On peak cult in general see Rutkowski, *Cult Places* 152–88; P. Faure, "Cultes Populaires dans la Crète Antique", *BCH* 96 (1972) 390–402; Dietrich, *Origins* 290–307; Burkert, *Griech. Rel.* 58–61, with references to earlier discussions in the notes; D. Levi, *PdP* 181 (1978) 294–313. A.A.D. Peatfield, 'The Topography of Minoan Peak Sanctuaries', *BSA* 78 (1983) 273–9.

[161] *AR* 1968/69, 34 f. & fig. 48; P. Warren, *Myrtos* (1972).

[162] Pyrgos III probably and Pyrgos IV certainly, with shrine, G. Cadogan, "Pyrgos, Crete, 1970–77", *AR* 1977/78, 70–84.

[163] J. D. S. Pendlebury, *The Archaeology of Crete*, London 1939, 306; V. Desborough, *The Last Mycenaeans and their Successors*, Oxford 1964, 172.

[164] *AR* 1977/78, 77.

[165] E. g. Karphi and Petsophas, cf. *P.d.P.* (1978) 297 n. 4.

[166] E. g. Pyrgos III (MM, Old Palace period – MM IIIA), *AR* 1977/78, 76.

[167] E. g. Rutkowski, *Cult Places*, 152–88.

settlement, every acropolis, from the massively impressive Ryzenia (Prinias) and Gortyn in Crete to the acropolis of Athens in Greece, should be included in a list of peak cult sites. How specialised was the cult in type One? That is almost impossible to say, but the separation of the sacred area from the settlement suggests a distinction in cult. It seems clear that the isolated peak cult had been closely related to that obtaining in caves in Crete. Many peak sites were almost identical with rock shelters which belonged to the category of cave cult[168]. Quite illuminating in this respect is the discovery of a deep fissure with votive offerings in the sacred precinct of the peak sanctuary on Mount Jouktas[169].

In Mycenaean Greece the nearest parallel to the second type, that is a peak cult associated with a settlement, is the cult on the summit of Mt. Kynortion at Epidauros. This has been compared with Minoan peak cult by the excavator and others[170]. The double axes, which have been found in the sanctuary, do suggest a strong link with Crete, although other typically Minoan cult equipment of peak sites is missing like tables of offering, Minoan figures of worshippers, models of separate limbs etc.[171]. North-east of the classical temple there stood an open-air altar. Its date was about the seventh century B.C., but it was constructed on the remains of a similar Mycenaean altar. Perhaps Mycenaean remains beneath the earlier 6th century temple also belonged to a sanctuary at the spot, to judge from the ceramic fragments from there. Other Mycenaean votive finds, like large wheel-made animals and 'Phi' figurines, can only be associated with the general area[172]. Altar and sanctuary, if there was one, were part of the Mycenaean settlement on the summit of Mt.Kynortion. The

---

168 *PdP* (1978) 296.
169 *BCH* 102 (1978) 636; *PdP* (1978) 305.
170 V. Lambrinudakis, "Remains of the Mycenaean period in the sanctuary of Apollo Maleatas", *SCABA* 59–63, with references to the preliminary excavation reports, discussion on p. 64; "Staatskult und Geschichte von Epidauros", *Archaiognosia* I (1980) 39–63; J. Bintliff, *Natural environment and human settlement in prehistoric Greece*, Oxford 1977, 152; Rutkowski, *Cult Places*, 260 n. 2.
171 See Hägg in *Thalassocracy* 120–1, who believes accordingly that there was no Minoan-type cult on Kynortion. A. Peatfield describes Apollo Maleatas' sanctuary as a hill-top shrine in the discussion of Hägg's paper p. 122.
172 *AR* 1974/75, 10; 1975/76, 12; 1976/77, ('77/78) 28; 1978/79, 17f.; *BCH* (1978) 672.

historic cult on the site of course belonged to Apollo Maleatas as apotropaeic and healing god, hence the proximity of Asclepius' worship there. No archaeological sign survives, however, which might point to continuity of cult on Kynortion. The Mycenaean altar might have triggered off the renewal of cult in the 7th century B.C.[173], although the apotropaeic figure of Apollo suggests that the salient features of the old peak and community deity had been preserved in Epidauros as well as, for example, in Laconian Amyclae[174]. And this is after all the main point, namely that the cult of Apollo on Mt.Kynortion was that of the community god and directly linked with that of his ancient predecessor.

A number of Zeus' historic peak cults in Greece, like that on Hymettus, show the characteristics of Minoan type One, that is an isolated *temenos* or shrine high on the mountain peak and divorced from any settlement. On Hymettos there was a sacred enclosure containing an open-air altar[175], probably that of Zeus Ombrios[176]. Many high peaks functioned as weather indicators to the Greeks according to Theophrastus[177], which explains Zeus' title of Ombrios here and in his cult on Mt. Parnes[178]. But this type of cult appears to have been an historical development in Greece[179], and it is remarkable that, apart from these two instances, Ombrios and the identical title of Hyetios, though common in Greece, were not associated with mountain tops[180]. Beside Ombrios, Pausanias also mentions local epithets of Zeus, like Hymettios, Parnethios and Anchesmios whose image stood on Mt. Anchesmos in Attica[181]. Still more interesting memories of prehistoric peak cult are brought to life by an altar to Apollo on Hymettus, although his title of Proopsios is

---

[173] *AR* 76/77 ('77/78) 28.
[174] See *Historia* 20 (1971) 520; *Kadmos* 14 (1975) 136; BICS 25 (1978) 2f.
[175] Langdon, *Sanct. of Zeus* 1.
[176] Paus. 1, 32, 2.
[177] *De signis Tempestatum*, 3, 43 (Mt. Parnes); 1, 24 (Oros); 2, 34 (Mt. Athos); *cf.* Langdon, *op. cit.* 81.
[178] Paus., *ibid.*
[179] *Cf.* Nilsson, *Gesch.*³ 1, 393.
[180] The cults of Ombrios and Hyetios have been collected by A.B. Cook, *Zeus*, Cambridge 1940, III, 525–70; *cf.* the author's exhaustive discussion of Zeus' connection with rain, III, 248–881.
[181] 1, 32, 2.

less than helpful. But, again according to Pausanias, Zeus Ombrios shared a common altar with Zeus Apemios on Mt. Parnes, that is the apotropaeic "Averter of Ills"[182].

The many martial finds on Hymettus of bronze knives, shields and iron daggers[183], are not particularly enlightening concerning the nature of Zeus' cult; but they do recall the finds in the Minoan caves of Arkalokhori and Psychro[184]. But if Pausanias' account is reliable, the cultic remains and the titles on Hymettus and elsewhere in Attica, and that probably means Greece in general, were the product of a mixture of new ideas with old traditions. Beside Zeus the Weather- and Raingod and Zeus Hypsistos, the supreme Olympian, peaks in the main continued to be remembered as the place where Zeus was thought to have been born and where he died[185]. These were the traditional aspects of Minoan cave and peak cult which manifestly survived strongly enough in Greece to hold their own next to later concepts, and of course in Greek myth throughout its history[186]. The important inference can then be made from the foregoing discussion that, although caves and peaks had been and continued to be considered sacred in Crete, the Mycenaeans and their successors generally preferred to adopt the cult without, however, retaining the original cult site. Greek caves were unimportant in historic cult: the haunt of monsters like Lamia and the Harpies[187], or the home of Pan and the Nymphs who occasionally through age-old memory still received gifts as "Geburtsgöttinnen"[188]. But otherwise the rites had been transferred to new homes probably as early as the Mycenaean age.

In Crete both cave and the closely related peak cult had been

---

[182] Pausanias, *ibid.*, mentions a second altar on Hymettos in honour of Zeus Semalios, "Giver of Signs".

[183] See *Hesperia Suppl. XVI* (1976), Append. B, 100f., for a description of finds and references to excavators' reports.

[184] Rutkowski, *Cult Places* 139f.

[185] For a list of the evidence see Cook, *Zeus* 1 (1914), 124–163; *Zeus* II (1925), Append. B, 868–987; *cf. Hesperia Suppl. XVI*, 81.

[186] See Dietrich, *Origins*, 14f.; 16f.; 109f.; 120; 303.

[187] *BCH* 102 (1978) 632 and n. 14.

[188] At Pitsa, for example, near Corinth, the 7th – 3rd century B.C. Votives included terracotta figures of pregnant women, *AA* (1934) 194; (1935) 197f.; Nilsson, *Gesch.*³, I, 248. For similar finds on peak see Levi, *PdP* (1978) 297.

"domesticated" before the end of Middle Minoan[189] although, of course, both continued in a number of their original locations[190]. The move to new quarters, which echoed an astonishingly similar

---

[189] Levi, *PdP* (1978) 296; 311, most recently discusses the connection of both types of cult.

[190] In Crete some fifty sanctuaries have been identified within the last decade as well as over forty caves, which witnessed cult at different times of the Bronze Age and beyond, and twenty-five open air sanctuaries; P. Faure, "Cultes Populaires dans la Crète Antique", *BCH* 96 (1972) 401; 425. *Cf. AR* 1974/75, 27 and 28. There may be another one in the "Gorge of the Dead" near Kato Zakro, *A. P.* 1975/76, 31 f.; *BCH* 100 (1976) 723; Faure, *BCH* 102 (1978) 639; Doro Levi, *PdP* 181 (1978) 294–313, who rightly counts the rock-shelters among the cult caves (p. 296). All the evidence of the known Cretan caves has been collected and discussed in a recent study by E. Tyree, *Cretan Sacred Caves: Archaeological Evidence* Diss. Colombia 1974. This careful survey of the remains from caves which might have witnessed cult shows up the difficulty of reaching conclusions from only the extant archaeological evidence much of which has either never been published or lost since it was discovered. Again the earliest demonstrable cult implements, which have been found in caves, belong to MM I, but other types of artefacts and remains prove habitation of, and burial in, caves from Neolithic and Early Minoan. If we accept the reasonable thesis that cult accompanied, or arose from (Tyree p. 114), habitation and burial, should we deny the very real possibility that these fragments of pottery, domestic implements and animal bones from periods earlier than Middle Minoan were used in religious ceremonies?

At the other end of the scale, cult continuity beyond the end of the Bronze Age has generally been assumed on archaeological grounds for at least four caves at Phaneromeni, Psychro, Skoteino, Amnisos. However, with the possible exception of Psychro, there is no published Protogeometric material from any one of these caves suggesting that the cult had been temporarily suspended before Geometric (Tyree 118). Other caves, which had been used in both the Bronze Age and in historical times, also show sometimes quite extensive gaps in the chronological sequence of their remains. But this does not of course always signify that cult was merely "reactive" at these sites after prolonged intervals, or even that a new cult was instituted at an old locality. Important indications of basic continuity can be found in the persistence from Minoan to Geometric times of the same types of offerings in cave cult. Cult vessels and votives, including human and animal figurines, as well as implements, weapons and also double axes (Tsoutsouros Cave) continued in the same forms until the eighth century B. C. (Tyree 125; 127; 128; 132; 138; 139). There were some minor changes and omissions without, however, any obvious effect on the nature of the cult. By Geometric times *kernoi* and *rhyta* shapes had disappeared, for example, and so evidently had horns of consecration (Tyree 140). But only two examples of the latter, both from the same cave (Patsos), have ever been discovered in connection with cave cult (LM III,

development in Anatolia more than a millennium earlier[191], left distinct traces in the dedication of stalagmitic concretions in the Little Palace at Knossos for instance[192]. Most probably it was the positive aspect of the goddess, her life-giving powers, which went to the new temple or sanctuary, for there are indications that the part of cave cult, which was concerned with death, also found another home in specially constructed tombs. These were built in Crete, at least from the beginning of the Bronze Age, and they witnessed some form of cult even then[193], but the first conclusive evidence of the transfer of cave cult to cave-like tomb dates from the beginning of Middle Minoan in the shape of more anthropomorphic concretions. Examples have come to light in the Apesokari Tomb in the Mesara[194]. It would probably be wrong to interpret such changes as signalling a centralization of cult in the new palaces, tombs and so on, because the old sites continued to be visited[195]. The development at that time

---

Tyree 106). In the seventh century the orientalising style dominated in the manufacture of votives which, though, most likely belonged to the same type of cult. This, as far as one can judge from all the evidence, in historical times continued to be concerned with birth, fertility and vegetation cult in general, although possibly new deities and nature spirits became involved. Perhaps, too, there was less solemn mystery in the chthonic ritual during the Classical age which seemed to favour grander caves with more impressive natural concretions (Tyree 159).

The dangers of relying exclusively on the archaeological evidence can be illustrated with the history of cult in the Idaean Cave. Whatever the divine title of the Minoan figure may have been, Zeus was worshipped in this cave from Geometric onward. However, no classical cult objects have been found there, suggesting a break in Zeus' cult between the fifth century and the Hellenistic age when it flourished again until Roman times (Tyree 219 with references). But a fifth century Gortynian inscription, which refers to Zeus' trieteric festival at his cave on Mount Ida, proves cult continuity through the Classical age (IC IV. 80. Cf. R.F. Willetts, Cretan Cults and Festivals, London 1962, 243; Tyree, 147). The present large-scale excavation by J. Sakellarakis is producing evidence of use of, and cult in, the cave from Neolithic through Minoan (MM silver axe (unpublished), kernos etc.) and Mycenaean times linking up with the historic cult of Zeus.

[191] See Dietrich, Origins 165.
[192] Origins 92; 110; 170f.; 183; 304.
[193] See I. Pini, Beiträge zur Minoischen Gräberkunde, Wiesbaden 1968, 29ff.; 31f.; 34; K. Branigan, "The earliest Minoan Scripts – the Prepalatial background", Kadmos 8 (1969) 2.
[194] C.R. Long, "Shrines in Sepulchres?", AJA 63 (1959) 59; 63f.
[195] Branigan, Kadmos 8 (1969) 2f.

rather suggests the existence of the same basic cult which was celebrated in different types of sacred area[196].

The confusion, or interchangeability, is illustrated by a cult site like Kato Symi Viannou in southern Crete. Seen from the modern village of Symi, the imposing peak leaves no doubt in one's mind that this was an isolated peak cult of our first category. The site is of considerable importance to the history of Greek and Cretan religion, because it is one of very few which preserved the unmistakable signs of cult continuity at least from the Late Bronze Age until the third century B.C.[197]. South of the Hellenic altar, which stood in the sacred area and succeeded another altar from Protogeometric, was a multi-room shrine complex from the end of the Middle Minoan (MM IIIB/LM IA)[198]. Another shrine, north of the Hellenic altar, was built much later, in the second century B.C. in fact, but witnessed essentially the same cult which had been observed on the summit for centuries, as the old cult implements, stone altar, and ancient tables of offering continued to be employed in the ritual[199]. In other words, the worship of Aphrodite and Hermes, in whose honour the cult was celebrated in historical times, not unlike Dionysus at Ayia Irini on Keos[200], preserved and carried on an old religious tradition. This point, as well as the divine nomenclature and the curious male and hybrid figurines, which have turned up on the site, have far reaching implications for later Greek religion.

The Bronze Age complex of cult buildings, on the peak at Symi, included some eleven or more rooms and an open paved court which in the Iron Age provided the area for altar and cult in the open air. However, in Late Minoan times, that is contemporary with the Mycenaean age, the arrangement of the sacred structures echoes that at Mycenae and elsewhere[201] and therefore appears to reflect the

---

[196] Doro Levi believes, *PdP* 181 (1978) 311 f., that an earlier common cult was only later departmentalized in different cult sites.

[197] See the reports in *AR* 1972/73, 30 f.; 1973/74, 36 f.; 1974/75, 28; 1975/76, 30; 1976/77 (1977/78), 64; 1978/79, 38; *BCH* 97 (1973) 398; 98 (1974) 707 f.; 99 (1975) 685; 687; 102 (1978) 754.

[198] Also probably preceded by an earlier structure.

[199] *AR* 1973/74, 36 f.; *BCH* 98 (1974) 707 f.

[200] See Dietrich, *Origins* 221; 226; Burkert, *Griech. Rel.* 65, with full references to excavation reports.

[201] See above p. 23.

practice of "domestic" rather than peak cult[202]. This conclusion is reinforced by a good many of the offerings from there: they seem more at home in the so-called "domestic" shrines. Doro Levi, for example, compares the *kernoi* and conical vases from Symi with those found in the sanctuaries of the Rural Villa at Kannia near Gortyn[203]. Quite clearly then cult tradition was more important than the actual site in all three main categories of domestic, peak and cave cult.

From what has been said earlier on, the same principle applied on the Greek mainland in Mycenaean and later times. The mixture of Greek and Cretan material at Symi can only bear out this same point. A good deal of otherwise puzzling archaeological evidence can be plausibly interpreted on the same grounds, that in Greek belief tradition outlived the original cult site. To begin with a Cretan example: a curious feature in the Late Minoan villa at Slavokambos (LM IA-B) consists in some natural rock which was allowed to protrude above the floor level of two rooms, at least one of which had been set aside for cultic purposes[204]. This natural outcrop in one of these rooms retained the marks of past burnt sacrifice, that is charcoal together with burnt animal bones, as well as offerings of bowls and sherds stuck into the crevices of the rock[205]. The last feature in particular rules out any secular use of the room[206]. Both rooms had been subterranean chambers originally, and the rock with its offerings recalls the scene of both cave and peak cults[207].

The shrine at Sklavokambos was evidently intended to reproduce a cave or rock shelter. No stalagmitic concretion of human or any other shape has survived. But quite clearly the natural rock itself was

---

[202] *Cf. AR* 1976/77 (1977/78) 64.

[203] *PdP* 181 (1978) 303; "La Villa Rurale di Gortina", *Boll. d'Arte* (1959), 237 ff.

[204] Rooms 15 & 19, see Sp. Marinatos, *Aph. Arch.* 1939/1941 (1948), 69 ff.; Rutkowski, *Cult Places* 101 f.

[205] Room 15.

[206] *E. g.* a kitchen, according to Marinatos, *Aph. Erch.* (1948), 76, after previously identifying the room with a sanctuary.

[207] *E. g.* Psychro Cave, *Origins* 82. N. Platon compares rock fissures and sacrifice with peak sanctuaries, *KC* 8 (1954) 425 f. Rutkowski discusses these rooms in his chapter on Minoan/Mycenaean crypts, all of which he believes to have been in secular use. Both Rooms 15 & 19, he argues, must have been used for domestic purposes, *Cult Places*, 102.

felt to possess the same sacred properties as had been in the cave. The Minoan example therefore admirably explains related, but less obvious, features in Mycenaean sanctuaries, notably the bare rock in the somewhat later sanctuary in the Citadel House at Mycenae[208]. This was below ground: its somewhat tomb-like effect can be judged by the two contemporary, but better preserved, subterranean cult rooms in Thebes. They had been cut into the natural sandstone and, with their frescoes, benches and the like, were distinctly similar to the Mycenaean rooms[209]. In Mycenae the rock chamber was next to the *megaron*-shrine, or temple, and beyond the platforms with the large goddess idol. The rock's prominent position in the whole complex underlines its undoubted cultic significance[210]. But the rock itself was screened from view by a wall and may have been a kind of inner sanctum. In historical times the *adyton* became a particular feature of temples which were dedicated to chthonic deities who received funerary cult. A case in point are the temples of Artemis at Brauron, next to a cave at the foot of the Braurion acropolis, at Halae and Aulis[211]. In Mycenae no trace of offerings has been found on or near the rock nor any evidence of sacrifice, most idols having been discovered in the upper "deposit" room. Nevertheless, the equation of rock = cave = *adyton* of the *megaron*-shrine strongly suggests itself. If this conclusion is correct, the rites within this Mycenaean "temple", at the end of the Mycenaean age, perpetuated a cult that had been celebrated on mountain peaks and in caves by the Minoans.

The shrine in Mycenae seems a particularly good example of the survival of an older tradition in new surroundings, but there might well be others which until now have gone undetected. The small chamber west of the Mycenaean West Shrine at Phylakopi, for

---

[208] See above p. 19.

[209] Excavated by Spyropoulos, *AAA* 4 (1971) 161 ff.; *B.C.H.* 96 (1972) 694; Schachermeyr, *D. Ägäische Frühzeit*, vol. 2, 172.

[210] Lord W. Taylour, *Antiquity* 44 (1970) 274; cf. *A.J.A.* 75 (1971) 266; Schachermeyr, *op. cit.*, vol. 2, 112, "Der linke Hinterraum liess z. T. den gewachsenen Felsen offen, was wohl kultische Bedeutung hatte".

[211] I. Travlos, "Three Temples of Artemis Aulis, Tauropolos and Brauron", (in Greek) *Neue Forschungen in griechischen Heiligtümern (Sympos. Olympia, 1974),* 197–205; L. Kahil, "La Déesse Artemis: Mythologie et Iconographie", *Gr and It,* 77.

example, possessed the remarkable feature of a niche containing four wheel-made bull votives together with a grotesque head in the east wall[212]. The niche and bull figurines could also be remnants of a cave cult transferred to new surroundings, on analogy with identical practices, elsewhere in the Aegean, but ultimately deriving from Anatolia in the Neolithic Age[213]. The relationship of niche and chamber, where stood the large goddess figure with upraised arms, with the main West Shrine at Phylakopi, was not unlike that of *megaron*-shrine and idol with the small rock chamber at Mycenae. In Neolithic Çatal Hüyük the niche was generally in the eastern wall, *i. e.* that part of the shrine which had been given over to the ritual celebration of death[214]. The Melian shrine, too, had its niche in the eastern wall of the adjacent chamber, while the natural outcrop of rock at Mycenae formed the north/eastern corner of the small alcove beyond the main shrine. The location might well be fortuitous in both cases, nor is there any sign in the remains of the Mycenaean sanctuaries that they witnessed scenes of funerary ritual. Without written records nothing can be certain.

The traditions connected with chthonic cave cult did, however, tenaciously survive into historic times, and generally in the worship of Demeter. For example the significance of the natural rock, which was allowed to project above the floor of the Eleusinian Telesterion, has caused endless debate for the past 150 years[215]. The rock actually marked the site of the ancient *anaktoron*[216], within which occurred the central ceremony of the Mysteries, and therefore symbolically represented a cave. The exact procedure of the rites of the Eleusinian Mysteries remains unknown, but the famous light, and the hierophant's fire ritual within the "cave", suggest the setting for an annual reenactment of birth and renewal[217]. The scene with its elements recalls the myth of Zeus' periodic rebirth in a cave

---

[212] *Antiquity* 52 (1978) 10. *Cf.* above p. 21.
[213] Dietrich, *Origins* 105 ff.; 182; 221.
[214] See the previous note.
[215] G. E. Mylonas, *Eleusis and the Eleusinian Mysteries*, third print. Princeton 1974, 83 f.
[216] *Ibid.*
[217] Plut., *prof. virt.* 81 e; *IG* II/III² 3811; Burkert, *Griech. Rel.*, 430.

accompanied by a great flame of fire[218]. The "Palace" and Telesterion stood on the site of an earlier Mycenaean building, or "temple"[219], of about the same date as the Mycenaean and Melian sanctuaries[220], and very probably continued the Mycenaean cult[221]. If this is correct, the Mycenaean Megaron B already witnessed the traditional cave cult in the symbolic setting of a sanctuary. It would not be unreasonable to conclude, then, that the symbolism of the rock in Eleusis and Mycenae, and possibly even that of the wall niche in Phylakopi, conveyed the same cultic message.

In fact, the association of birth and cave, of goddess and divine associate, strongly continued to permeate Eleusinian cult. When the tyrant Peisistratus enhanced the lustre and importance of the Mysteries, he not only constructed the new Telesterion, but actually added a nearby cave to the sanctuary area. He also built a "Plutonium" within the cave[222] which was restored some two centuries later[223]. Demeter had another temple and "Megaron" in Arcadian Lycosoura together with ancient Mystery rites[224]. This "Megaron", too, played the part of a subterranean chamber, or cave, although it was no more than an open sacred area. The altar within it, however, incorporated a natural rock which still bears the traces of sacrificial ashes[225]. The Arcadian myths of Demeter were ancient,

---

[218] Anton. Liber. 19. The identification of the *anaktoron* with a cave is discussed in greater detail in my paper on "The Religious Prehistory of Demeter's Eleusinian Mysteries" in *La Soteriologia dei Culti Orientali nell'Impero Romano, Atti Coll. Intern. Rome 1979*, Leiden 1982, 445–71.

[219] Megaron B. See Mylonas, *Eleusis* 33f. Desborough doubts the cultic use of Megaron B, *Last Mycenaeans*, 44.

[220] LH III; perhaps LH IIIC, Desborough, *Last Mycen.* 43.

[221] On the "pros" and "cons" of cult continuity in the Eleusinian Telesterion see Dietrich, *Origins* 140ff. & n.46. See also now J. Coldstream, *Geometric Greece*, London 1977, 331ff.

[222] Mylonas, *Eleusis* 96; 99f.; 103; 104.

[223] Nilsson, *Gesch.*³ 1, 471, ascribes the reconstruction of the Plutonium in the fourth century to a conscious piece of "Atavismus" at a time when Pluto's place in cult had already been usurped by Kore. In fact Demeter/Kore probably always existed side by side with the male figure.

[224] According to Herodotus, 2, 171, only the Arcadians preserved their Mysteries after the "Dorian uprising".

[225] K. Kourouniotes, *AE* (1912), 146; 150; *cf.* Mylonas, *Eleusis* 83f. See also F. Studniczka, "Altäre mit Grubenkammern", *Jahreshefte d. österreichischen archäologischen Instituts* 6 (1903) 123ff.; 7 (1904) 239ff.

dark and confused[226]: they emphasized her nature as a chthonic goddess who was associated with animals and the cave[227]. Demeter's theriomorphic leanings, as well as her affinity with Artemis, obviously were central elements in the Mysteries at Lycosura, for the rites revolved about the figure of Despoina, the Mistress, whom Pausanias identified with Kore, Persephone[228].

An interesting side-light on this discussion is that many of Demeter's temples shared the feature of an inner sanctum, or *adyton*, with those of Artemis, also therefore visibly retaining the link with caves. Demeter's temples were commonly called *megara*[229]. There is some evidence that *megaron* was a Semitic loan word deriving from the Hebrew *mecara* meaning "cave"[230]. Hesychius records the tradition of *megara* describing subterranean dwellings or pits[231]. Certainly, in classical Greek usage, a *megaron* meant the inner room within a temple[232], or the entire building: this being its exclusive significance in Herodotus[233]. Some of Demeter's temples actually retained *adyta* or *megara* in the form of subterranean rooms. Examples have been excavated in Priene[234] and in Cnidus[235]. In these

---

[226] See Dietrich, "Demeter, Erinys, Artemis", *Hermes* 90 (1962) 129–148.

[227] She hid in a cave after the rape of Persephone, Paus. 8,42,2.

[228] Paus. 8,37,8f.; Nilsson, *Gesch.*[3] I, 479; Burkert, *Gr. Rel.* 418.

[229] At Megara, Paus. 1,39,5; on Paros, Herod., 6,134; Delos, *Inscr. de Delos* 440 A, 41; and in the Piraeus, *IG* II, 1177, 6f. Of course the Megaron at Lycoscoura really belonged to Despoina, Demeter's daughter (Paus. 8,37,8; *cf.* Eur., *I. T.* 1462f.); just as the *heroon*, which succeeded the cave at the foot of the Brauronian acropolis, belonged to Iphigenia where she was associated with Artemis, Paus. 1,33,1. Cult at the site dates from Neolithic to the end of Mycenaean but no sign of historic cult survives there before about the middle of the eighth century B.C., Kahil, *Gr and It* 76f. *Megaron* – temples were not exclusive to Demeter but could for example belong to Aphrodite, Dionysus (Paus. 8,6,5) or the Couretes (Paus. 4,31,9).

[230] H. Lewy, *Die Semitischen Fremdwörter im Griechischen*, Berlin 1895, 94; H. Frisk, *Griechisches Etymologisches Wörterbuch*, Heidelberg 1970, 189.

[231] Hesych. μέγαρα· οἱ μὲν τὰς καταγείους οἰκήσεις καὶ βάραθρα.

[232] Frisk, *ibid.*

[233] H. Cary, *A Lexion to Herodotus*, Oxford 1843, *q. v.;* E. Powell, *A Lexicon to Herodotus*[2], Cambridge 1938, *q. v.*

[234] *Priene* 1904, 154f., cited by Nilsson, *Gesch.*[3] I, 463 n. 12.

[235] Newton, *Halicarnassus, Cnidus and the Branchidae*, II, 283, cited by Nilsson, *Griechische Feste von religiöser Bedeutung mit Ausschluss der Attischen*, Leipzig 1906, 320 n. 1.

cases, like the historic cave at Eleusis, the *megara* with their offerings and rites more explicitly continued the religious traditions which survived only symbolically at Lycosura, in the Eleusinian *anaktoron*, and indeed in the Late Bronze Age shrine at Mycenae. The same was true of some of Demeter's festivals such as the Thesmophoria in Attica, Potnia and in Cnidus. On those occasions real caves or substitutes were used in the celebrations[236]. Also ceremony and offerings quite manifestly expressed the celebrants' concern for the renewal of life[237]. In Demeter's recently excavated sanctuary in Cnidus, too, the prolonged cultic tradition, the terracotta bull figurines, as well as the cave within the *temenos*, tell their own story[238].

In sum, historical Greek linguistic and traditional, together with the archaeological evidence, indicate that even in the case of peculiarly Minoan sites, like caves and peaks, the cult content was shared with the people of the mainland. The Cypriot remains of Mycenaean temples brilliantly illustrate this community of Minoan/Mycenaean religious forms and substance.

Evidently the actual physical site did not greatly matter: it was not essential to the performance of the cult. This was true in Mycenaean Greece at the end of the Bronze Age, but also, and even earlier, in Crete judging from the "mixed" architecture, cult paraphernalia and offerings in so-called "domestic" and peak and cave sanctuaries. Accordingly the conclusion suggests itself that there was much common ground in Minoan and Mycenaean belief and cult practice. The archaeological data from Greek, Cretan and Cycladic shrines do not seriously contradict this view, although they certainly highlight some clearly defined local variations of divine names, architectural forms and the like.

In this shared religion furthermore there is little doubt that Crete represented the senior partner in the sense of having been the major contributor. Crete became fully integrated in the Greek world from the Geometric age but nevertheless conservatively preserved her

---

[236] The Athenian Thesmophorion was ἐπὶ, ὑψηλοῦ which was a common location for a cave, schol. Arist., *Thesmoph.* 585; *cf.* Hesych, ἄνοδος.

[237] B.C. Dietrich, "A Religious Function of the Megaron", *Rivista Storica dell' Antichità* 3 (1973) 5 ff.

[238] *AJA* 77 (1973) 413–24.

Minoan heritage[239]. In mainland Greece changes were more noticeable at the end of the Dark Age, but Bronze Age religious traditions survived in considerable strength too, lending their names and form to a number of Greek religious institutions. The continuity of a common Minoan/Mycenaean religion remained palpable in places like Kato Symi or at Ayia Irini on Keos, as did their painless transformation into archaic and classical Greek religion.

However, it seems clear now that religious ideas also survived, though less obviously, when removed from their old sites. A significant indication of the longevity of common religious concepts in the Cretan and Greek world appears from the fact that gods and cults could be moved to a new site, as at Delphi, or even from one country to the other. A case in point is the cult of Artemis Orthia in Sparta[240]. Often continuity of tradition was much older than the history of the actual cult site.

Numerous theories have been proposed to explain the cultural similarity of Crete and Greece during the Mycenaean age. No doubt there will be others. But whatever the historical reasons for this community may be, the fact of common religious observances at the time deserves recognition. It is worth remembering also that the names of gods and festivals on both Knossian and mainland documents had been written by Mycenaeans, or at the behest of Mycenaeans[241]. But there are still some old and a few new questions to be answered. One concerns the extent to which the substance of cult and cult figures survived into historical times even at a site which had perhaps seen uninterrupted worship through the break of the Dark Age. Another allied question is that of the origin and significance of divine names and functions as they appear in the classical pantheon in the light of the common Minoan/Mycenaean religious past.

Finally, if there did in fact exist an identifiable chronological phase of primarily Cretan inspired Minoan/Mycenaean religion in the western Aegean, it would be useful to know how this phase related to

---

[239] *Cf.* the recent study of A. Kanty, *The Late Minoan III Period in Crete. A Survey of Sites, Pottery and their Distribution (SIMA)*, Göteborg 1980, 326.

[240] On both Delphi and Artemis Orthia in Sparta see ch. II.

[241] S. Hiller – O. Panagl, *Die frühgriechischen Texte aus mykenischer Zeit*, Darmstadt 1976, 289.

earlier religious forms in the Neolithic period of Greece. No doubt the answer would add to our understanding of historical Greek religion and the problem of overall continuity. New excavations have produced examples of male figures, hybrids and the like which differ from the commonly drawn Minoan/Mycenaean picture of goddess, male *paredros* and the ubiquitous figure of the bull. Behind these finds lies the explanation of our last question which is now on the way to becoming one of the most fascinating problems in the history of Greek religion.

Tradition in the History of Greek Religion

Greek religion is a loose term which conceals some major *a priori* assumptions. It assumes that the Greeks of the archaic and later ages practised a religion which could be defined and localised on geographical, ethnic and indeed chronological lines. However, the classical Greeks did not live in isolation but borrowed ideas from all manner of sources near and far.

Ancient religions tended to be more tolerant of the beliefs of others than has been the case of the Christian Church. Settlers, traders, conquerors took over foreign gods and cult and made them their own. When Cyrus sacked Babylon in 539 B.C. he also adopted its gods. City gods performed important political functions which could prove useful to the newcomer or invader. His own similar system of guardian, apotropaeic figures of "state" cult ensured the ready integration of the divinities from other cultures with which he had been in contact. Extreme cases perhaps were Etruscan and Roman religions whose official cult in some respects could be said to have been extensions of Greek religion. The latter of course itself evolved as a consequence of several traditions of which the Aegean, European, and Minoan/Mycenaean constituted the three most significant elements.

Accordingly the period of Greek renaissance at the end of the ninth and in the eighth century B.C., following the obscure centuries of the so-called dark age, was one of renewed prosperity rather than of a new culture. Older traditions managed to survive in their original form, and quite commonly in a mixture in which the earlier elements had been combined to produce cult forms to suit the new age. The reasons for the Greek revival are complex and need not detain us in detail: they became manifest in a renewed sense of outward looking expansionism of the mainland communities. In consequence communication with the east was strengthened encouraging the import of oriental art and a new system of writing to replace the old Linear script which may have perished in the west centuries earlier[1].

---

[1] N. G. L. Hammond, *A History of Greece*², Oxford 1967, 93 ff.; A. M. Snodgrass,

Some new divine figures arrived in the same movement, and perhaps a few older ones returned as well, which had once been familiar in the Bronze Age. In Greece the growth of sanctuaries and temples during the period was startling. Within a hundred years, and before the end of the 8th century, the number had increased from barely ten to over seventy[2]. At the same time large stone temples replaced the earlier humble structures throughout the Greek world from Samos to Eretria and Perachora[3]. Certain deities and cult localities came into prominence assuming pan-Hellenic importance like Zeus and Hera at Olympia, and Apollo at Delphi and Delos[4]. The causes for this process of selection, from which arose the unified Olympian pantheon, were primarily due to the effect on tradition of political and literary forces. The dissemination of Homeric epic greatly determined men's attitudes to their gods and cult[5].

Cultural continuity across the dark age is difficult to prove but nevertheless likely despite social changes and new institutions in the early Archaic age. The members of the communities were the same after all and their religious beliefs would hardly have materially altered. What does remain uncertain is the extent and quality of transmission; was it direct or recovered from memory? Did it exclusively spring from the Minoan/Mycenaean world? The subject of continuity is contentious. The camp is divided between those relatively few who would deny any kind of survival from the past in classical Greek religion and those who see Greek culture as the result of a continual evolution. Most, who would like to believe in continuity, surrender in the face of the fragmentary archaeological evidence. It seems impossible to assess the history of survival and change from the second to the first millennium B.C. solely through the archaeological picture which rarely reflects social, political or religious events[6]. There are many sites of proven continuity of use

---

The Dark Age of Greece, Edinburgh 1971, 421; *Archaic Greece*, London 1980, 78f.; J. N. Coldstream, *Geometric Greece*, London 1977, 358.

[2] See Coldstream, *Geom. Gr.* 317 and fig. 101.

[3] Snodgrass, *D.A.* 408–12; 421; *A.G.* 58–60; Coldstream, *G.G.* 317ff.

[4] Snodgrass, *D.A.* 421; *A.G.* 56.

[5] *Cf.* Coldstream's summary of the main "manifestations" of Greek renaissance in the eighth century B.C., *G.G.* 367.

[6] For a bibliography of the discussion see F. Gschnitzer, "Vocabulaire et Institutions: La Continuité Historique du deuxième au premier millenaire", *Colloquium*

and settlement, particularly in areas which were more or less exempt from the disturbances at the end of the Bronze Age. And although religious worship often continued to occur in such places, on the evidence it is impossible to be sure of where, how, and for how long. Equally inadmissable as evidence should be sites like Olympia where the oldest area of cult, the Pelopion[7], albeit occupied in Mycenaean times, had not been preceded by a Bronze Age sanctuary[8]. This still leaves a respectable list of a) sanctuary areas with a break in the material remains for the dark age, but where cult probably continued unabated into historical times, and b) sites where continuity of cult can actually be archaeologically attested through the ages in Greece, the Aegean islands, in Crete and Cyprus. Examples of the first category are Eleusis, which appears to have enjoyed continuous worship despite the absence of material remains during the dark age[9], Aphaea's sanctuary in Aegina[10], the Samian Heraeum[11], Zeus' Dictaean Cave[12], and Spartan Amyclae[13].

The two cases of Hera's cult on Samos and the Spartan Amyclae are particularly interesting in that the archaeological evidence, or rather its absence, tells a false tale. Cult continuity in both places is assured through other sources, namely the continuing Bronze Age tradition of terracotta votives of the goddess and her bull on Samos[14],

---

Mycenaeum, Acts of 6th Intern. Coll. on Mycen./Aegean Texts, Chaumont sur Neuchatel (1975), Geneva 1979, 111 n. 2. To this should be added V. Desborough, *The Greek Dark Ages,* New York 1972, 278–287; Coldstream, *G.G.* ch. 13 & 14; W. Burkert, *Griechische Religion der archaischen und klassischen Epoche,* Stuttgart 1977, 88–98; E. Vermeule, *Götterkult,* Göttingen 1974, 73–76; J. Hooker, *Mycenaean Greece,* London 1977, 209–11; L. A. Stella, *Tradizione Micenea e Poesia dell'Iliade,* Urbino/Rome 1978, *passim;* L. Baumbach, "The Mycenaean Contribution to the Study of Greek Religion in the Bronze Age", *Studi Micenei ed Egeo-Anatolici, Fasc. 20, Incun. Graeca vol. 70,* Rome 1979, 143–160, with further modern literature.

[7] H. V. Herrmann in *AM* 77 (1962), 18 ff.
[8] Snodgrass, *D.A.* 397; Coldstream, *G.G.* 331.
[9] Coldstream, *G.G.* 331 f.; Dietrich, *Origins* 140 ff. For the view that the break in evidence also signalled a break in cult, Snodgrass, *D.A.* 395.
[10] Coldstream, *ibid.,* but see Snodgrass, *ibid.*
[11] Again contrast Coldstream, *G.G.* 333 with Snodgrass, *D.A.* 398.
[12] Coldstream, *ibid.* and Snodgrass, *D.A.* 401 are in agreement. The latter admits continuity in Crete but not on the mainland on archaeological grounds.
[13] Coldstream, *G.G.* 331, contrast Snodgrass, *D.A.* 395.
[14] Desborough, *G.D.A.* 280.

and the prehistoric figure of Apollo Hyacinthus at Amyclae[15]. The number of sites with unequivocal monumental evidence of unbroken cult is steadily growing in Greece, Crete and elsewhere in the Aegean. The most astonishing must be the temple at Ayia Irini on Keos which began in the Middle Bronze Age and witnessed worship until Hellenistic times[16]. But other examples are equally convincing, notably the precinct of Apollo Maleatas on Mt. Kynortion, near Epidaurus[17]. At Phocian Kalapodi, a few miles from the ancient Atalante, the presence of some 12 Mycenaean levels of LHIIIC (in the sacred precinct near the later Geometric and archaic cult area and sanctuaries) suggests possible cult activity before the end of the Bronze Age[18]. Outstanding examples of continuity on Crete are the "peak" sites at Gortyn, with its eight Subminoan sanctuaries and the ninth century temple[19], and at Kato Symi[20]. In Kition, on Cyprus, Temple IV preserved enough tangible evidence to prove its continuing usage from the thirteenth to the fourth century B.C.[21], while recent excavations at Palaipaphos have turned up the remains of a twelfth

---

[15] Desborough, *ibid.;* Coldstream, *ibid.;* Dietrich, "The Dorian Hyacinthia", *Kadmos* 14 (1975), 133–42.

[16] Desborough, *G.D.A.* 280F.; Snodgrass, *D.A.* 395; Dietrich, *Origins* 140, with references to archaeological reports; J. L. Caskey, "The Bronze Age Temple at Ayia Irini in Keos and its later History", in *Gr and It 209.*

[17] Beneath the Classical temple of Apollo the remains of an Archaic sanctuary have been found above those of Mycenaean buildings. Northeast of the temple an open-air altar came to light during the excavations of 1976 whose lower part is of Mycenaean date and the upper from the seventh century B.C., Mycenaean finds (EH & LH) include fragments of stone vases, seal stones, beads, bronze axes, spear heads, "phi" figurines and fragments of wheel-made animals. Evidently the site was inhabited until the seventh century, and might subsequently have been revived again under the tyrant Procles after a brief interval, *BCH* 102 (1978) 672; *JHS A.P.* for 1977/78, 28.

[18] R. C. S. Felsch and others, "Apollon and Artemis oder Artemis und Apollon? Kalapodi 1973–77", in *AA* (1980) 38–123. However, there appears to be a gap between IIIC and the 9th century B.C., p.47.

[19] *Cf.* another sacred area from LMIII onward on the eastern slope of the acropolis, G. Rizza – V. S. M. Scrinari, *Il Santuario sull' Acropoli di Gottina*, Rome 1968, II, 99–152.

[20] For the history of excavation by Dr. A. Lembessis see above ch. I n. 197

[21] *BCH* 98 (1974) 866f.; 99 (1975) 831; 102 (1978) 916, the report notes similarities with Enkomi and oriental models.

century Mycenaean sanctuary underneath Aphrodite's historical temple there[22].

These examples are drawn from a wide area and constitute solid arguments, as strong as material evidence can make them, for continuity of a sacred site. Physical survival, however, does not necessarily entail that the same cult endured as well. That would generally have to be proved by other means. Of course it is possible to overstate the case in both directions. On the one hand, architectural continuity as at Eleusis, the continued use of the same altar or altar site, and of the same cultic implements as at Gortyn, Symi and Mt. Kynortion, are powerful indicators of enduring religious beliefs. The same must obviously be true of the growing number of sanctuaries, or sacred precincts, like Symi and Ayia Irini on Keos, which may never have been entirely abandoned by worshippers from the Bronze Age to classical times and later. On the other hand, such examples are in the minority compared with sites which by all outward signs suffered a break in usage.

The contrast between the tenuous material resources at the end of the Bronze Age and the imposing structures of the 8th century suggest a gap between the two periods. Perhaps the new age created a revival of interest in the forgotten past. It did happen that under the influence of Homeric epic cults were instituted at rediscovered Mycenaean settlements and tombs in honour of the kings of a glorious Heroic Age. Obvious examples of this process appear to be the eighth century cults of Agamemnon near Mycenae and of Menelaus and Helen at Therapne[23]. Sometimes Mycenaean tombs were rediscovered during the Geometric age and honoured with a new cult. The tholos tomb at Menidi in Attica for example attracted hero cult at the time and worshippers placed their offerings in the *dromos* leaving the old main chamber undisturbed. Other examples of this practice have turned up at Marathon, Mycenae, near Corinth, amongst others including several examples in the west in Messenia[24]. Even the ruins of Bronze Age settlements attracted sanctuaries in historic times out of respect for the heroic past. Snodgrass cites the Geometric

---

[22] *BCH* 98 (1974) 874f.; 102 (1978) 922.

[23] J. M. Cook, *Geras A. Keramopoullou* (1953) 112–118; *BSA* 48 (1953) 30–68; T. H. Price, *Historia* 22 (1973) 129ff.; Coldstream, *JHS* 96 (1976) 8ff.

[24] Snodgrass, *D.A.* 192ff.; 397; Coldstream, *G.G.* 347 with further refs.

structures and massive votive deposit which had been associated with
an Early Helladic house outside Athens as an example[25]. There is no
doubt that several of these cults testify to a new interest in the past
and were responsible for much of Greek hero cult of the eighth
century[26].

However, this type of cult was far from unknown even before
Homeric epic returned to Greece. Occasionally there were links with
the dark age or earlier periods. The worship of Odysseus in the Polis
cave on Ithaca, or that of Academus in Athens, are probable instances
of enduring traditions. The material evidence provides a narrow view
of what was new or old in religious tradition. There is no hint for
example of cults which continued in the dark age but which were
moved to a new site, as happened at Delphi[27]. Sometimes a new
foundation of the Geometric age, without a trace of an earlier history,
nevertheless continued the substance of traditional cult. In the absence of literary sources proof is awkward. It is fortunate therefore
that a few cases did survive of links between the Greek mainland and
Cretan sites with a fully attested unbroken history of use from
prehistoric times. One such seems to be the remarkable likenesses
between the dedications and cult installations at Gortyn and the
sanctuary of Artemis Orthia whose archaeological history on the
Spartan site did not start before the tenth and possibly as late as the
eighth century B.C.[28]. The Gortynian altar on the east slope of the
acropolis had parallels with the seventh century altar of Artemis in
Sparta[29]. But far more important are the correspondences between
the votives in both places. The representations of the goddess in
Sparta are identical in nature to those of the Gortynian model, the
sole difference in both centres being due to the exigencies of local
manufacture[30]. Best known in Artemis' sanctuary are, of course, the
many grotesque and other masks. But all other types, which have

---

[25] Snodgrass, *D.A.* 398; 439 n.2 37 for references; *cf.* Desborough, *G.D.A.* 278.

[26] *Cf.* the inscription on a late Archaic sherd from Mycenae, του ἥρωος ἐμι, L. H.
Jeffery, *The Local Scripts of Archaic Greece*, Oxford 1961, *174 no.6, pl.31.*

[27] *BCH* 96 (1972) 899 ff.; Desborough, *G.D.A.* 279; Dietrich, *Origins* 224; Coldstream, *G.G.* 330.

[28] Desborough, *G.D.A.* 278; Snodgrass, *D.A.* (8th cent.). Site and finds are reported
by R. M. Dawkins, "The Sanctuary of Artemis Orthia", *JHS* Suppl. 5 (1929).

[29] Rizza-Scrinari, *Santuario* 148.

[30] Rizza-Scrinari, *Santuario* 250.

been observed in Gortyn, have also been found in the Spartan sanctuary, including the multiple figures, like the nude Aphrodite[31], and the many lead figurines of the armed "Athena"-type[32], as well as the mixture of human and animal, and male and female representations. These, like the masks, suggest other, non-Minoan sources of influence. More plainly visible survivals of Minoan/ Mycenaean practices, as elsewhere in Crete, Greece and on Samos[33], were provided by the continuing tradition of wheel-made votive terracottas of the goddess and her animals[34]. It follows that the Spartan cult brought together Minoan and older Neolithic forms, but it could hardly be described as a new institution in the true sense of the word, even though the actual cult buildings belonged to the age of the Greek renaissance.

The material evidence can not, however, define the nature of the goddess, distinguish between the possibly differing aspects of her worship in various religions, or trace the origins and development of her cultic tradition. The Gortynian goddess came to be known as Athena. By the middle of the seventh century the Athena figure had fully developed from the Minoan-style cylindrical statuette and is easily recognized in *e.g.* an expressive head with archaic features[35]. From this evolved her typical image of Athena Polias with shield and helmet[36]. Accordingly, name apart, her nature as City-goddess seems firmly grounded in the Minoan age. Artemis Orthia, on the other hand, despite the relatively recent cult at Sparta, presents a far more primitive aspect. It is precisely in this respect that the archaeological evidence proves unreliable. Very rarely do the material remains of a sanctuary identify the divinity who was worshipped there, at least before the eighth or seventh century. Again certain, or probable, continuity of votives, cult implements *etc.* on their own do not prove that the same deity remained "in residence" in the cult, nor does material continuity inevitably reflect an equivalent survival of cult

---

[31] *E.g.* Dawkins, "Art. Orthia" Pl. XXXVI, 1–7.

[32] Dawkins, *op.cit.* Pl. CXCVI, 2–16.

[33] See above n.14.

[34] Desborough, *G.D.A.* 282f.; Dietrich, *Origins* 210; 218; 221; Coldstream, *G.G.* 333.

[35] Rizza-Scrinari, *Santuario* 231, fig.308; Pl. XXI, No. 118.

[36] Many examples have been found on the eastern slope of the acropolis near the altar in its second phase (4th cent.), Rizza-Scrinari, *op.cit.,* Pl. XLIV–XLVI.

content. Geometric cult names, with a few exceptions like Aphaea in
Aegina, lacked unimpeachable ancestries in the Minoan and
Mycenaean world with its predominantly invocatory divine titles.
But even those which do can not as a rule be shown to have survived
in the same sanctuary in the dark age.

There is no proof of continuity of cult figure, as well as cult, at least
by archaeological means. It is possible to be fairly confident of the
long history of Zeus' cult in the Dictaean Cave, at least from the 11th
century B.C. The same does not, however, apply to Hermes and
Aphrodite at Symi, although the former may have been known at the
time in Pylos[37] and perhaps even at Knossos. Again Athena's name
appears to precede even the Bronze Age, and yet at Gortyn it has no
clear history prior to the 7th or 6th century[37a]. Did the community
goddess in Kition and Palaipaphos receive worship from the
Mycenaean settlers already? Was she known then as Aphrodite or
Wanassa? Change of divine name seems implied in Ayia Irini, on
Keos, where Minoan statues, or at least one of the heads, continued to
be revered in Geometric times, but under the name of Dionysus, to
judge from graffiti and a votive kantharos from 750 B.C.[38]. And yet
Dionysus' name was known in Pylos in the 13th century B.C. (Xa
102) and therefore perhaps also to the contemporaries of the early
statues at Ayia Irini. On Delos the Mycenaean cult site lay beneath
Artemis' archaic temple which had been carefully aligned with the
prehistoric sanctuary. But by this time, about 700 B.C., Apollo had
become the chief deity on the island[39]. Apollo certainly looks like a
later intruder. In Delphi his votives did not begin before 800 B.C. and
were divorced from the Mycenaean remains below the temple of
Athena Pronaia[40]. For once literary tradition appears to corroborate
the archaeological picture by recording Apollo's takeover of cult at
Delphi from Ge[41]. Apollo's name has not been read on the Linear B
tablets. Nevertheless the god was probably known to Mycenaean cult

---

[37] Tn 316.
[37a] See below p. 79.
[38] Keos K4365. Dietrich, *Origins* 226; Coldstream, *G. G.* 76; 330.
[39] Dietrich, *Origins* 223f.; Coldstream, *G.G.* 215.
[40] Coldstream, *G.G.* 178. On Apollo at Delphi see Dietrich, *Origins,* Append. II;
      BICS 25 (1978) 1–18.
[41] Aesch., *Eum.* 1ff.

in the Bronze Age at Amyclae near Sparta and in Cyprus[42]. Clearly change in cult, or conversely continuity of tradition, have to be established by other means.

Some sort of continuity seems unavoidable with the survival of the Greek language which was a precondition for the transmission of past ideas, although perhaps not a decisive feature on its own[43]. But continuing language, clan and community groups constituted the basis of the survival of older traditions through the dark age[44]. The latter, at least in nucleus, must have been founded on a kinship system with a central community deity in prehistoric times[45]. The religious vocabulary in Linear B leaves no doubt of enduring tradition. The tablets treat some Olympian names as common currency in Mycenaean times, and even reveal family relationships between them. In Pylos for example Drimios received offerings as son of Zeus[46]. To what extent the same names centuries later described identical gods with identical functions is of course another matter which cannot be resolved on linguistic grounds. More significant for this reason are the general Greek terms for god, all the gods, Divine Mother and the like which already appeared on the Mycenaean tablets[47].

The continued use of technical vocabulary signals the survival of the same institution[48]. For example, *temenos*, both in Linear B and in Homer, was a technical term for a piece of land over which the king, amongst other nobles, had juridical control. The word accordingly described a social institution which must have begun in the Bronze

---

[42] The evidence has been discussed in *Kadmos* 14 (1975) 133–42, and in "Some Evidence from Cyprus of Apolline Cult in the Bronze Age", *RM* 121 (1978) 1–18.

[43] A. Morpurgo Davies, "Terminology of Power and Terminology of Work in Greek and Linear B", *Colloquium Mycenaeum*, Geneva 1979, 104; Gschnitzer, *Coll. Mycen.*, Geneva 1979, 112.

[44] On community groups in the dark age see Dietrich, *Origins* 242–66.

[45] *Ibid.*

[46] PY Tn 319; *dirimijo diwo ijewe*, S. Hiller–O. Panagl, *Die frühgriechischen Texte aus mykenischer Zeit*, Darmstadt 1976, 296.

[47] *teo, pasi teoi, matere teja*, Hiller–Panagl, *Texte* 292.

[48] Gschnitzer, *Coll. Mycen.*, Geneva 1979, 114. The paper by Morpurgo Davies, *Coll. Mycen.*, Geneva 1979, 87–108, despite its greater emphasis on the areas of cultural disruption in essence concurs with Gschnitzer's views on religious continuity, 105 n.65. Professor Morpurgo Davies underlines the numerous lexical losses between the Mycenaean and historical Greek, while nevertheless conceding a limited continuity in those areas where organisational and technical terms survived in use.

Age[49]. There are other lexical survivals concerning objects of use, crafts, craft names like oil, spices, the making of arms, chariots, and particulary the working of metals: silver, gold, lead and bronze. These terms continued through the ages and effectively guaranteed an enduring tradition. Similar links in political, juridical and other social terminology make it difficult to explain such coincidences as borrowings from the past by a new society[50]. The same continuity of tradition applied in the still more conservative sphere of religion. It is quite astonishing that much of the religious terminology of later times had already been fixed in Linear B. There are familiar terms such as *hagnos, hieros, hiereus,* or evidence of blood and animal sacrifice which were practised in Minoan/Mycenaean times[51]. The evidence from Pylos alone suggests that the sacrificial ritual remained essentially the same from Mycenaean times. Cultic officials also kept the same names, as did religious institutions, months and festivals in a number of cases. Months on Knossian tablets, and in Pylos on the mainland, were called after the same adjectival principle as in historic Greece. There was, for example, a month of the festival of Zeus[52], or the month of the festival of Pakijane[53], and the like[54]. In fact the month of Dios (Zeus), which occurred on a Knossian tablet[55], was paralleled in historic times in Aetolia, Thessaly and Macedonia. The more unusual month of Lapatos, also cited in Knossos[56], survived in Arcadian Orchomenos[57]. The principle of naming the months of the calendar after the major gods and their festivals was at least as old as the Mycenaeans. The tradition remained in historical times, despite the almost countless local variations[58].

Unfortunately the linguistic evidence is inadequate to identify

---

[49] Gschnitzer, *Coll. Mycen.,* Geneva 1979, 112.
[50] Gschnitzer, *op.cit.* 121. Morpurgo Davies also poses the question, but leaves it open, *op.cit.* 105.
[51] Stella, *Trad. Micenea,* 79f.; Gschnitzer, *Coll. Mycen.* 115f.
[52] KN Fp5: *diwijojo meno.*
[53] *pakijanijojo meno* PY Fr 1224.
[54] *karaerijo meno, deukijojo meno, amakato meno, etc.,* see Hiller–Panagl, *Texte* 313; Gschnitzer, *Coll. Mycen.* 116.
[55] KN Fp 5.
[56] KN Fp 13, *rapato meno.*
[57] E. Schwyzer, *Dial.* 667; A. E. Samuel, *Greek and Roman Chronology,* 1972, 64f.
[58] Burkert, *Gr. Rel.* 343–46.

beyond reasonable doubt particular festivals which continued in later times[59]. However, the distribution of a number of major Greek festivals suggests their great antiquity. This seems to be especially true in the case of the festivals of Artemis, Demeter, Poseidon and Apollo. Artemis and Apollo were the only Olympians with special days on all Greek calendars[60] which means that both transcended the narrow boundaries of localised and tribal-oriented cult[61]. The Artemisia for example was common to Dorians, Ionians, north-west Greeks and Macedonians[62]. The Thesmophoria enjoyed an equally wide distribution among Dorians, Ionians, Arcadians, Aeolians and north-west Greeks[63]. Such common festivals, which also include the Apaturia, Anthesteria, Thargelia, Boedromia, Metageitnia and Apellai, must therefore have been instituted at least before the migrations at the end of the Bronze Age[64]. Some, like the Boedromia, Artemisia and Metageitnia, may have begun in the Mycenaean age, that is in the thirteenth or twelfth centuries B.C.[65]. Others, together with their gods, most probably were much older than that. This is particularly true of Poseidon and his Poseidea and Demeter and her festivals like the Thesmophoria. None of the festivals, however, could have been newly founded in Geometric times either through nostalgic memory or fresh religious impulse.

---

[59] M. Gérard-Rousseau, *Les Mentions Religieuses dans les Tablettes Mycéniennes*, Rome 1968, *ad loc.*; J. K. Promponas, *The Athenian Festival Thronoelkteria and its Survival into Historical Times*, Athens 1974 (Greek); Hiller–Panagl, *Texte* 312; Burkert, *Gr. Rel.* 87.

[60] The sixth and seventh respectively, *cf.* Hesiod, *W and D* 770f. (Apollo's birthday). W. Schmidt, *Geburtstag im Altertum*, R.V.V.7, Giessen 1908, 88ff.; M. P. Nilsson, *Die Entstehung und Bedeutung des griechischen Kalenders²*, Lund 1962, 38f.; J. D. Mikalson, *The Sacred and Civil Calendar of the Athenian Year*, Princeton 1975, 18f.

[61] *Cf. BICS* 25 (1978) 1–18.

[62] For this and the following examples see J. Sarkady, "Die Jonischen Feste und die Jonische Urgeschichte", *Acta Classica Debrecen* 1 (1965) 11–20; "Heortologische Bemerkungen zur Dorischen Urgeschichte", *A.C.D.* 5 (1969) 7–19; *cf.* 8 (1972) 3–9.

[63] Herodotus' remark, 2, 171, that the Thesmophoria came to an end with the arrival in Greece of the Dorians, should be seen in the context of his notice in 9, 97, that the first Ionian settlers took Demeter's worship with them to Miletus. In other words, the migrations at the end of the Bronze Age extended an old cult eastward from the mainland of Greece.

[64] *Cf.* Burkert, *Gr. Rel.* 346.

[65] *A.C.D.* 1 (1965) 16.

Their antiquity remains manifest in the enduring tradition of name and associated divinity. Sometimes, however, tradition is obscured by physical alteration of a sanctuary's lay-out. New forms could signify fundamental changes in cult, god or even the conception of the god's presence in the place. But the material evidence on its own is never decisive. The archaic temple for example appeared to break with Mycenaean tradition[66]. It was divorced from any dwelling and therefore no longer part of a 'private', 'domestic' cult within a royal palace. More recently free-standing, separate temples have been identified in the Minoan and Mycenaean world, so that historians have been compelled to move away from the narrow definition of domestic cult in the Bronze Age. It still remains to be established whether the concept of the temple as the home of the god or his image was new in the archaic age or had also been foreshadowed in Mycenaean times. The signs point to the latter of the two and cast doubt on Drerup's widely accepted history of the classical Greek temple. His view had the added merit of explaining the paradox of a new temple whose architectural form nevertheless derived from prehistoric models. The Greek temple, according to Drerup[67], evolved from the Mycenaean *megaron,* that is the actual dwelling and dining quarters where meals were taken and where sacrifice occurred about a central hearth/altar[68]. This 'Versammlungstempel', a kind of concerted Mycenaean dwelling place, was distinct, however, from the home of the deity. The sequence of events in the dark age is said to have progressed in three stages. During the early post-migration centuries divine worship was practised in caves or trees, or in the ruins of Mycenaean buildings. From the 10th century altars were added to such natural sites together with 'Brandopfer', and the area was then enclosed within a *temenos.* Finally, and beginning, with the eighth century, the Greeks fashioned statues and built 'houses' for them. Thus there was nothing traditional in this last step[69], since such

---

[66] "Das griechische Normalheiligtum", Burkert, *Gr. Rel.* 94. But see ch. I p. 23 and n. 145.

[67] H. Drerup, "Griechische Architektur zur Zeit Homers", *AA* (1964) 180–219; *Griechische Baukunst in geometrischer Zeit, (Arch. Hom.),* Göttingen 1969.

[68] G. Gruben, *Die Tempel der Griechen*³, Munich 1980, 30; *cf.* Snodgrass, *D.A.* 408.

[69] Gruben, *op.cit.* 28.

divine houses were inevitably preceded by open-air cult areas and ash-altars like that in the Altis at Olympia[70].

However, some temples do not conform to Drerup's model. The earliest Samian Heraion, for example, with its elongated shape and central line of columns would have been awkward for social gatherings and communal meals[71]. These were held in specially constructed *oikoi* or *hestiatoria*. The first such building in the Delian sanctuary was Geometric or earlier[71a]. Architecturally they were hard to tell apart from temples, but they differed in function. Most temples were not equipped to deal with meals inside the *cella*. Only a few, like the Apollonion in Neandria or in Cretan Dreros, had an internal altar for sacrifice and feasting and with facilities for washing out after the ceremonial banquet[71b]. It seems that Drerup underestimated the complexity of tradition and sophistication of pre-archaic temple building. Separate shrines are known to have been in use in the Bronze Age in Myrtos, at Mycenae, Tiryns, at Phylakopi, on Melos, Ayia Irini on Keos, in Delos (Temple), amongst others[72]. Other elements of Geometric cult were equally popular then already. There is evidence of sacred areas in the open from many places, some of which continued in the dark age, such as Ayia Triada in Crete and

---

[70] Coldstream, *G.G.* 321.

[71] Snodgrass, *Archaic Greece*, 61 f. The second temple (7th century) dispensed with this internal colonnade altogether. But a double colonnade returned to Rhoikos' (6th century) and later temples, Gruben, *Tempel*, 326–40; H. Gallet de Santerre in *BCH* 108 (1984) 678.

[71a] On the Delian Pre-Oikos see *BCH* (1984) 676 n.37.

[71b] G. Roux, *Études déliennes* 542; Gallet de Santerre in *BCH* (1984) 688.

[72] P. Warren, *Myrtos*, Oxford 1972, 81 ff. Nine other Cretan temples, from Early to Late Minoan, are discussed by S. Hood in "Minoan Town Shrines?", *Greece and the Eastern Mediterranean in Ancient History and Prehistory* (Studies F. Schachermeyr 1977), 158–172; J.C. van Leuven, "The mainland tradition of sanctuaries in prehistoric Greece", *World Archaeology* 10 (1978) 139–148; B. Rutkowski, "Religious Architecture in Cyprus and Crete in the Late Bronze Age", *Cyprus and Crete* 224; *Sanctuaries and Cults in The Aegean Bronze Age*, 17, fig. 2, no. 54; 20; 23, fig. 7; 24, no. 54; 25, fig. 8; BCH 103 (1979) 601 (chronological periods at Ayia Irini, Keos); W. Taylour, *Antiquity* 43 (1969) 91 ff.; 44 (1970) 270 ff.; *AJA* 75 (1971) 266 ff.; *Ergon* from 1970; *JHS Arch. Rep.* 1968–1973 (Mycenae); *AR* 1975/76, 25 f.; 1977/78, 52–54; C. Renfrew, *Antiquity* 52 (1978) 7–15; *Mycenaean Seminar, Classical Institute, Proceedings*, March 1979 (Phylakopi); *AR* 1977/78, 26 f.; 1978/79, 16; *BCH* 101 (1977) 548; 102 (1978) 666–668; 103 (1979) 559 (Tiryns).

Ayia Irini on Cyprus[73]. Other sites in the same category have come to light at Kato Symi, on Mt. Jouktas, both in Crete, and on the mainland, notably on Mt. Kynortion near Epidaurus[74]. In conservative Cyprus the tradition of open-air sanctuaries, whose form was subject to eastern and Aegean influence, endured strongly from the Bronze Age to archaic times[74a]. Often the sacred precinct also had an altar on which offerings were burnt in good Greek fashion[75]. It is another question, of course, whether all these elements had already been combined in the same sort of cult in the Bronze Age. There were stylistic differences in the Bronze Age sanctuary which may have been reflected in the cult. The most obvious of these consists in the multiple, more agglutinative, type of the former contrasting with the free-standing single cult structure of the historic Greek temple[76]. The Minoan/Mycenaean 'temple' was less manifestly the home of one deity or its image. Quite generally more than one idol or statue was dedicated in the sacred chamber on ledges, shelves or niches[77]. It nevertheless remains possible, indeed probable, that these constituted minor, not to say cosmetic, differences in an ongoing tradition.

One tablet from Pylos[78] refers to temple bronze[79], using the standard Greek word for 'temple' *(naos)*[80]. *Naos* in the Bronze Age

---

[73] Desborough, *G.D.A.* 281.

[74] *BCH* 102 (1978) 754; *AR* 1977/78, 64; *PdP* 181 (1978) 302 (Symi); *BCH* (1978) 758 (Jouktas peak); 672 (Mt. Kynortion).

[74a] For a discussion of these sanctuaries with reference to Kourion see ch. IV, 126–142.

[75] Since the first discovery of a "Brandaltar" at Mycenae, *Ergon* (1972) 60ff.; *AR* 1972/72, 13f.; *cf. AR* 1973/74, 9, others have turned up in Symi, on Jouktas, in Dreros, see previous note, and as far afield as Kition in Cyprus (IIIB, oval altar in Temenos A, *BCH* 97 (1973) 651. *Cf.* the burnt sacrifice in a tomb at Argos, *BCH* 102 (1978) 664.

[76] Gruben, *Tempel* 27.

[77] *Cf.* Burkert, *Gr. Rel.* 94.

[78] PY Jn 829.

[79] *Kako nawijo.*

[80] The discussion of *nawijo* = "ship" *versus* "temple" in J. Chadwick – L. Baumbach, "The Mycenaean Greek Vocabulary", *Glotta* 41 (1963) 223, with references, has now been ended in favour of the latter meaning, L. R. Palmer, *The Interpretation of Mycenaean Greek Texts,* Oxford 1963, 284; *Mycenaeans and Minoans²*, London 1965, 110; J. Chadwick, *Documents in Mycenaean Greek²*, Cambridge 1973, 513; S. Hiller, "Kako Nawijo", *Colloqu. Mycen.* Geneva 1979, 192; 194; A. Leukart,

text, and in later Greek, is best read as meaning home, dwelling, in which case the Macenaeans were no strangers to the concept of the deity residing in a specially built home. The legend *chalkinaos* on the tablet recalls the Spartan temple of Athena Chalkioikos, or Chalkinaos according to a Hesychian gloss[81]. It seems that the Spartan temple of Athena followed in the same tradition as the Pylian *chalkinaos*, both being regarded as the divinity's home[82]. Interestingly enough, *oikos/woikos* was also used by Mycenaeans with this significance, to judge from a recently discovered Theban tablet with the legend of *potnias woikonde*[83], that is, "to the temple/house of Potnia"[84]. Naturally, none of this evidence can be considered as conclusive, but it manages to cast doubt on present day dogma regarding the origins of the House of the God in classical times.

The last word has not yet been written on the beginnings of the Greek temple. It is a complex story in which, one suspects, the division between secular and sacred use of the community god's "dwelling" had not always been closely observed. This ambiguity probably existed in the case of the Mycenaean palace already which was given over to both kinds of function. The Throne Room, or Megaron, too, with its central hearth for cooking as well as for burnt sacrifice, was involved in the worship of the palace deity[85]. In fact communal banquets and symposia remained an important element in many Greek panegyreis and cults, including amongst others the Carian Komyria and Heraia[86], the festivals of Poseidon on Tenos and Mykonos[87], and those of Athena Itonia at Arkesin and Minoa on

---

"Autour de Ka-ko- Na-wi-jo", *Coll. Mycen.*, 1979, 185; and additional note on previous paper by Hiller, p. 194.

[81] Paus. 3,17,2f.; Hiller, *Mycen. Coll.*, 1979, 192, and further references to modern discussions in n.31.

[82] See Leukart's note to Hiller's paper, above n.80, p. 194.

[83] *potinija wokode*, TH Of 36.

[84] Leukart, *op.cit.* 185; 194, who also cites Chadwick, *TT* II, 89.

[85] It has been argued that the palace at Ano Englianos was primarily a sanctuary for the "Pylian deities and their priesthood", Gösta Säflund, "Sacrificial Banquets in the "Palace of Nestor"". *OpAth* 13 (1980) 244f.

[86] With feasts for men and women respectively, M.P. Nilsson, *Griechische Feste mit Ausschluß der Attischen,* Leipzig 1906, 28f.

[87] *Ibid.* 81f.

Amorgos[88]. Such "Festschmäuse", or drinking bouts, generally signalled the culmination of a ritual which began with a sacred procession and sacrifice to the god. There are clear indications of symposia in Geometric Greece[89]. In fact *pompe* and ritual banquet were familiar features of Minoan/Mycenaean cult judging from contemporary frescoes. Also the many *kylikes* which have been found in Knossos and in Mycenaean cult buildings of Aphaea, on Aegina, at Ayia Irini, on Keos, and in the Citadel House in Mycenae had once been used for this purpose. Room 19 (west of the Megaron) in Nestor's palace at Pylos has yielded the remains of almost 3000 drinking cups. Together with the finds of many other cooking utensils from the same palace the evidence suggests that cultic banquets and drinking bouts were celebrated in Pylos, in LHIIIB, and possibly earlier in Knossos, and elsewhere[90]. Accordingly the preparation and consumption of food in divine ritual, the confusion of secular and sacred usage of a divine sanctuary, were not features which evolved in post Bronze Age Greece. They began much earlier and perhaps as early as Minoan/Mycenaean times.

Some basic concepts of Greek religion evidently bridged the gulf of the dark age. But it is unlikely that the Minoans and Mycenaeans were responsible for all aspects of traditional beliefs. Greek religion was far too complex for that and indeed older than the Late Bronze Age. What is remarkable about Minoan and Mycenaean culture, however, is the homogeneity of the religion, the impression of one generally compatible system that in some respects interposed itself between the preceding ages and the archaic/classical Greek worlds. If this view is correct, then some religious traditions may have directly continued from Minoan/Mycenaean times, while others descended from even earlier practices in Neolithic Greece. Particular features of the latter might well have survived unofficially during the Bronze Age, or lain dormant. Minoan and Mycenaean culture ignored rustic

---

[88] *Ibid.* 89f. see also *OpAth* (1980) 244, and K. Kerenyi, *Antike Religion,* Munich and Vienna 1971, 43–67.

[89] Discussed by O. Murray in a paper, "The Symposium as Social Organisation" (2nd Intern. Symposium at the Swedish Institute in Athens, 1–5 June 1981, *The Greek Renaissance of the Eighth Century B.C.; Tradition and Innovation)* Stockholm 1983, 195–9.

[90] *OpAth* (1980) 238; 244; 245f.

Neolithic practices rather like the Homeric poets who scorned the cults of Dionysus and Demeter. In any event, the reemergence of older traditions in the Geometric age disturbed the picture of direct transmission of religious beliefs from the Bronze Age suggesting the arrival of novel ideas which clashed with what had immediately gone before. This is not to say that the Minoan/Mycenaean world was entirely self-contained and uniform excluding older or foreign ideas. Far from it. The Mycenaeans most probably used, adapted, and continued traditions then, too, although the return of these to public worship in the Iron Age threw them into greater prominence and contrast with the immediate past.

Some Mycenaean religious institutions, gods and festivals, had the ring of old established tradition even then. For example the Mycenaean Megaron A in Apollo's sanctuary at Thermon provided alignment and style for the 10th or 9th century B.C. Megaron B, and ultimately fathered the Doric and Ionic temple[91]. Megaron A belonged to the category of typically Mycenaean long rectangular structures, and yet its builders had given the temple curved sides, thereby consciously imitating older Helladic forms[92]. There is a mixture of architectural styles, the Mycenaean adapting older forms which were fully taken up by the later Greeks once more. There is no way of deciding whether such tenacious architectural tradition reflects on other cultural factors. A clearer impression of pre-Mycenaean traditions in Greek thought can, however, be had from some festivals, cult localities and cult practices which, though also present in Mycenaean religion, seemed alien to it. The Thesmophoria has already been mentioned as an ancient common festival from pre-migration times[93]. Some of its features offer grounds for suspecting even pre-Mycenaean origins. The Thesmophoria was an exclusive women's festival and concerned with fertility. The rites included offerings of piglets and replicas of phalli which were cast into subterranean caverns, or *megara*, to be retrieved after they had decayed, in order to be consecrated and ultimately mixed with the seed corn to give strength to the soil and ensure the "rebirth" of the

---

[91] Coldstream, *G.G.* 324.
[92] Gruben, *Tempel* 27; 33 and Fig. 25.
[93] See above p. 38, and Nilsson, *Griech. Feste* 313ff.; L. Deubner, *Griechische Feste*, repr. Berlin 1956, 50ff.; H. W. Parker, *Festivals of the Athenians*, London 1977, 82.

new corn. The various features of the historic Thesmophoria festival presented a mixture of Mycenaean and earlier elements with the emphasis on the values and practices of the Stone Age[94].

A similar case could be made out for other festivals, particularly those in honour of Poseidon and Artemis. The Artemisia, too, and the Poseidea, were not narrowly tribal or localised festivals but common mainly to the Ionians in Attica and the Arcadian communities. Since, with the development of the Argolid during the Mycenaean age, Arcadia became isolated, or at any rate did not maintain its close communication with the Attic Ionians, the formation of these festivals belonged to an earlier age. Their importance declined in Mycenaean times, because they are not mentioned on the tablets from centres like Knossos and Pylos. There is another point of some significance in this context. The festivals had no connection with Athens, nor surprisingly did they concern the goddess Athena, or even involve the most important Athenian heroes like Theseus or Erechtheus. Such curious omissions from Ionic celebrations explain themselves, if one assumes the festivals to have come into being prior to the rise into importance of Athens as a Mycenaean centre. This "urban" development had the effect of pushing them into the background, until, after the collapse of the Mycenaean world, certain aspects of the cult of Artemis, Poseidon and Demeter reemerged into the foreground of Greek affairs[95]. Athena's position in Classical Athens, and her festivals therefore, appear to reflect Mycenaean tradition in the main[96]. Historically this point is most interesting, because like Poseidon, Demeter, and Artemis, Athena outside Athens was probably older than the Mycenaean pantheon.

---

[94] E. Simon, *Die Götter der Griechen*², Munich 1980, 92; Burkert, *Gr. Rel.* 38; 365–70. On the probable significance of the "caves" in this and related festivals, like the Skira, see Dietrich, "A Religious Function of the Megaron", in *Rivista* 1–12. On the caves in Minoan/Mycenaean cult see Dietrich, *Origins* 109f.

[95] Sarkady, *A.C.D.* (1965) 16f.

[96] This partly appears from the peculiarities of the Ionic-Attic calendar which, unlike that of other Greek states, formed the names of its months from the genitive plural of its festivals. And these were of the kind attested in Linear B, -on from -a endings, E. Schwyzer, *Griech. Grammatik,* Munich 1939, 488; Hiller – Panagl, *Texte* 312; Burkert, *Gr. Rel.* 87; 376. Unfortunately the calendar turns out to be an unreliable guide to the age of the festivals, *e. g.* Poseidea – Posideon, on the eighth day of the month, Deubner, *Feste* 214f.; Mikalson, *Athen. Calendar* 89.

The Hyacinthia was one of three known exclusively Dorian festivals[97]; and yet the name Hyacinthus, like that of Athena, was non-Greek and pre-Mycenaean[98]. The name of the cult locality, too, was non-Greek. Laconian Amyclae could have been a Cypriot word[99], or rather it was oriental in origin[100]. The actual rites were typical for a god of vegetation, however, and therefore familiar to the Minoans and Mycenaeans, even though aspects of the cult could well have been much older[101]. Thus already before Apollo's take-over, which probably fell within the Bronze Age, the festival contained a complex variety of elements from the east, from Minoan/Mycenaean cult, and ultimately perhaps from Neolithic tradition. The Dorian connection of the Hyacinthia[102] should also have antedated the Mycenaean age[103].

The evidence of temples and festivals shows how the Mycenaeans partly identified with earlier traditions and handed them on to their descendants, and partly formed a separate cultural unit between historical and Neolithic Greek tradition. Greek myths, as Nilsson has shown[104], were tied to Mycenaean centres. But these were almost invariably sited in Neolithic settlements so that, as Burkert suggests, some myths may in fact be as old as the inhabitants of the earliest settlements[105].

Apart from inter-state sanctuaries, like the Panionion at Mycale, or pan-Hellenic religious centres in Delphi, Olympia and Dodona in Epirus, the majority of archaic Greek temples stood on the acropolis of the new city-state. This was so in Athens, Corinth, Sparta, Miletus, Smyrna and similar examples. Other politically united communities in central and western Greece placed their sanctuaries within a central district, or town, as at Thebes and Arcadian Tegea[106]. Curiously

---

[97] The other two are the Geraistia and Karneia.
[98] On the name see L. Deroy, "La Valeur du Suffixe Préhellénique -nth- d'après quelques Noms Grecs en -nthos", *Glotta* 35 (1956) 185 ff. References to further discussions in *Kadmos* 14 (1975) 135; Burkert, *Gr. Rel.* 47 n. 27.
[99] *Glotta* (1956) 185. *Cf.* ch. IV, p. 161.
[100] Burkert, *Grazer Beiträge* 4 (1975) 70 f.; Dietrich, *RM* 121 (1978) 7.
[101] *Kadmos* (1975) 133–42; Burkert, *Gr. Rel.* 47.
[102] For the Hyakinthides see *Kadmos, ibid.*
[103] *Cf. A.C.D.* (1969) 13.
[104] M. P. Nilsson, *The Mycenaean Origin of Greek Mythology*, Berkeley 1932, 35–186.
[105] *Gr. Rel.* 41.
[106] Snodgrass, *Arch. Gr.* 55.

though a few early sanctuaries had been constructed outside towns. Hera's temples were some of the oldest in the Greek world, and in Argos, Olympia and on Samos, they had been erected on the sites of Neolithic and Early Helladic settlements[107]. Apparently in such cases a strong religous tradition managed to stay alive resisting geographical change through the ages, and indeed successfully defying the centralising movement of archaic synoecism. The extreme conservatism may not have extended to the substance of the cult which was bound to alter and develop. On Samos, for instance, we know from the surviving votives that Mycenaean practices had left their mark, so that here and elsewhere in similar sanctuaries a certain amount of syncretism must have occurred. It is worth noting, however, that many of these "outside" shrines belonged to areas which were relatively remote from Mycenaean urban areas. For example Apollo's archaic seats of worship in Thermon, on Mt. Ptoon, on Delos and at Phanae were mostly "outside" major settlements. His most famous site at Delphi also falls into this category. The same applies to Artemis' cults at Lousoi and Mavriki in Arcadia, even at Sparta, Aulis, Pherae and Brauron[108]. Conversely Athena's sanctuaries tended to be within the city and generally on its acropolis, from Athens to Sparta, Gortyn, Lindos, Emporio, and Miletus in the east. Accordingly her nature as City-goddess in the archaic age of Greece predominantly reflected that of a Mycenaean guardian and community goddess.

Much of archaic religion then presented a mixture of Mycenaean and older traditions which, though partly accepted within the Mycenaean system, in the main continued in outlying areas where

---

[107] C. W. Blegen, *Prosymna. The Helladic Settlement preceding the Argive Heraeum*, 1937; J. Milojčič, *Samos I: die prähistorische Siedlung unter dem Heraion*, 1961, 27–30; 68; Burkert, *Gr. Rel.* 41; Coldstream, *G.G.* 328.

[108] The geographical location of such archaic sanctuaries outside Mycenaean towns does not, of course, exclude the possibility, indeed strong probability, of Mycenaean cults having been practised there. This applies to Apollo's cult near Sparta, in Thermon, and on Mt. Kynortion, for example, Dietrich, *Origins* 222, and equally to Hera's cult on Samos, *ibid.* 225. These areas were peripheral to the urban sphere of Mycenaean influence, and the population also continued to recognize and honour older religious practice. The cult place of Apollo Maleatas, for instance, had been sacred from Early Helladic times, *Praktika* 1948–1951, *cf. Origins* 222.

pre-Mycenaean community groups, or clans, more successfully managed to preserve aspects of such ancient practices during the Mycenaean era. There has been much debate about the origins of the Greek *phyle*-system. There is no evidence of it in Mycenaean documents and most tribal names appear to be confined to the Dorians and Ionians. Hence *phyle, phratry, genos* divisions, though a dominant factor in historical Greek politics, are generally held to have begun during the dark age[109]. Nevertheless common cults and festivals, like those discussed earlier on, which transgressed dialectal and tribal boundaries, may have come in peripheral territories within the Mycenaean system and ultimately reappeared during and after the dark age[110].

The precise composition and names of such early prehistoric communities are quite uncertain. However, Neolithic traditions showed up in common every-day Greek cult practices. It was no accident that sacrificial victims were chosen from those animals which had first been domesticated in the west in Neolithic times, namely cattle, sheep and pigs[111]. All of these may have been at home in some areas, like northern Crete, as early as 6000 B. C.[112] Thus the piglets, which were thrown into the underground caves in Thesmophoria, fitted in with Neolithic custom, as indeed did the phalli. Both kinds of offering, however, were quite uncharacteristic of Minoan/ Mycenaean cult which accordingly appeared out of step with the rest of the Mediterranean and Europe in the fifth pre-Christian millennium[113]. Pigs and phalli were used once more in historic Greek cult, as were masks and other features of special cultic significance. These included the curious bisexual figures which were prominent in many

---

[109] Most recently, Snodgrass, *Arch. Greece* 25–27. See also Dietrich, *Origins* 245 ff. for possible traces of a related community structure in the Mycenaean system.

[110] Against this must be set Snodgrass' observation, *ibid.*, that the tribes survived only in the *polis* and not the *ethnos*. Naturally it would be impossible to make out a case for the survival of the actual terminology of *phyle, genos, etc.* On the possibility of the pre-Mycenaean existence of tribal groups and common cults see J. Sarkady, "Outlines of the Development of Greek Society. In the Period between the 12th and 8th Centuries B.C.", *Acta Antiqua and Scientiarum Hungaricae* 23 (1975) 118 f.

[111] P. Phillips, *The Prehistory of Europe*, London 1980, 149.

[112] D. H. Trump, *The Prehistory of the Mediterranean*, London 1980, 39.

[113] Phillips, *Preh. of Eur.* 169; Trump, *Preh. of the Med.* 75.

parts of the Mediterranean world in the Stone Age and which also played a role in historic Greek myth and religious life.

Animal and human masks, phallus, or ithyphallic figurines, were practically universal throughout Neolithic times from Mesopotamia, the Zagros Mountains, Iran, Guran in western Asia[114], to Cyprus[115], Yugoslavia[116], along the Danube[117], in Greece in Thessaly[118], Sesklo[119], Corinth[120], Tiryns[121], and elsewhere. Both mask and phallus belonged to basic chthonic cults of fertility in which the generative powers of Nature were invoked and celebrated. Both also possessed protective and apotropaeic powers: the mask as a type of Gorgoneion, and the phallus as a territorial stone of demarcation which was intended to frighten off intruders[122]. In Neolithic times phalli were also frequently placed in tombs. Examples from the sixth millennium B.C. have turned up at Guran, in western Asia, and in Mesopotamia[123]. Quite often in Phrygia and Smyrna phalli were placed above graves as stones, or stone markers. This custom was not confined to the east[124], but had been at home everywhere in the Mediterranean including Greece in pre-Mycenaean times, so that there can be no question of the Greeks in this case having imported foreign habits from Asia Minor, Mesopotamia or Egypt[125]. Such gifts combine the same generative with apotropaeic and purificatory

---

[114] *CAH²*, I, 1, Cambridge 1970, 264; 272; 278; 436.

[115] J. Karageorghis, *La Grande Déesse de Chypre et son Culte,* Lyon 1977, 17; *BCH* 104 (1980) 772.

[116] Bosnia, Danilo Culture, *CAH²*, I, 1, 598f.

[117] Chalcolithic Vinça Culture, M. Gimbutas, "The Mask in Old Europe from 6500–3500 B.C.", *Archaeology* 27 (1974) 266; *The Gods and Goddesses of Old Europe,* London 1974, 66.

[118] Achilleion, *Archaeology* (1974) 264.

[119] *BCH* 102 (1978) 704.

[120] Middle Neolithic, *C.A.H.³,* I, 1, 599.

[121] Early Helladic and pre-Mycenaean ithyphallic figurine, *Tiryns V,* Pl. 12, 1–2; F. Schachermeyr, *Die Ägäische Frühzeit,* I, Vienna 1976, Pl. 28 a & b.

[122] Burkert, *Gr. Rel.* 171, with further literature on the Gorgo-head in n.54; 243. See also his discussion in *Structure and History in Greek Mythology and Ritual* (Sather Class. Lect. 47), Berkeley 1979, 39f.; H. Herter, "Phallos", in *Der Kleine Pauly* vol. 4 (1979) 701.

[123] *CAH²*, I, 1, 264; 272.

[124] Examples from Italy in Herter, *Kl. P.* 4, 705.

[125] This has been suggested by Nilsson, *Gesch.* I³, 594, and implied by Herter, *ibid.*

powers, a significance which in fact survived in historic times in many aspects of belief and legend from herms to apotropaeic stone markers. Pausanias records the strange story of Orestes' being cured of his madness, that is purified of his blood guilt, while sitting on such a phallic tombstone near Arcadian Megalopolis[126]. The phallus was thought to incorporate divine power, it was not originally a deity in its own right. The change from divine symbol to object of worship was a secondary stage which probably had not yet occurred in the Stone Age[127]. In any event this entire tradition appears to have bypassed the Mycenaean age.

The mask, too, was placed in graves from the very early times. The meaning of this custom is not too clear, although it may have been connected with ideas of rebirth as well. If true this would explain the purpose of the many skulls of the dead, and the plaster models of faces with inlaid eyes of shells, which were put in shrines in the city of Jericho as early as the eighth millennium B.C.[128]. Elsewhere in the cult of the living the mask served as a convenient means for a change of identity[129]. Almost countless examples survive from the Neolithic Mediterranean of ritual masks as such instruments of incarnation. In the course of cultic ritual the worshipper or priest, by donning the mask of a god, temporarily assumed his characteristics: he actually became one with him[130]. Interestingly enough this ready metamorphosis was not confined to anthropomorphic form. Animal masks were at least as common and carried the same power: the wearer did not merely imitate the animal to influence its behaviour[131], but he assumed its very identity and nature. The narrow boundary between all living creatures in Neolithic cult was most graphically expressed in Anatolian religious art[132]. The curious affinity between man and

---

[126] The *Daktylou Mnema*, Paus. 8,34,2. On the identification with a phallus, see A. Dieterich, *Mutter Erde, ein Versuch über Volksreligion*, 1905, 105; G. Kaibel, *Nachrichten G.d.W.*, Göttingen 1901, 490, cited by Nilsson, *Gesch.* I¹, 202 n.9.

[127] *Cf. Kl.P.* 4, 701.

[128] Trump, *Preh. of the Med.* 25.

[129] *Cf.* Burkert, *Gr. Rel.* 169f., who cites K. Meuli, *Handwörterbuch des deutschen Aberglaubens* 5, 1932/33, 1744–1952.

[130] Gimbutas, *Archaeology* 27 (1974) 269; *Gods and Goddesses of Old Europe*, 66.

[131] Nilsson, *Gesch.* I³, 53.

[132] *E.g.* Çatal Hüyük, J. Mellaart, *Earliest Civilizations of the Near East*, London 1965, e.g. 97 and fig. 81; *The Neolithic of the Near East*, London 1975, 108f., fig. 61; Dietrich, *Origins* 103.

animal never quite disappeared: it was sometimes echoed in Minoan religion[133]. But there must have been some fundamental departure then from Stone Age practice, as the Bronze Age cult did not seem to make use of the mask as an implement of representation or invocation[134].

In Neolithic art the animal mask and human wearer were shown as mixed creatures, part bull part man, or a combination of woman and bear, woman and bird, or again as man and goat. Chalcolithic Vinça Culture provided many examples of such combinations in Europe[135]. Evidently mask and head were synonymous which explains the significance of *e. g.* the magnificent large heads from Predionica and Priština in southern Yugoslavia of about the fourth millennium B.C.[136]. In Cyprus the earliest surviving examples of bull masks come from Vounous at the beginning of the Bronze Age and therefore are somewhat later. The necropolis was in the north of the island and strongly influenced by Anatolian customs at the time[137], reflecting common beliefs which had been brought to the island by eastern immigrants since the Neolithic period. In any event, ritual masks and heads of bulls, some of them hollowed out to serve as masks,

---

[133] *E. g.* goddess and bull, Dietrich, *ibid.* 110 f.; 116; 117 ff. *etc.*

[134] There are few exceptions. Possibly the 13th century stucco head from Mycenae belonged to this category, Tsountas in *Ephemeris* (1902) I, Pl. 1–2; *P.M.* III, 519, fig. 364; *AJA* (1936) 205; Sp. Marinatos – M. Hirmer, *Kreta, Thera und das Mykenische Hellas*³, Munich 1976, Pl. LVI–LVII ("Göttin oder Sphinx"). One should also mention the 12th century head from Asine and the fragmentary Tiryns head (13th century B.C.), see Dietrich, *Origins* 151 for references to modern discussions; *cf.* R. V. Nicholls, "Greek Votive Statuettes and Religious Continuity, c. 1200–7000 B.C.", in *ACE*, 6 f. The famous head from Ayia Irini on the island of Keos came from a Minoan statue but was set up within a separate terracotta ring-base as an independent cult image only later in the eighth century, *Hesperia* 33 (1964) 330 & Pl. 60e. More directly related to other Mediterranean forms appear to be the gold and electron death masks from Circle A and B at Mycenae, Marinatos – Hirmer, *op.cit.* 171 and figs. 184–9; Pl. XLVIII. They were all of males, kings or princes presumably, and had few, if any parallels in later Mycenaean times. One possible exception is the gold mask from the sanctuary at Phylakopi. On this see *Antiquity* 52 (1978) 7–15.

[135] Gimbutas, *Archaeology* (1974) 268.

[136] See previous note.

[137] H. W. Catling, "Cyprus in the Neolithic and Bronze Age Periods", *CAH*², Cambridge 1966, 25 f.; V. Karageorghis, *The Ancient Civilization of Cyprus*, London 1969, 109 ff.

continued in use in Cyprus throughout the Bronze Age. Examples from the Late Bronze Age have been found in Enkomi[138], and in the 12th century Temple V at Kition, where clay votive masks have turned up together with two life-size masks of bearded men[139]. Mask and head continued to be important to Cypriot cultic ritual even after the Bronze Age, as witness for instance a female (goddess) figure with ram's mask from a Geometric tomb at Kition[140]. The same site, but from c. 800 B.C. has also turned up the hollowed-out heads of bulls. In Tamassos the archaic temple of Aphrodite/Astarte similarly preserved ritual masks[141].

All these, as well as the many archaic and classical votives of miniature masks[142], tell the same story of continuing religious tradition in Cyprus from Neolithic/Chalcolithic times through the Bronze Age and into the archaic and classical periods. Bull head and mask therefore were not part of a peculiarly Cypriot bull cult, but fitted into a wider Mediterranean context[143]. Hence Cyprus also produced examples of the same type of blend of human and animal figures as the Neolithic European "Bird-woman", "Goat-man", "Bear-woman", and the like[144]. The Geometric figure with ram's mask from Kition has already been mentioned. Other examples were excavated many years ago, including a stag-headed figure[145], a "Bird-man" from Amathus[146], and a "Bird-woman", amongst others[147]. More recently the discovery in Amathus of a splendid archaic limestone statuette of a "Bull-man", that is a male figure sporting the head of a bull, completes the picture[148].

---

[138] J.-C. Courtois, *Alasia I* (1971), 183; 186 and fig. 2.
[139] *BCH* 99 (1975) 835; 100 (1976) 877; 879.
[140] Geometric I/II, V. Karageorghis, *Scripta Minora 1977–1978*, London 1977, 15.
[141] *BCH* 102 (1978) 923.
[142] V. Karageorghis, in *Harvard Theological Review* (1971) 262, figs. 6–7; Y. Calvet, *Report of the Dept. of Antiquities*, Cyprus (1976) 148 ff.
[143] For a different view see Burkert, *Gr. Rel.* 170.
[144] See above n. 137–141.
[145] Now in New York, J. L. Myres, *Handbook of the Cesnola Collection of Antiquities from Cyprus*, Metropolitan Museum of Art, New York 1914, No. 1030.
[146] Head of falcon, *ibid.* No. 1268.
[147] In the Louvre, inv. no. N 2656.
[148] The figure has been dated in the 6th century B.C., A. Hermary, "Statuette d'un "Prêtre" Masqué", in *BCH* 103 (1979) 734–41.

In contrast with the Cypriot evidence Minoan/Mycenaean religion appeared to have interposed itself between Neolithic and archaic Greece in the west, because the use of masks and heads was discontinued for a time until it resurfaced once more in force in the later age. The most illuminating example comes from Despoina's temple in Arcadian Lycosoura, namely from Demophon's group of marble sculptures of Demeter, Artemis and Despoina[149]. A fragment of the veil of either Demeter or Despoina shows female figures on its border with the heads of various animals: a horse, ram, pig and the like[150]. Also quite unambiguous in this context are the terracottas of human figures with the heads of cow, sheep, and ram, which came to light in the *megaron* of the temple[151].

It is not generally realised that the famous Minotaur first appeared in Greek iconography in archaic times. The monstrous figure of a man with the head of a bull was not familiar from Minoan and Mycenaean art[152]. The myth of the Minotaur was relatively young in the west. Its central theme of Theseus' killing of the Minotaur seems to have been an Athenian invention of the archaic age[153]. Whatever the historic background to the tale may have been, its final form was un-Minoan. Mixtures could arise from any number of compounds which were haphazardly thrown together. The Cypriots for example borrowed a stylistically Minoan type of votive to create other unearthly "Mischwesen". At Ayia Irini the goddess type with

---

[149] Paus. 8,37,3f.

[150] G. Dickens in *BSA* 13 (1906/7) 356ff.; Nilsson, *Gesch.* I³, 236; 479 and Pl. 31,2; Dietrich, "Demeter, Erinys, Artemis", *Hermes* 90 (1962) 139. Dickins, p. 393, wrongly identifies the figures as animals in human dress.

[151] *BCH* 23 (1899) 635f.; *AE* (1912) 156ff.

[152] Hermary in *BCH* (1979) 740.

[153] See the discussion in Nilsson, *The Mycenaean Origin of Greek Mythology*, Berkeley 1932, 163f.; 169. The Minotaur was probably not Minoan in origin. There is no evidence of a bull-headed god in Minoan/Mycenaean religion. Nilssons's theory that the myth arose from Minoan bull games or bull hunting, is unconvincing, *op.cit.* 176; *Gesch.* I³, 297. The myth contains a mixture of different traditions and assumed its final form in archaic times or later. There is an interesting theory that "Mischwesen" like Centaurs were invented when men first saw riders mounted on horseback, H. Nash, "The Centaur's Origin: A Psychological Perspective", *The Classical World* 77 (1984) 273–91. The same story could not explain the origin of Minotaurs and other more wayward hybrids.

upraised arms was joined to a male beast at the lower end[154]. It is not a Minotaur, the mixture is wrong and the compound creature again un-Minoan to a degree. It was the phantastic result of popular imagination which had been stimulated by the coming together of different religious and artistic traditions. There was no direct antecedent for them nor was there any need for one. Precisely the same applied to the history of a more famous "Mischwesen", namely the Centaur, which also had no parallel in Minoan/Mycenaean cult, or in the east, or anywhere else, but began its existence in Geometric times. The oldest example was found at the Lefkandi necropolis[155]. Perhaps it, or a similar figure, became the standard model for myth and art in archaic times[156].

Mask and head, whether benign or repulsively apotropaeic, could equally well represent a divinity on its own without being worn by any worshipper. Many different types have survived from Neolithic Europe[157]. It is difficult to be certain whether the mask was felt to be part for the whole in these cases, or whether it carried divine power in its own right. However, when it reappeared in archaic Greece, it was generally used in particular kinds of chthonic ritual involving the enactment of an *anodos,* or in the celebration of the related mystery cults, or again in certain protective apotropaeic rites which included the ithyphallic herm. The detached head as representative of the whole deity enjoyed a much wider vogue of course in all periods, from the examples at Jericho to the eighth century head on an old Minoan statue at Ayia Irini on Keos, and to the early fifth century mask of Artemis on the temporary altar at Phocian Kalapodi[158]. But in many cases the connection with chthonic cult remained noticeable[159]. Another demonstrably un-Mycenaean feature, which

---

[154] In Medelhavsmuseet, Stockholm, N. 1775; 1690. Karageorghis, *Scripta Minora* 27 and Pl. XII, 1 *and* 2.

[155] *AR* 1969/70, 9, and cover picture.

[156] *Cf.* Burkert, *Gr. Rel.* 269 and n.10. On Centaurs in Cyprus see below ch. IV, 144–5.

[157] They have been classified and discussed by Gimbutas, *Archaeology* (1974) 263–265.

[158] This was used during the period between the Archaic and Classical temples there to ensure continuity of cult after the Persian destruction of the site, R. Felsch, *AA* (1980) 92–94, and figs. 73; 76.

[159] See the discussions in H.R.W. Smith, *Hesperia, Suppl. VIII* (1949) 375ff.; B. Schmaltz, *Das Kabirenheiligtum bei Theben* V (1974) 131f.

linked Neolithic with archaic and classical Greek, seemed to be these special combinations of mask and phallus, and mask with aniconic pillar or pole. Sometimes, but not invariably[160], pillar and phallus were the same, in which case they expressed the generative and protective power of Nature. Examples are legion, like the ithyphallic figurines with goat or bull masks from Fafos I[161]. They must have been the direct ancestors of the classical Greek ithyphallic masked satyrs. They, too, were types rather than specific individual figures[162].

At other times the sexual nature is less obvious. Mask and pillar rather convey the impression of semi-iconic cult statues, with the mask identifying the divinity as well as its numinous power. Such types also have their almost exact replicas in historical Greek cult, and above all in the cults of Dionysus and Hermes, the latter in his non-ithyphallic herms, and even of Aphrodite. Among many masked figurines of the Sesklo Culture of about 6000 B.C. the excavators of Thessalian Achilleion in northern Greece also recently discovered masked heads on the necks of vases, and a cylindrical stand with a mask which could be slipped over the top[163]. This remarkable "set" in particular recalls the Theban figure of Dionysus Perikionios[164], as well as the god's detachable mask and pole from the Anthesteria or Lenaea festivals. They were depicted on many vases. During the celebration of the Choes for example, the mask was carried separately in a *liknon* and attached to a pole wreathed with ivy, the whole constituting the semi-iconic representation of the god[165]. The pillar, which simply functioned as a stand for the mask, was non-phallic in these cases, although in classical times a symbolic connection with tree and cult is quite probable in view of the figure of Dendrites, and the (much later) evidence for the practice of hanging masks in trees in

---

[160] Gimbutas believes that the cylindrical shape of such figures was intended to represent the phallus, *Archaeology* (1974) 265.

[161] Vinça Culture, c. 5000 B.C., *Archaeology* (1974) 268 and figs.

[162] The classical types emphasized the figures' grotesque, ridiculous and obscene properties, Burkert, *Gr. Rel.* 171.

[163] Gimbutas, *Gods and Goddesses* 61; *Archaeology* (1974) 264 and figs.

[164] Schol. Eur., *Phoen.* 651; *cf. Orph. Hymn* 46.

[165] Nilsson, *Gesch.* I³, 208; 572; 587, Pl. 37,1; 38,1. Deubner. *Att. Feste* 130 and Pl.20,1, ascribes a similar example on a r.-f. stamnos from Naples to the Lenaea. *Cf.* ch. III n.137.

honour of Dionysus[166]. But in essence it was the mask which formed the most important part of the ritual on its own and together with the phallus, in what was primarily a chthonic cult and, with a few known exceptions, in contrast with Minoan/Mycenaean religious practice.

The ithyphallic male figure has turned up in Minoan Symi and Pyrgos[167], a phallus in Kumasa[168], and various bisexual figures on sites like Kamilari and the Mycenaean sanctuary at Melian Phylakopi[169]. Sometimes "grotesques", as at Symi and Phylakopi for instance, suggest the possibility of masked figures. These sparse examples show that the Mycenaeans were aware of Neolithic beliefs but largely chose to ignore them. Their reoccurrence in archaic Greece in part reveals a renewed and more representative popular interest which was allowed to come to the fore after the centralised "urban" Mycenaean culture had ended. Minoan/Mycenaean tradition had, however, left its mark on older cults even so, and also the further impact of other eastern, as well as European, traditions led to new religious forms in the historic age.

The Neolithic content of certain festivals of Artemis and Demeter, like the universal Thesmophoria, has already been noted. A number of Demeter's cults seem sunk in antiquity, such as her rites at Chthonia and her secret ceremony within a circle of stones in Hermione[170]. The same is especially true of her Arcadian cults. Quite often, however, later cult reshaped Neolithic ideas to suit its more modern purposes. Sometimes the elements of the resulting blend remain distinguishable, and one is bound to wonder what the worshipper had found so attractive in the more primitive, but universally shared, religion of the Stone Age to neglect the more immediate past. In Arcadian Pheneus, for example, an old chthonic

---

[166] Verg., *Georg.* 2, 387; Serius, *ad loc.* and on *Aen.* 6, 741; Athenaeus 78 C, reports a similar practice on Naxos. On this aspect of Dionysus' cult see especially J. Harrison, *Prolegomena to the Study of Greek Religion*, repr. New York 1955, 424–431.

[167] Sitting figure, *AR* 1977/78, 83.

[168] Cited by B. Rutkowski, *Cult Places in the Aegean World*, Warsaw 1972, 173 n. 55.

[169] A group in the tholos at Kamilari, J. A. Sakellarakis, *Herakleion Museum* (Guide), 1979, 53 and fig. 15073: men with breasts. C. Renfrew in *Antiquity* 52 (1978) 7–15, *cf.* ch. IV, 143.

[170] Paus. 2,35,4ff.; 34,10; *cf.* similar ancient rites 7,22,4; 9,38,1. Burkert, *Gr. Rel.* 38: 308.

cult with mask and *anodos* became associated with the rites of mystery cult[171]. Central to the ancient chthonic celebrations was a rock-like structure of two stones surmounted by a spherical container which housed the mask of Demeter. The priest put this on and "beat" the beings below the ground *(hypochthonioi)* with sticks. The whole scene was the enactment of a primitive fertility rite in which the nether forces were summoned to rise from below. The old part and nucleus of the cult was the rock and mask[172]. Subsequently the ritual came to be incorporated in the mysteries of Demeter Thesmia and Eleusinia[173]. Now the rock held the *hieros logos* which was taken out and read to the initiate at the Greater Rites. The content of the mysteries, with their emphasis on "rebirth" and "regeneration", continued the Neolithic cult in spirit, but form and aims were new and more sophisticated[174].

The apotropaeic mask soon declined into grotesque hobgoblin shapes in licentious country performances, dances, or was used to frighten the superstitious[175]. But as an instrument of ancient chthonic cult it preserved at least traces of its numinous religious powers in the worship of other figures like Artemis, whose archaic and classical festivals had links with Neolithic practices, too. In the case of the Spartan Artemis Orthia Minoan ideas impinged on older concepts[176]. Elsewhere in Laconia Neolithic cult survived more clearly identifiable in the ritual dances in which girls wore masks and phalloi in her honour as *lombai* or *bryllichistai*[177]. No doubt the masks of the Cypriot goddess Aphrodite/Astarte in her archaic temple at Tamassos belonged to the same kind of cult[178], since Neolithic traditions managed to live on intact in Cyprus during the Bronze Age[179].

The dances of the Laconian maidens in honour of Artemis lead on

---

[171] Paus. 8,15,1 ff. On the festival see Nilsson, *Feste* 343 f.
[172] The Kidaris dance most probably belonged to the same ancient fertility ceremony, Athen. 631 D.
[173] Nilsson, *Gesch.* I³, 477 f.
[174] *Cf.* Nilsson, *ibid.* 163 n. 1.
[175] See *e. g.* Burkert, *Gr. Rel.* 169 ff.
[176] See above p. 47.
[177] Hesych., λόμβαι; Nilsson, *Feste* 186; *Gesch.* I³, 162; Burkert, *Gr. Rel.* 170 f.
[178] *BCH* 102 (1978) 923.
[179] See above p. 65.

to another ancient cult characteristic of mask and phallus, apart from their more obvious connection with chthonic fertility. Both were commonly worn in rites which confused the division between man and animal, and even between male and female sex. Girls put on phalli and masks, human figures donned animal heads and masks, female figures sported masks with beards and the like, as in Ayia Irini on Cyprus[180]. Ambiguities of this kind again were typical of primitive belief[181] and can be traced to many early cultures of the Mediterranean from Malta to Cyprus, and from Greece to the Near East[182]. Numerous Neolithic figurines have been found at Ayios Epiktitos and Chirokitia in Cyprus, both male, female, and of indeterminate sex, wearing beard and sometimes phallus[183]. In Mesopotamia, at Eridu, odd female figures have turned up with male genitals, lizard heads and *polos*[184]. Bisexual, in the sense of supra-sexual, divine nature strongly survived in the east in the bearded Ishtar figure and her male counterpart of Ashtar[185], and thence *via* Cyprus, in the divine pair of Aphrodite-Aphroditos[186] and the figure of the bearded Aphrodite[187]. The same history lay behind the ritual exchange of clothes in the Athenian Aphrodite cult[188]. Bisexual figures occurred sporadically in Minoan/Mycenaean cult, as in the Kamilari group[189], or in the male figure with breasts from the shrine at Phylakopi[190], but they seemed to be exceptional concessions to earlier and foreign customs.

The oriental nature of Aphrodite's bisexual nature once again

---

[180] Karageorghis, *Scr. Minora* 20, who compares similar examples from Gournia and Gortyn.
[181] *E. g.* F. R. Adrados, "Les Institutions Religieuses Mycéniennes" *Acta Mycenae (Proc. 5th Intern. Coll. on Mycen. Studies, Salamanca 1970)* (S. Ruipérez ed.) I, Salamanca 1972, 187.
[182] On Malta see J. D. Evans, Malta, London 1959, 140 ff. Examples are from the Bronze Age.
[183] J. Karageorghis, *La Grande Déesse,* 15 ff.
[184] *CAH* [3]I, 1, 1347.
[185] In the Old Testament, *Jer.* 7,18; 44, 17–19, she is called the "Queen of Heaven". See A. Caquot, *Syria* 35 (1958) 45–60, on this topic.
[186] Paeon, *F.G.H.* 757 F1.
[187] See Burkert, *Gr. Rel.* 238, with further modern literature.
[188] Philochorus, *F.G.H.* 328 F 184.
[189] Above n. 169.
[190] Above n. 169.

illustrates that, though Neolithic cult features survived in archaic Greece, they were modified through the impact of diverse religious observance. The best known of these, we have noticed before, was the popular celebration of the mysteries. And these therefore represented the most up-to-date means of ensuring the regeneration of Nature, man and animals. The clash of traditions also gave birth to astonishing new creatures of myth like the Centaurs which became important from Geometric times[191]. It seems quite probable that even the popular nature and fertility god Pan, owed his origins to the same kind of source, namely the combination of man and animal, that is masked, figure[192]. His myth connected him with Hermes, but also with Dionysus, and his cult betrayed some Minoan/Mycenaean influence through cave cult. Other well-known figures in classical times were the ithyphallic Silens and Satyrs who had similarly begun life as men with animal masks. Their chief contribution, however, was to myth and the origins of Greek drama rather than to religious worship. Probably the central figure, which embraced all aspects, from the mysteries to the rebirth of the Divine Child and to dramatic performances, was Dionysus. Together with Hermes, he was predominantly associated with mask, pillar and phallus. As "Masken" and "Hermengott" both were all but indistinguishable in archaic art[193]. The semi-iconic nature of mask and pole in Dionysus' cult as Perikionios has already been noticed, and also the identification of his mask with the god himself. The Dionysiac worshipper achieved his highest aim of fusion with the god by putting on his mask.

Again various traditional strands combined to produce the historic form of Dionysus' cult: concepts of regeneration which mixed with more oriental ideas like the orgiastic identification of the worshipper with the divine figure. Many of these found the mask a convenient implement for their ritual purposes[194]. The mask could be human, as

---

[191] See above p. 67.
[192] R. Herbig, *Pan, der griechische Bocksgott*, Frankfurt 1949; F. Brommer, *P. W.R.E.* Suppl. VIII, 949–1008; W. Pötscher, *Kl.P.* 4, 444–447; Burkert, *Homo Necans. Interpretationen Altgriechischer Opferriten*, Berlin 1972, 103; 255.
[193] J. Marcade, "Hermes Doubles", in *BCH* 76 (1952) 605.
[194] On the mask in Dionysus' cult see W. Wrede, "Der Maskengott", *AM* 53 (1928), 66ff.; H. Jeanmaire, *Dionysos. Histoire du Culte de Bacchus*, Paris 1951, 6; 11; 39; 43; 483; Nilsson, *Gesch.* I³, 162; 571; Burkert, *Gr. Rel.* 252.

in the type of performances which led to classical drama[195], or animal. The god's affinity, not to say interchangeability, with the bull was impressively preserved in Thespian and Elean cult particularly[196] and generally conveyed by mask, head, or the horns of a bull[197]. A splendid fifth century B.C. example has recently been discovered in the sanctuary of Demeter and Kore on Acrocorinth[198] In Dionysiac cult the phallus was equally important and could, like the mask, be representative of the whole god. Either phallus or mask therefore was carried in the *liknon* during the celebration of the mysteries or the Anthesteria and Lenaea Festivals[199]. In Methymna there was a cult of Dionysus Phallen. Fishermen had caught a wooden mask or head in their nets and were ordered by Delphi to honour the god[200]. The mask served them as cult image *(xoanon)*[201].

Almost exactly the same story was told of Hermes Perpheraeus in Thracian Aenos. Fishermen caught in their nets and set up Epeios' wooden image of Hermes. Coins from Aenos show that it was the head or mask of the god[202]. It may well be that Phallen's story was modelled on that of Hermes Perpheraeus[203]. The point of both accounts, however, was the combination of mask, pole/phallus, that is fertility, regeneration and apotropaeic protection, all of which provided the reason for the closeness of the two gods. They met on the same grounds in the Attic Anthesteria on the second and third days of the festival, despite the contrast between the joyful Choes,

---

[195] Nilsson, *Gesch.* I³, 572.

[196] Dietrich, *Origins* 117 n.284.

[197] Plutarch, *Is. et Osir.* 364F.

[198] Bearded Dionysus with bull horns. The mask had an attachment for fitting to a pole, *Hesperia* 43 (1974) 290f.; Pl. 59.

[199] See Herter in *Kl.P.* 4, 703 for sources. *Cf.* above p. 68.

[200] Paus. 10,19,3.

[201] Hence the alternate reading of "Kephalen" for "Phallen" which Nilsson accepts, *Gesch.* I³, 82f. and 593 n.6, because he does not believe that Dionysus was phallic. However, the correct reading is cited by Eusebius, *Pr. Ev.* 5.36. p.233d, from Oenomaus, *cf.* Theodor., *Gr. aff. cur.* 10, 141. The verse response, which Oenomaus quotes, could well be genuine, see J. Fontenrose, *The Delphic Oracle,* Berkeley 1978, 347, Q 241.

[202] Ch. Picard, *Rev. Numism.* 6 (1942) 1ff. The story of the discovery in the *Diegeses* of Callimachus, Norsa *and* Vitelli eds., Florence 1934; *Callimachus,* ed. R. Pfeiffer, 1949, I, 193.

[203] The date suggested for this Delphic response in Oenomaus is c. 200 B.C., Fontenrose, see n.201 above.

when Dionysus' mask was attached to a pole, and the gloomy
Chytrae of chthonic Hermes[204]. It is surprising, therefore, that the
statues of both Dionysus and Hermes in Classical times were rarely,
if ever, ithyphallic[205], until it is remembered that the fully
anthropomorphic image replaced the semi-iconic mask and phallus.
And it was the latter combination which carried the divine power in
the past cult[206]. Later on the masked figures, which surrounded the
god, were generally ithyphallic, but not Dionysus. Often the phallus
on its own played an important part in cult, particularly in the
mysteries, and it embodied the ancient divine power. The story is the
same in the case of Hermes. Phallus and mask were features of the
herm rather than of the Olympian Hermes. Quite clearly the classical
figures of Dionysus and Hermes had become detached from such
primitive origins. But the old Neolithic ideas lived on almost
independently in the mask, herm and phallus. Their use in cult was
extremely popular of course and led to a canonical type of the herm in
Greek art in the 6th century B.C. or perhaps even later. The form
may have been new[207], but hardly the substance of belief, as the herm
as cultic image was very old indeed[208].

---

[204] See Nilsson in *Eranos* 15 (1916) 181 ff.; Deubner, *Feste* 121 f. On the atropaeic
nature of the Aiora rites see Dietrich, "Dionysus Liknites", *Class. Quarterly* 8
(1958) 244–48. On the connection of Choes and Chytrai and masks, Marcade, in
BCH (1952) 602; 607. Suidas mentions a common offering to Hermes and
Dionysus on the second or third day, *s.v.* χύτροι· πᾶν σπέρμα ... Διονύσῳ καὶ
Ἑρμῇ. Nilsson thinks that Dionysus' name was later "eingeschwärzt", *Gesch.* I³,
594 f. n. 7.

[205] Hermes Orthannes in Athens probably, U. v. Wilamowitz-Mollendorff, *Der
Glaube der Hellenen*, repr. Darmstadt 1959, I, 83. Otherwise the god is generally
shown in this form only later, *e. g.* in Gaul and elsewhere, Herter, *RM* (1976) 220
n. 99. Nilsson is not prepared to admit any instance of an ithyphallic Dionysus,
Gesch. I³, 593, although a case could be made out for Dionysus Thyonicas and
Orthos, both of which were probably phallic, *Kl.P.* 4, 703. The same may apply to
Enorchus on Samos.

[206] For examples see R. Forrer, *Strasbourg-Argentorate 2*, Strasburg 1927, 722 f.;
BCH (1952), Fig. 7; 11; below ch. III, p. 108–9.

[207] J. F. Crome, *AM* 60/61 (1935/36) 304 ff.; 62 (1937) 149, and P. Devambez, *Rev.
Arch.* (1968) 139 ff., believe that the form of herm was invented at the same time as
its canonical type. Their theory is clearly refuted by Herter, *RM* (1976) 203 .n 35.

[208] R. Lullies, *Würzburger Jahrb.* 4 (1949/50) 126 ff.; E. van Hall, *Over den oorsprong
van de grieksche grafstele*, Amsterdam 1942, 124 ff.; K. Schefold, *Die Bildnisse der
antiken Dichter, Redner und Denker*, Basel 1943, 196; Herter, *ibid.*

There has been much debate whether the archaic herm derived from Hermes' or Dionysiac cult, because in form both were identical[209]. In fact, although consistently used in Dionysiac cult and processions, herm and phallus seemed to fit the god less easily, as it were; Nilsson suggested that Dionysus' possible eastern origins could have been responsible for his association with the phallus which enjoyed lively and widespread worship in Phrygia, Smyrna and other areas of Asia Minor[210]. But of course it had been very much at home in Greece too in cult which in historical times fell into the province of Artemis and Demeter amongst others[211]. Dionysus' origins, and even the etymology of his name[212], are notoriously obscure, because they were rooted in different geographical areas and religious traditions. Nonetheless his connection with vegetation cult and the rites of return, rebirth, was ancient and universal[213]. There is little evidence, and less likelihood, that Dionysus existed in aniconic or even semi-iconic form, e. g. as Perikionios, in Neolithic times[214]. His affinity to the bull and tauromorphism, and his nature as Divine Child and paredros of the Nature Goddess, ally him more closely to Minoan/Mycenaean cult[215]. His name in fact occurs on the Linear B tablets from Pylos[216], and continuity of Minoan/Mycenaean traditions is also implied by his appearance in the sanctuary at Ayia Irini on Keos[217]. It is difficult to avoid the conclusion that Dionysus' herm

---

[209] H. Goldman, *AJA* 46 (1942) 58–68, believes in one form for both which, however, according to him was essentially Dionysiac. Marcade, *BCH* (1952) 605, merely emphasizes the common form of both. Herter, *RM* (1976) 221 f. and n.102 (with references) singles out the stone herm of Hermes as the original form from which those of other gods evolved, including the predominantly wooden herm of Dionysus and Priapus.

[210] *Gesch.* I³, 590–94; *cf.* Herter, *Kl.P.* 4, 704.

[211] Nilsson left the question unresolved, *ibid.* 594, "Die Frage muß unentschieden bleiben".

[212] Probably at least in part non-Greek, see the discusssion and references in Burkert, *Gr. Rel.* 253 f.

[213] W. F. Otto, *Dionysus, Mythos and Kultus²*, Frankfurt 1948, 71 ff., aptly defines his nature as "der Kommende". The literature on this aspect of the god in Nilsson, *Gesch.* I³, 582 ff.

[214] This appears to be implied by Goldmann, *AJA* (1942) 58 ff.; but see Herter, *RM* (1976) 222 n.102.

[215] See Dietrich, *Origins* 238 f.

[216] PY Xa 102; 1419.

[217] See above p. 48, p. 67.

had been borrowed from that of Hermes[218], and that the mask and
phallus in Dionysus' cult represented a mixture of Bronze Age
Mycenaean ideas with Neolithic tradition.

This is not the place to examine the origins of Hermes beyond his
manifest Neolithic parentage. His position in Minoan/Mycenaean
religion is uncertain, and his credentials in Linear B remain subject to
dispute[219]. The etymology of his name is also unknown. It may be
pre-Greek, a Grecised form of a foreign, even non Indo-European,
word, or it may have been brought to Greece by Greek speaking
migrants[220]. Hermes obviously derived from *herma* which, whatever
its precise linguistic origin, signified a stone. This had the same
apotropaeic, chthonic, as well as procreative power as the phallus.
Quite probably both were identical since the Neolithic Age[221]. In
Cyllene, and probably in Arcadia, the home of many conservatively
preserved cults, Hermes was actually worshipped in the form of a
phallus[222]. According to Herodotus, the god's characteristic
ithyphallic herm was Pelasgian[223]. Therefore, if he was known to the
Minoans and Mycenaeans, they adopted his figure from the earlier
inhabitants of Greece. It is now quite impossible to establish the date
and locality for the different stages from unshaped to semi-iconic
stone, with head and phallus, and eventually identification with
Hermes[224]. It is enough to understand Hermes' Neolithic ancestry
and his connection with fertility and rebirth. These qualities
incidentally were also reflected in his function as Psychopompus.
The title could not have been acquired late in the god's development,

---

[218] This was proposed already by Gerhard over a century ago, in *Gesamm. Ak. Abh.* 2 (1868) 126 ff.

[219] M. Gerard-Rousseau, *Atti e Mem. 1° Congr. internz. di micenologia 1967*, Rome 1968, 594 ff.; *Les Ment. Rel.* 856; A. Heubeck, *Aus der Welt der frühgriechischen Lineartafeln*, Göttingen 1966, 100; *cf. Gnomon* 43 (1970) 812; Hiller – Panagl, *Texte* 293.

[220] Herter, *RM* (1976) 197 ff. with full discussion of the evidence, such as it is.

[221] J. Wiesner, *Olympos,* Darmstadt 1960, 58 f.; Herter, *ibid.; Kl.P.* 4, 701–6; Burkert, *Gr. Rel.* 243.

[222] Paus. 6,26,5.

[223] Her. 2,51,1.

[224] See Herter in *PWRE* 19, 1688 ff., together with the full literature; *RM* (1976) 202 f. and n. 31.

in view of Hermes' role as "Guide of Souls" in the ancient Anthesteria festival already[225].

Quite possibly Hermes had been given his name as early as the Stone Age; but in any event, it was his cult which most directly led back to the stone herm and no doubt to the use of mask and phallus. When other gods, like Dionysus and even Aphrodite[226], borrowed the herm for their own festivals, it still conveyed the same basic significance as carrier of apotropaeic and life-giving powers. This was true of new cults in the archaic and classical age, no less than of those which had survived from the past. In other words, the date of foundation of a cult did not materially affect the religious tradition of the herm. Its revitalising powers extended over all of Nature: its vegetation, men and animals. The atavistic lack of distinction between all three categories seemed to survive to some degree in particular areas of cult including mystery rites. Hermes in fact was more immediately concerned with the well-being of animals rather than with the growth of plants. He was the Nomios who increased Phorbas' flock of sheep in the *Iliad*[227], or who, according to Hesiod, could cause the farmer's herds of goats, sheep and cattle to increase[228]. Dionysus' powers, on the other hand, extended beyond his association with the bull to include the growth of vegetation and the vine in particular. The last function he might conceivably have exercised already in Mycenaean times[229].

Despite different origins, Dionysus and Hermes met on similar cultic grounds. The two factors, however, which allied them most intimately, concerned their nature as Divine Children and their involvement with the periodic ceremonial celebration of rebirth[230].

---

[225] Wilamowitz, *Glaube* I, 165, who elsewhere insists on this characteristic being a secondary development, p. 156. The herm as grave marker, or stele, points to the same idea of rebirth. For a discussion of this much disputed point, see Herter, *RM* (1976) 216 f. n. 87. For a different view see also Nilsson, *Gesch.* I³, 388 ff.

[226] Herter, *ibid.* 204 and n. 36; 37.

[227] Homer, *Il.* 16,179 ff.

[228] Together with Hecate, Hes., *Theog.* 444 ff. Apollo has similar powers in Callimachus, *H.* 2, 50 ff.

[229] K. Kerenyi, amongst others, connects *wonowatisi*, on Pylos tablet Xa 102, 1419, with wine. He believes that Dionysus was god of wine in Mycenaean Pylos already, *Atti e Mem. 1⁰ Congr. Intern. di Micenol., Rome 1967*, 1968, II, 1021 ff.

[230] On Hermes, Dionysus and others, like Zeus, as Divine Children, see Nilsson, *M.M.R.²*, 533 ff.; Gesch. I³, 315 ff.; Dietrich, *Origins* 14 ff.; 88 ff.; 172 ff. See also,

These were features of Minoan and Mycenaean cult. To them we must now add the ultimately Neolithic herm, mask and phallus which both gods equally shared in archaic times. Thus when older religious practices returned to favour in Geometric and later Greece, they clashed with this heritage from the Bronze Age. The resulting mixture was destined to lead to quite new forms like mystery cults behind which lay Neolithic elements no less than the Minoan/Mycenaean figure of the Divine Child and basic features of cave cult which itself had found novel more sophisticated meaning in Bronze Age worship.

The reason why crude cult paraphernalia like mask, phallus and the like reappeared at this time is difficult to define. One suspects political causes in some measure. The collapse of the Mycenaean urban system released older religious elements which had temporarily remained concealed. Again social and political developments of the archaic age fostered such ancient popular cults, like Demeter's festivals with their phalli, piglets and various unpleasant cult practices[231]. Some of these seem genuine survivals from pre-Mycenaean times, particularly in remote areas like Arcadia which may have been less subject to Mycenaean cultural dominance. After all the people from the same province also failed to distinguish clearly between Demeter and Artemis as well as their "doubles", Kore and Despoina[232]. More commonly, however, and certainly in the case of Dionysus and Hermes, the confluence of Neolithic with Bronze Age traditions managed to create a potpourri of religious syncretism which was so finely blended as to obscure the various evolutionary stages.

If one places this kind of cultic mixture beside more direct survivals from the Minoan/Mycenaean Bronze Age, and also takes into account the impact of other European and oriental cultures, one begins to comprehend the dynamism of Greek religious development which in

---

with special reference to the youthful Hermes, *RM* (1976) 231f. Apollo is also an interesting member of this group. His youthful adventures were not copied from Hermes. "Apollon wird verhältnismäßig früh jugendlich", Herter, *RM* (1976) 232 n.134; *cf.* Burkert, "Apellai und Apollon", *RM* 118 (1975) 11.

[231] *Cf.* Snodgrass, *Arch. Gr.* 42ff.; 131f.; 194f.
[232] See Dietrich, "Demeter, Erinys, Artemis", *Hermes* 90 (1962) 129–148; Nilsson, *Gesch.* I³, 480; 496f.

its variety can convey the impression of being new and untraditional in the archaic age. Two examples will serve to illustrate the point, one from the fascinating but difficult history of Greek divine nomenclature, and the other from cult. Consider for example the Old European and Minoan/Mycenaean elements which culminated in the different aspects of the classical Athena. The goddess probably began as a localised pre-Greek figure[233]. Her name first came into prominence in the cult of Mycenaean Athens[234]. Athena does occur once in Minoan Crete, where it clashed, however, with the more usual Minoan/Mycenaean invocatory title Potnia[235], and the Cretan toponym *triton*[236]. The epithet Tritogeneia could have linked Athena with Knossos[237], but the myth surrounding Triton and Tritogeneia is complex[238] reflecting a pre-Minoan religious tradition which had also been localised in many other places[239]. In Mycenaean urban development she became a community and city goddess[240]. Nilsson's typical palace goddess, however, may not have been identified with the armed figure of Athena before the 7th or 6th century B.C., judging from the fully representative iconography from Subminoan to Geometric and archaic at Gortyn[241].

Recent discoveries have made it easier to assess the effect of this

---

[233] On the suffix -*ene* see Hoffmann – Debrunner, *Geschichte der griechischen Sprache* I³, 1953, 70; O. Szemerenyi, "The Origin of the Greek Lexicon", *JHS* 94 (1974) 155; Burkert, *Gr. Rel.* 220.

[234] Sarkady, A.C.D. (1965) 16f. Perhaps the Mycenaean imported Athena to Egypt (Neith, Herod. 2,28, *etc.*), Schachermeyr, *Äg. Frühz.* II, 88.

[235] *atana potinija* KN V 52.

[236] *tirito*, Hiller – Panagl, *Texte* 298.

[237] Trita = Knossos in a well-known Hesychian gloss, *q. v.*

[238] E. g. P. Grimal, *Dictionnaire de la Mythologique Grecque et Romaine*, Paris 1958, 57; 340f.; 463, with ancient sources.

[239] Outside Crete, *e. g.* Thessaly, Arcadia, Boetia, Libya. Sources in R. F. Willetts, *Cretan Cults ans Festivals*, London 1962, 282. See also Wiesner, *Olympos* 38f.

[240] Of course it is possible, though unlikely, that *atana* in V 52 was nothing but a toponym, see especially L. R. Palmer, *Mycenaeans and Minoans²*, London 1965, 131.

[241] The development of the armed Athena figure with shield, spear and helmet has been traced and discussed by Rizza-Scrinari, *Santuario Gortina*, Pl. 11, no. 59 (7th cent.); Pl. 14–16: 4th cent. terracottas of the armed goddess, and stylistically related to 6th century heads of the armed Athena from Papoura, *B.C.H.* 102 (1978) 631.

meeting of different religious streams and the surprisingly haphazard direction in which older traditions could develop. Kato Symi in southern Crete was the site of uninterrupted worship from Minoan until Roman times[242]. A typical Minoan peak and domestic cult[243], with traces of mainland and eastern influence, evolved there without significantly changing its nature. The Minoan cult paraphernalia continued in use in the Iron Age, even the votive figurines retained their strong Minoan strain[244]. By the 7th or perhaps 6th century B.C. the chief figures there were known as Aphrodite and Hermes. The development of the familiar Hermes-type can be followed from the many dedications from Daedalic to the 5th century B.C. and Hellenistic times, when the cult names first appeared in inscriptions[245].

Hermes' ancestry is clear. His presence in Mycenaean religion is possible but problematic. Aphrodite's name is certainly missing from the Linear B texts. Nor do her nature and cults, despite a recently expressed view[246], appear particularly Minoan. Once Sappho calls on her in Crete[247]. Her involvement in Ariadne's myth on Cyprus[248] and Delos[249], also testify to the great age but not origin of Aphrodite's association with the island. She was Kypris and Kyprogenes[250], because Mycenaean settlers first met her on Cyprus and identified her with their *Wanassa*. She had been the Golgian at Golgoi, or the Paphian at Paphos, or simply the Cypriot at Amathus, since the end of the Bronze Age[251]. The name Aphrodite, like Amyklaios, Amyklai[252], is best explained as a Greek transliteration of a Phoenician

---

[242] Reports in *JHS AR* from 1972/73 – 1978/79; see ch. I n. 197

[243] Doro Levi in *PdP* 181 (1978) 294–313. See ch. I p. 32–3.

[244] *AR* 1978/79, 38.

[245] *BCH* 99 (1975) 685 & 687.

[246] G. Pugliese-Carratelli, "Afrodite Cretese", in *S.M.E.A.* 20 (1979) 131–141.

[247] δεῦρύ μ' ἐκ Κρήτας, Frg. 2 (Page). There is an interesting discussion of different traditions and elements in the origins of Aphrodite by P. Friedrich, *The Meaning of Aphrodite*, Chicago 1978, ch. 2, pp. 9–54.

[248] Paion in Plutarch, *Thes.* 20.

[249] Paus. 9,40,3.

[250] Hesiod, *Theog.* 199; *Hom. Hymn Aphrod.* 10,1.

[251] *ICS*, 103 f.; 112–15; 206 n. 1; 245; 259–62; "Remarques sur les Cultes Cypriotes à l'Europe du Bronze Récent", in *East and Med*, 116. Cf. ch. III, p. 116.

[252] Dietrich, in *RM* 121 (1978) 7 f.

title[253]. *Aporodita* may well have been coined from *Astort* in the early Iron Age, certainly before the sixth century[254]. The strong eastern trait in her nature was never totally obscured in any of her cults.

Plutarch records that the association of Aphrodite and Hermes was ancient[255]. A few of their cult titles sound late and derivative, like Peitho on Lesbos[256], Machanitis, the Tricky, in Megalopolis[257], and Psithyros in Athens[258]. Elsewhere they were an old pair, at Argos[259], Athens[260], and on Delos[261]. In the last two Aphrodite was worshipped in the shape of an aniconic herm, as a kind of female Hermes. Her common ground with Hermes, like other figures with herms, was also fertility, reproduction and the aspects of vegetation cult in general[263]. But different features of this were more prominent in the cults of various regions and periods. Occasionally the combination of Aphrodite's oriental background and bisexual nature and the phallic pre-Greek Hermes figure produced strange results. One outlandish

---

[253] Perhaps Astort, as on a 9th century B.C. inscription from Kition, A. Dupont-Somner, "Une Inscription Phénicienne archaique récemment trouvée à Kition, Chypre", in *Mem. Ac. Inscr.* 44 (1970) 15. This seems the most plausible etymology. The meanings of Greek divine names are notoriously obscure, see Burkert, *Gr. Rel.* 283. Few are obviously Greek, or even Indo-European words. Aphrodite's name is not counted among them, although attempts at finding Greek derivations continue. The latest is in Friedrich, *Aphrod.* Append. 6,201f.

[254] O. Masson, IC.S., Paris 1961, 243,3. See further on the likely etymology of Aphrodite, J. E. Dugand, "Aphrodite – Astarte", in *Annal. de la Fac. des Lettres et Sciences Humaines de Nice,* 21, 1974, 80; J. Karageorghis, *La Grande Déesse* 109. The myth of Aphrodite's birth and genealogy always betrayed her eastern nature, Wiesner, *Olympos* 21.

[255] Plut., *Coniug. Praecept.* 138D.

[256] Inscription in Keil, *Philologus* Suppl. 2, 579.

[257] Paus. 8,31,3.

[258] Harpocration, *q. v.*

[259] Tradition of ancient *xoana* of Aphrodite and Hermes, Paus. 2,19,6. See also L. R. Farnell, *Cults of the Greek States,* Oxford 1909, V,12; 63, for other examples. For the common association of Aphrodite and Hermes in cult and art see also H. Thiersch, *Sitz. Ber. Heidelberg,* 1913, 4, 37; D. M. Robinson, *Olynthus 10* (1941) 6; E. B. Harrison, *The Athenian Agora 11,* Princeton 1965, 38; A. Lembesis, *AAA* 6 (1973) 104.

[260] Aphrodite Urania *en kepois,* Paus. 1,19,2.

[261] Paus. 9,40,3f.

[262] Herter, *R. M.,* 204 n. 37.

[263] See above p. 77. Cf. Nilsson, *Gesch.* I³, 503.

example in Hellenistic belief is the Hermaphroditos whose cult appealed to the superstitious man of Theophrastus[264].

At Symi, and on another peak site at Pyrgos[265], Aphrodite and Hermes replaced the Minoan pair of goddess and male associate. They had brought with them ancient traditions, and by the 8th century B.C. their cult recalled pre-Greek forms but in Minoan dress. The many votives include an ithyphallic Hermes figure[266], which can only be paralleled from Pyrgos[267], a Geometric figure with whip, a bisexual bronze figurine holding a conical cup and standing on a Cypriot-type ingot[268], and finally a 'Gorgon' mask but on a 5th century ring[269]. These were found together with the more usual Minoan artefacts of goddess and bull figurines, horns of consecration and similar cult implements, including numerous terracotta minia-ture bronze shields familiar from finds in the Idaean Cave and Gortyn[270].

What sort of cult would possess all these elements from vastly different times and places? Clearly the basic nature of Aphrodite and Hermes made them compatible with the Minoan peak and cave cult which revolved about death and renewal. The tradition of this cult remained alive in the historical myth and cult of the new figures. The evidence is well known regarding Hermes[271], and Aphrodite, espe-cially in her Cnidian cult[272]. At Symi remains of votive tripods, like those from the Idaean Cave, suggest the same association with death

---

[264] Theophr., *char.* 16,10. A phallic herm with female head and breasts. Wilamowitz was not convinced that such a figure had any standing in religious belief or cult, *Glaube* I, 94 n. 1, "Was später die Kunst gebildet hat, geht sie allein an." Herter, *RM* 201 f. and n. 26; Burkert, *Gr. Rel.* 238; 337. *Cf.* Nilsson, *Feste* 370 n. 1; 374. Cretan androgynism, *ibid.* 370 n. 4, most likely derived from eastern practice. On this subject see also ch. IV, p. 143.

[265] Hellenistic shrine to Aphrodite and Hermes at Pyrgos V, *AR* 1977/78, 83.

[266] *PdP* 181 (1978) 304.

[267] Presumably of Minoan date, *AR* 1977/78, 83.

[268] *E.g. BCH* 101 (1977) 648; 102 (1978) 754; *AR* 1978/79, 38.

[269] *BCH* 99 (1975) 485 & 687.

[270] *BCH* 99 (1975) 685; 687; *P.d.P.* (1978) 304; St. Alexiou, *Minoische Kultur*, Germ. trans. Göttingen 1976, 109 f.; Wiesner, *Olympos* 41, distinguishes between the oriental and Minoan armed goddess with lance and shield.

[271] Dietrich, *Origins* 87; 187.

[272] I.C. Love in *AJA* 77 (1973) 419.

and rebirth[273]. The Minoan ritual appears in a number of scenes with a divine epiphany, various cult implements, and not infrequently a tree, as part of the ceremony[274]. A typical scene was engraved on the LMI bronze votive tablet from the Psychro Cave[275]. Quite remarkably just such a tree epiphany may have survived on an early sixth century cut-out plaque from Symi depicting a young Hermes sitting in what looks like a Tree of Life[276]. He was either Ledrites, or more probably Kedrites[277], like Artemis Kedreatis whose image was placed in a cedar tree[278].

Cave, epiphany, the periodical return of gods in Classical and Hellenistic religion primarily belonged to mystery cults in the service of Demeter rather more frequently than of Aphrodite. Dionysus, too, often, but not invariably, replaced Hermes[279]. A fifth century pelike from Camirus, for example, shows our pair together. Aphrodite appears from below flanked by an ithyphallic Pan and by Hermes brandishing a stick or whip, recalling the so-called "flagellant" from Symi. The scene is an *anodos,* and Hermes is engaged in beating the ground in order to summon the nether deity[280]. It is quite conceivable that the ritual descended from a cult like that at Symi and

---

[273] On the function of the tripod cauldron as an instrument of rebirth, see Ch. Uhsadel-Gülke, *Knochen und Kessel,* Maisheim 1972 (*Beitr. z. klass. Philol.* no. 43). See also the discussion with further literature, in Dietrich, *BICS* 25 (1978) 6f.

[274] Dietrich, *Origins* 83; 91; 171; Burkert, *Gr. Rel.* 78; 81; 85.

[275] A. Evans, *The Palace of Minos at Knossos,* London 1925, I, 632. Fig. 470; Nilsson, *Gesch.* I³, Pl. 7, 3; Dietrich, *Origins* 83; 171.

[276] *AR* 1974/75, 28 and Fig. 53. On tree epiphanies in Greek and other religions *cf.* M. Eliade, *Traité d'Histoire des Religions,* Paris 1949, 243f.

[277] Epithet on a third century A. D. votive inscription which had been wrongly read as *Dendrites.* See G. Daux, *BCH* 100 (1976), 211–13. Daux considers an initial *Lamda* for *Kappa* "invraisemblable", *i. e.* Hermes of Ledrae, Ledroi or Ledron in Cyprus. But see the 7th century B.C. tribute list of Asarhaddon and Assurbanibal which reads *Li-di-ir.* On the adjectival form Ledrius in Cyprus see *Rev. Phil.* 32 (1958) 93. See also *PWRE* (1924) "Ledroi", 1125–27; and Schwyzer 1, 500 on -*ites* as a common locative suffix. Carratelli, *SMEA* 20 (1979) 131f., connects the epithet with Crete.

[278] Paus. 8,13,2.

[279] See C. Bérard, *Anodoi. Essai sur l'Imagerie des Passages Chthoniens,* Rome 1974, especially ch. 7–9 on Aphrodite and Hermes in such rites of return.

[280] Bérard, *Anodoi* 59; 110; 131; 157; Pl. 18, 63. Flagellant figurine at Symi, *AR* 1976/77, 64. On the classical rite of beating the ground on such occasions, as in the cult of Demeter Kidaria in Pheneus, see above p. 70 and n. 171.

arose from a mixture of Neolithic as well as Minoan/Mycenaean tradition. A Minoan *anodos* scene has been identified on a cup from Phaistos[281]. But whatever the mechanics of the divine epiphany, its significance could hardly have altered much. Hence the continued use of the tripod in such ceremonial, as seen on an Early Geometric funerary pithos lid from Fortetsa, near Knossos, with an *anodos* from beneath a tripod[282], and a seventh century B. C. bronze mitra which was found in the ruins of Aphrodite's temple at Axos[283]. Already by Geometric times it seems impossible to tell Minoan apart from pre-Bronze Age tradition at Symi.

Tripos and associated remains lead us back to the Cyprus connection which is most impressively revealed by the 8th century figure on an ingot[284]. The workmanship is Minoan but the religious significance is undoubtedly oriental/Cypriot like the 'Barrengott' and '-göttin' from the Mycenaean settlements at Enkomi and Kition[285]. These figures and the 'Warrior god' will be discussed in chapter IV. The bisexual characteristics of the Symi figure is also Cypriot and ultimately oriental like Aphrodite's similar nature[286]. In the western Aegean metallurgy was first practised in Crete since the Early Bronze Age or earlier. The copper ore was imported from Anatolia or Cyprus[287], and by the early second millennium B. C. Cretan craftsmen were skilled enough to cast monumental bronze

---

[281] C. Kerenyi, *Eleusis. Archetypal Image of Mother and Daughter*, London 1967, XIX–XX; 1. Chirassi, *Elementi di culture precereali nei miti e riti Greci*, Rome 1968, 104 and Pl. 31; 123.

[282] The god's identity remains uncertain, D. Levi, *Hesperia* 14 (1945) Pl. 28,3; *AJA* 49 (1945) 310, Fig. 20; *BICS* 25 (1978) 7.

[283] *AJA* 49 (1945) Fig. 15; H. Hoffmann, *Early Greek Armorers*, Mainz 1972, 37, identifies the figure as Athena, Aphrodite seems more probable.

[284] *AR* 1978/79, 38 and Fig. 50.

[285] The figure has been much discussed. Modern literature in H.-G. Buchholz, "Beobachtungen zum prähistorischen Bronzeguss in Zypern und der Ägäis", *Cyprus & Crete* 84 n. 39. H. Catling, *Alasia I,* 1971, 15; V. Karageorghis, *Kition: Mycenaean and Phoenician Discoveries in Cyprus*, London 1976, 74. See below ch. IV, 160–169.

[286] See p. 86. *Cf.* similar figurines from Ayia Irini in Cyprus and from Phylakopi on Melos, ch. IV, pp. 143–4. The Minoan "content" is shown by the upraised arms of the upper female halves which recall the typical Minoan goddess idols.

[287] Phillips, *Preh. of Europe*, 202.

statuary[288]. The Symi figure, not to say divinity, on an ingot therefore is an important reminder that in Crete, as in Cyprus, the metal industry was intimately connected with the welfare and prosperity of the community and formed a central part in its religious belief.

These points are reflected in myth which equated metallurgical skill with magic, and which preserved the memory of this country's connection with the province of the Great Mother Goddess[289]. For instance the Idaean Dactyls remained firmly anchored in eastern and Cretan tradition as workers of magic and the inventors of metal work[290], as well as the children of the Cretan Rhea in the west and of the Idaean Mother Goddess in the Troad[291]. The Dactyls were identical with the dwarf-like Telchines, Couretes, Corybants and similar creatures of Cretan myth[292], all of whom were renowned for their powers of magic and skill in metal technology. Cretan tradition was so strong in fact that it managed to reverse the order of the transmission of metallurgy to run from west to east[293].

In Cyprus metal workshops were placed in the physical protection of the Aphrodite/Astarte temples at Kition and Athienou[294], and later

---

[288] An MM life-size mould for a hand has been found by the Italian excavators at Phaistos, C. Laviosa, *Ann. S. Arch. Atene* 45/46 (1967/68) 499; Buchholz, *Acts. Nicosia* 1979, 82.

[289] J. G. Parr, *Man, Metals and Modern Magic,* 1958, on the connection of magic with metal work in antiquity.

[290] Clem. Alex. 1,16,75,4 pp. 48–9; Herter, *P. W.R.E.* V A1 (1934) 221; R. J. Forbes, *Bergbau-Steinbruchtätigkeit-Hüttenwesen,* in *Archaeologia Homerica,* Göttingen 1967, 29; Buchholz, *op. cit.* 77 f. They were called *Goetes* in the 7th century B.C., Burkert, *RM* 105 (1962) 36; 39.

[291] References collected in Grimal, *Dict. Myth.* 113.

[292] Dio. 5,55,2; Strabo p. 654; Eust. on *Il.* 9,525, p. 771 f.; P. Realacci, "Telchines, maghi nel sogno delle Transformazione", in *Magia, Studia di Storia delle Religioni, Mem. R. Garosi,* Rome 1976, 197–206; Buchholz, *Cyprus and Crete,* 78 f.; see also Herter, *PWRE* V A1, 203 f.; 223, on the Telchines, together with other related figures.

[293] Apollod. in Strabo 653 f.; *cf.* Athena Telchinia's move from Crete to Rhodes, Herter, *op. cit.* 203 f. "Als gebender Teil ist in diesem Fall Zypern anzusehen", Buchholz, *op. cit.* 85 n. 41. The author distinguishes between copper working, which moved from east to west, and the knowledge of iron working, which was transmitted in the opposite direction. He believes that tradition only reflected the secondary movement, *ibid.* 80.

[294] *BCH* 97 (1973) 656 (Athienou); 98 (1974) 866 (copper workings at Kition from LCIII).

still, in archaic times, at Tamassos[295]. The patron deities of the city's copper industry were shown standing on ingots[296]. They had evolved from a goddess of Nature and her associate who now in the new city symbolized the 'fertility' of the mines[297]. In historical times the pair were worshipped as Aphrodite and Hephaestus. Their cult association travelled west but was misunderstood, becoming the subject of ridicule in Homer[298].

It appears that the Minoans and Mycenaeans brought back with them this eastern Aphrodite figure, together with her new name. It is impossible to judge whether she was imagined as bisexual or associated with a separate male figure. In either case, however, her connection at Symi with the Minoan deities of peak and cave cult, and with the pre-Greek Hermes, shows a religious compound of startling range. Later tradition evidently did not concern itself with origins, but preferred to draw from those inherited elements which best suited its own interests, such as rebirth, initiation, and mystery rites.

The ease with which the worshipper in the Geometric age accepted such diffuse syncretism does explain some of the surprising divine metamorphosis in Greek religion. Epic literature, for example, allied Aphrodite, Goddess of Love and Beauty, with Ares, God of War and Strength. This pair competed with that of Aphrodite and Hermes and a third association of Aphrodite with Hephaestus. Of these only the first can be called "new", however. But then it did not really represent religious belief.

---

[295] *BCH* 97 (1973) 665; 98 (1974) 882; 100 (1976) 886; Buchholz, *op. cit.* 78 and n. 8. For similar practices in Anatolia, Syria and other eastern settlements in the Late Bronze Age, see Karageorghis, *Kition* 75.
[296] *BCH* 96 (1972) 1059; *AJA* 77 (1973) 53; Karageorghis, *op. cit.* 74f.
[297] Karageorghis, *op. cit.* 170.
[298] Dietrich, "Views of Homeric Gods and Religion", *Numen* 26 (1979) 134.

Divine Concepts and Forms

The Greeks had the good sense to borrow ideas about the gods and many of the gods themselves from other cultures. Very few Olympians were, so to speak, autochthonous on Greek soil. The origin of practically all of them remains obscure except in the accounts of cosmogonic myth. And this, too, in substance, was lifted from the east.

Some divine notions they preserved from Neolithic times. Other figures and concepts derived from the Minoan/Mycenaean interlude during the later Bronze Age in the western Aegean. Yet others originated in the common Mesopotamian cultures of the third and second millenna B.C., or from Egypt, or indeed from the divinities of ancient Europe. But invariably Greek worship transformed these gods, made them their own, so that their historical background all but vanished from sight. 'Of the gods we know nothing', said Socrates in Plato's *Cratylus* (490d), 'either of their natures or of the names which they give themselves.' Others, like Herodotus[1], were more optimistic, but, despite much enlightened guesswork, no less ignorant than we are today about the history of the Greek gods. However, sometimes the knowledge of origins is only useful to antiquarians, and in the case of religious figures is but one aspect of their nature and meaning. It is far more important to try and understand the Greek conception of their gods in the archaic and classical age together with the notions underlying their iconographic representation of them. Certain inferences may then be drawn about the names and history of the gods.

The Greek gods were conceived of as personal beings in human shape. This belief in anthropomorphic gods the Greeks shared with other cultures some of which had contributed to Greek religious thought. However, the relationship between man and god was fundamentally different in east and west. When the Babylonian Marduk created man, he charged him

---

[1] Herod. 2,53.

'with the service of the gods
that they might be at ease'[2]

But the Greeks had no taste for servitude to mortal or immortal of
any shape or form. The Sumerian gods, despite their human shape,
remained vastly superior cosmic powers with only rudimentary
personal characteristics. The gods of Egypt, too, were devoid of
personality. The names of most major Egyptian deities are particularly
interesting in contrast with Greek practice because their meaning is
generally transparent. They translate as divine functions rather than
as personal titles. They describe the characteristic activity, or nature,
of a particular god and not his personality. The ithyphallic figure of
Min, for example, symbolized the generative force of nature[3]. Amun
means 'The Hidden One', that is the invisible god of the air. Chons
again translates as 'He Who Passes Through', namely the moon god
who moves across the sky[4].

There are worlds of difference between this conception of the gods
and that of the highly personal man-oriented figures of classical
Greek times. In this respect Greek gods appear to have been
exceptional in the Mediterranean world. I doubt whether it is often
understood that, with all their dependence on Greek divine myth and
tradition, Italian and Roman gods also lacked this peculiarly Greek
personal quality. In concept Italy was more closely akin to Egypt
than to Greece. The divine names also reflected functions which a
god performed or symbolized. But for their masculine or feminine
gender such titles remained lifeless abstracts. Sometimes a name
began as the adjectival description of a function. Parca, for example,
the goddess of birth, was formed from the verbal stem *par-, 'to give
birth', Genius from *gen-, 'to produce', Aius from the root *ag-, 'to
speak', and so on. Even the venerable Ceres, goddess of corn, and the
equivalent of the Greek Demeter in myth, owed her name to the
verbal stem *ker-, 'to grow, let grow, to nurture'[5]. Contrast that
etymology with the personal nature of Demeter, whatever the

---

[2] Babylonian *Creation Epic* Tablet VI, lines 5–8, *ANET*[3] (1969) 68.
[3] H. Frankfort, *Ancient Egyptian Religion*, Harper Torch Book. 1961, 25–6.
[4] S. Morenz, *Ägyptische Religion*, Stuttgart 1960, 22.
[5] G. Radke, *Die Götter Altitaliens*, Münster 1965, 37; 59; 85–6; 138 with further
    modern literature.

meaning of her name[6]. The Romans thought nothing of elevating participial *nomina agentis* to divine status. *Pollens, valens,* or *gens* easily became the gods Pollentia, Valentia or Geneta[7]. They were inanimate forms, all of them, no less than value concepts like Virtus, Victoria, Spes, Honos and the like, all of whom received cult in Roman Italy. It would be wrong to describe such figures as personifications because they lacked a true persona unlike the similar literary creations in Homer and Hesiod. Eris, Hebe, Charis may not have been ancient figures of cult but the two poets endowed them with genealogies and gave them life by fitting them into a family relationship. Eris was among Hesiod's primordial forms, mother of Toil, Pain, Hunger and of other similar personifications[8]. She was also sister of Ares like Hebe[9]. They were allegories like Homer's Prayers[10], or his invention of Charis as Hephaestus' wife because, as one scholiast put it, it is right that Skill, *techne,* should be together with Grace, *charis*[11]. Even when Hesiod split Eris into the two figures of Good and Evil Strife as a kind of moral paradigm for men, neither lost her family ties[12]. The institution of a cult to lifeless ideas or values was extremely rare in Greek religion and generally late. The famous altars in Athens to Pity, Shame, and Good Repute, *Eleos, Aidos,* and *Pheme* were probably not set up before late Hellenistic times[13].

The opening verse of Pindar's Sixth Nemean Ode speaks of one and the same race of men and gods. Bury rightly comments that the poet wished to insist on the 'ultimate primal unity' of both[14]. Men were drawn into the same family of gods and men[15]. The poet was speaking figuratively, of course. He pointed to the close bond

---

[6] The old explanation as *Ge Meter,* "Mother Earth", is no longer accepted, *e. g.* W. Burkert, *Griech. Rel. d. archaischen und klassischen Epoche,* Stuttgart 1977, 247–8.

[7] = Italian Genita, *deívaí gentaí* on a tablet from Agnone, Vetter, *Handb. d. ital. Dial.* I, no. 147.

[8] Hes., *Theog.* 225–32.

[9] *Il.* 4, 441; Hes., *Theog.* 922, sister of Ares and Eileithyia.

[10] *Il.* 9, 502.

[11] Hom. *Il.* 18, 382–3.

[12] Hes., *W. and D.* 11–26. For the probable relative chronology of this passage and *Theog.* 225–32 see M. L. West's ed. of the *Theogony,* Oxford 1966, 44. Cf. his discussion on the genealogy of abstract divine concepts on pp. 31–4.

[13] H. Dörrie, "Gottesvorstellung", *RAC,* fasc. 89 (1981) 117.

[14] Pindar, *Nem. Odes,* J. R. Bury ed., London 1890, 103.

[15] *E. g. Il.* 1, 544; *Od.* 1, 28; 20, 201.

between the two worlds without suggesting that a blood relationship existed between Zeus and men[16], any more than Lactantius intended to be taken literally in his definition of a Christian's *pietas* as *nihil aliud quam parentis agnitio*[17]. First and foremost Zeus' title marked out his 'paternal' dominance over all gods and men[18]. But beyond that even the metaphorical membership of one common family implies that man also shared unity of nature and form with the gods. This oneness could actually be looked at from both sides: either the gods were anthropomorphic or men were theomorphic[19].

It is a question of attitudes. The Judaic Yahwe was also imagined as anthropomorphic. But he was too far removed and divinely spiritual to be represented in physical form. Man was made in His image[20] and acted as a symbol of his God. Man strove to be righteous and just. In other words, the relationship was God-oriented, God-focal, to coin an ugly anthropological term. The Jewish attitude to Yahwe is paralleled elsewhere, in ancient Persian Zoroastrianism, for example. The righteous king was the earthly symbol and image of Ahura Mazda[21]. The God himself, however, existed without material form and therefore could not be shown[22]. Such eastern beliefs[23] contrast with Greek, or I should say Homeric, gods who were fashioned in the image of man. Concepts of the gods' moral superiority, or

---

[16] Ed. desPlaces, *Syngeneia*, Paris 1964, 21; C. Colpe, "Gottessohn", *R.A.C.* 89 (1981) 27–28.

[17] *Inst. Div.* III, 9.

[18] Cf. M. P. Nilsson, *Gesch. d. gr. Rel.* I³, Munich 1967, 417; Burkert, *Gr. Rel.* 204–5. For the same reason El has the title of "Father of Men" in Ugarit.

[19] J. Adam, *The Vitality of Platonism and other Essays*, Cambridge 1911, 124, "Anthropomorphism implies theomorphism". DesPlaces, *Syng.* 21, suggests that the notion of Zeus the Father gave rise to anthropomorphism. The reverse process seems more likely, however, namely that Zeus' fatherhood was only possible in an already established anthropomorphic pantheon.

[20] *Gen.* 1,26–7; 9,6; *Testament of Naphtal* 5,2; *Wisdom of Solomon* 2,23. Cf. A. Hultgard, "Man as Symbol of God", in *Religious Symbols and their Functions*, ed. H. Biezais, *Proc. Symp. on Rel. Symbols & their Funct., Abo 28th–30th Aug. 1978*, Uppsala 1979, 110–16.

[21] Cf. Plutarch, *Themistocles* 27.

[22] See Hultgard, *op.cit.* 114–5.

[23] For the confusion in the relationship between image and god in Babylonian religion, see H. Ringgren, "The Symbolism of Mesopotamian Cult Images", in *Proc. Symp. Åbo*, 105–9.

absolute moral standards, which man should seek to equal, complicated but did not fundamentally alter such epic values. In his *Protrepticus* Aristotle still recognizably preached the same. The formula *homo-deus mortalis* was clearly based on the ancient notion of the gods' living personality and their oneness with men[24].

Epic values do, of course, presuppose literary rather than cultic divine figures. Epic heroes were special men: they lived in the past, were better, stronger and larger than mortals of existing generations[25]. Also they were closer to, and more familiar with the gods, meeting with them and sometimes even sharing a common table with them[26]. The easy *perioche*, or communication, then between heroes and gods in the Homeric tradition belonged to a legendary past and not to the realistic present[27]. It would not be representative of ordinary men who were distinct from the hero with his divine or semi-divine qualities[28]. Nevertheless there is no doubt that the epic, that is the Homeric and Hesiodic, concepts of divinity and divine human relationship directed the accepted religious thought of Greece from archaic times. This is surprising for two reasons in particular. Firstly Homer's heroic figures were generally not the same as the hero of cult. Secondly Homeric epic could hardly be described as religious poetry[29] when compared with the older Akkadian, Hittite or Ugaritic epics some of which, like the Babylonian *Creation Epic,* constituted basic elements of cultic ritual and also contributed their ideas to the west[30].

The history of hero cult in Greece is not well understood[31]. The word *heros* itself has not been satisfactorily explained[32]; but the cultic

---

[24] Frg. 10c Ross = frg. 61 Rose³; Cicero, *de fin.* 2,40; *cf.* Dörrie, *RAC* 89 (1981) 137.

[25] *Il.* 5,304; 12,383; 449; 20,287 etc.

[26] Hes., frg. 82 Rzach; Paus. 8,24–5.

[27] See F. Pfister, "Epiphanie", in *P.W.R.E.* Suppl. IV (1924) 283–4; 291.

[28] Dietrich Roloff, *Gottähnlichkeit, Vergöttlichung und Erhöhung zum seligen Leben,* Berlin 1970, 3–101; 151.

[29] *Cf.* the view of P. Mazon, *Introduction à l'Iliade,* Paris 1942, 294.

[30] *E.g. Enuma Elish.* "The epic ... was ... the most significant expression of the religious literature of Mesopotamia", E. A. Speiser in *ANET³,* 60.

[31] See A. D. Nock, "The Cult of Heroes", in *Harv. Theol. Rev.* 37, (1944) 141–74; A. Brelich, *Gli eroi Greci,* Rome 1958; Nilsson, *Gesch.* I³, 184–91.

[32] H. Frisk, *Griech. etym. Wörterbuch,* Heidelberg 1960–70, I, 644–5; P. Chantraine, *Dict. étymol. de la langue grecque,* Paris 1968–417. The connection with Hera is only one of many often mutually exclusive ones (Nilsson, *Gesch.* I³, 350) and tells

hero was localised and tied to his tomb. Occasionally he preserved some attributes or functions of a god[33]. The Homeric hero had no religious pretensions, nor, with the exception of Ajax in Salamis, did he aspire to cult in his home[34]. For all his superiority in the legendary past during the Trojan War and before, he became indistinguishable from the common citizen of post-Homeric times[35] who now inherited the hero's closeness to the gods and his familiar attitude to them. The reason that Homer's and Hesiod's ideas successfully cut across inherited religious traditions, despite the secular nature of their poems, was mainly political. Through some, as yet not entirely explicable, cause the secular epic hero became identified with his cultic counterpart in the archaic age. The latter most probably was older than Homeric epic[36]. But, judging from the predilection for epic topics in art and the proliferation of hero cults at the time, the cultic hero changed under the impact of epic poetry after the eighth century B.C.[37]. Whatever his antecedents might have been, his title now, on analogy with the epic hero, helped to bring the gods closer to this world.

Hesiod's Fourth Race of Heroes were also known as *hemitheoi*[38]. The word occurs once in the *Iliad* with the same significance drawing attention to the hero's divine descent rather than his semi-divine nature[39]. Through his high origins the figure of the hero provided a link with the gods which could legitimize the worldly claims of the new ruling class. Each aristocratic family was able to boast of its ultimately divine connection through its legendary ancestral hero. Positions and land-ownership in the new state depended on such qualification[40]. Hesiod filled this need by constructing elaborate genealogical systems in the Heroic Catalogues which established direct lines of descent from god to the ancient kings of Mycenae,

---

nothing certain about the past of the goddess or the title *heros* in the Bronze Age, M. L. West, *Hesiod's Works and Days*, Oxford 1978, 371.

[33] Dietrich, *Death, Fate and the Gods²*, London 1967, 14–58; Burkert, *Gr. Rel.* 312–9.
[34] Dörrie, *RAC* 89 (1981) 96.
[35] Roloff, *Gottähnl.* 102–21.
[36] Burkert, *Gr. Rel.* 313–9.
[37] *Cf.* Colpe, *RAC* 89 (1981) 29–30.
[38] *W. and D.* 159–60.
[39] *Il.* 12.23. West, *W. & D.* 191; Colpe, *RAC* (1981) 29–30.
[40] A. Snodgrass, *Archaic Greece*, London 1980, 37–9.

Tiryns or Argos, and finally down to the rulers of the archaic age[41]. The very *polis* itself acquired a hero as founder, saviour, protector who received cult next to the community's city god[42]. Many hero cults grew about the tombs or sites of the Bronze Age from the eighth century onward[43]. Not all such heroes were drawn from Homer. Some might have been gods once, many others came from myths outside Homer like Theseus or Orestes. No doubt even some of the Homeric figures had been taken up by the epic poets from earlier times[44]. The fickle Helen of the *Iliad* and *Odyssey* may well have been a goddess once in Sparta[45]. Homeric views prevailed, however, and set the standard for man's conception of the gods.

In a sense the archaic Greek was irreverent enough to allow thoughts of political expediency to govern his notion of the gods. Homer insured that they should be conceived of as universal pan-Hellenic beings and not as localised cult figures. In fact locally bound cult and cult buildings are rarely mentioned in either *Iliad* or *Odyssey*. Apollo and Athena alone possessed temples by virtue of their universal nature as city gods. Hence Athena was also worshipped on the acropolis of the enemy city of Troy[46]. Hesiod's view of the gods followed very much along the same lines, albeit for somewhat different reasons. Cult gods were subordinate to general divine figures and concepts[47]. Small wonder that man's view of the gods was also eminently practical: he visualized them like himself in appearance but greater in power.

Everyone is familiar with Xenophanes' criticism of Homer's anthropomorphic gods. According to the epic poets the gods looked, acted and dressed like men[48]. His attack was directed not so much against the fact of anthropomorphism as the arrogance of imagining the gods in one's own form[49]. Thus the Thracians saw theirs as blond

---

[41] B. Snell, "Die Welt der Götter bei Hesiod", in *Entr. Fond. Hardt* I (1952) 97–126; Dörrie *RAC* (1981) 99–100.

[42] Dörrie, *op.cit.* 96.

[43] Snodgrass, *Arch. Gr.* 39.

[44] Even Achilles, perhaps, Burkert, *Gr. Rel.* 314.

[45] Herod., 6,61,3; *cf.* Burkert, *Gr. Rel.* 314; M. L. West, *Immortal Helen*, Inaug. Lect. London 1975.

[46] See E. Vermeule, *Götterkult*, Göttingen 1974 105–12; *AJA* 79 (1975) 294.

[47] *Cf.* Dörrie *RAC* 89 (1981) 99–102.

[48] Xenophanes, B11; B12; B14.

[49] W. Jäger, *The Theology of the Early Greek Philosophers*, Oxford 1947, 42–7.

with blue eyes, the Ethiopians black with snub noses[50]. If cattle and horses had hands and could paint with them, they would depict their gods in their own shape[51]. The modern theologian Martin Buber explains this anthropomorphism as man's need to preserve the 'sense of concreteness of the meeting with God'[52]. He is speaking of the one Christian God, of course, but his views, though no doubt unconsciously, seem tinged with Homeric man-oriented values. They envisage the possibility of direct confrontation between god and man in human form. There is a grave dilemma. How must such meetings be supposed to have occurred? Did the Greek worshipper fancy that he faced his god directly, or did the communication between human and divine take place on a purely spiritual level? The fact that the classical Greek considered his god to possess the same shape as himself certainly implies, in view of what has already been said, that he pictured the divine as a definite figure[53]. But that does not fully answer the question how real, how concrete was the meeting with the divine. Of course, one can take this question only so far because, Buber's definition notwithstanding, our Christian God, too, for most remains no more than a vague notion derived from the Renaissance conception of divine form modelled on human physical ideals. These incidentally are quite Homeric. The most perfect example and model for later ages has been Michel Angelo's painting of God in the Sistine Chapel in the appearance of a seated bearded man with great physical strength and beauty[54].

Since archaic and classical Greek thought drew so profoundly from the heroic epic world of easy human and divine *perioche,* and since the new aristocratic rulers claimed descent from the Olympian gods, one might reasonably suppose that direct epiphany of the gods in human form was not only possible but indeed common currency. However, contemporary art, cult, and to some extent literature suggest that this was not the case but that, as in our Christian world, direct confrontation between god and man was quite exceptional. I

---

[50] Xenoph., B16; B15.
[51] Xenoph., B15.
[52] Martin Buber, *Gottesfinsternis,* Zurich 1953, 19.
[53] O. Kerenyi, *The Religions of the Greeks and Romans,* trans. C. Holme, London 1962, 143.
[54] R. Holte, "Gottessymbol und soziale Struktur", in *Proc. Symp. Åbo 4.*

mean the appearance of the Olympian god of the *polis* before his worshippers. Visible epiphanies seem to have been reserved for lesser beings, namely the cultic hero, who personally aided his followers in their hour of need. Such was Echetlaeus, who was seen at Marathon wielding his plough and helping Athenians defeat the Persian foe[55], or Theseus, or Ajax and Telamon who were invoked at the battle of Salamis[56]. They appeared physically like Helen who was seen to come out of her sanctuary at Therapne in order to address and actually touch her worshipper[57]. These were more akin to the ubiquitous daemons, or daemonic powers, of popular superstition which roamed this world constantly ready to interfere in human affairs. They were invisible and wrapped in mist, according to Hesiod[58], while Penelope's suitors feared their presence concealed as beggars and strangers[59].

There is an amusing story in Herodotus[60] of how Peisistratus' supporters managed to bring the tyrant back to Athens. They dressed up a tall and attractive woman in armour, made her stand in a chariot in a striking pose and then pulled the car into Athens. They said that this was the goddess Athena who was personally conducting Peisistratus home to her acropolis. Herodotus described it as the 'silliest trick which history has to record', and he thought that the otherwise most intelligent Athenians should have seen through this foolish stratagem. Obviously the historian knew that Olympians did not regularly visit their subjects, least of all in the uniform of their statues. Perhaps Peisistratus simply played on the Athenians' superstitious fear, unless of course they wanted their tyrant back at any price. What makes Herodotus' comment so interesting, however, is its manifest lack of faith in the probability of the goddess' physical

---

[55] Paus. 1,32,5.

[56] Burkert, *Gr. Rel.* 317–8, with references to ancient sources. For examples of "epic" type epiphanies and heroic support in Greek literature see W. K. Pritchett, *The Greek State at War*, Berkeley 1979, III, 11–46.

[57] Herod. 6,61. *Cf.* the hero Astrabacus who had intercourse with Ariston's wife in the form of her husband, Herod. 6,69. The heroes Phylacus and Autonous pursued and killed the Persians, Herod. 8,38–9.

[58] *Works and Days* 252–5.

[59] *Od.* 17, 485–7. It is doubtful whether this belief was purely epic and literary invention, W. Kullmann, *Das Wirken der Götter in der Ilias*, Berlin 1956, 96.

[60] 1,60. *Cf.* Pritchett, *The Greek State at War*, III, 20–21.

appearance among her people. To stage the improbable can in fact be blasphemous, and so Socrates censured the poets for what he called their scurrilous practice of introducing Olympian gods in the theatre[61]. This was not only immoral but also unlikely.

There are many recorded instances of epiphanies. But with few exceptions they turn out to be the invention of patriotic or political propaganda[62]. Quite probably a Greek did not seriously expect to see a god in the flesh, as it were, and he therefore did not feel the need to picture his form with any precision. This is surprising in the light again of Greek dependence on epic values, and we should perhaps take another look at epiphanies in Homer. The special conditions of epic society apart, how unclouded in fact was even the Homeric hero's view of his gods, and how commonly did he meet him face to face? The answer is, very rarely. Direct confrontation with a god, presumably in his own anthropomorphic form, was quite exceptional in Homer, too. A mere handful of such meetings occur in both epics between Athena and her favourites Odysseus and Diomede, between Apollo and Achilles, Aeneas or again Diomede, or between the lesser divine intermediaries Hermes and Iris and Priam[63]. Otherwise for a god to meet man was *nemesséton,* that is improper[64], as if a barrier existed between the two[65].

In the vast majority of instances the arrival of a god on the scene remained unseen by men who did, however, suspect the work of a superior agency through observing the events or the exceptional valour of another fighter. But it is invariably the poet who announces the epiphany in both *Iliad* and *Odyssey* and not a member of the cast, not even a priest officiating at a ceremony or sacrifice[66]. The colourful

---

[61] Plato, *Rep.* 2,381d.

[62] Most recorded instances are Homeric in conception, *e. g.* Asclepius in Epidaurus *IG* IV²128, lines 57–78 (338 B.C.); *cf. SIG*³ 398 Apollo expels the Gauls from his temple in Delphi (279 B.C.) with Artemis and Athena, Diod. 22,9,5; Justin 24, 5–12; Athena appears at Ilion, Plut., *Lucullus* 10,4; Artemis Leucophryene to her priestess, *SIG*³557 *etc.*

[63] For a discussion of these instances see my paper on "Divine Epiphanies in Homer" in *Numen* 30 (1983) 53–79.

[64] *Cf.* Hermes' comment in *Il.* 24, 463–4.

[65] Athena removed the mist from Diomede's eyes so that he could tell gods from men, *Il.* 5, 127–8.

[66] E. Pax, "Epiphanie" *RAC* 5 (1962) 840; F. Schachermeyr, *Griechische Geschichte,* 1960, 92–3.

variety of such intervention in its different forms is most poetically illustrated by following Poseidon's extended *aristeia* in Books 13–15 of the *Iliad*. In this prolonged episode Poseidon seems closer to the human than the divine level. His efforts resemble those of other outstanding heroes like Achilles. And it becomes clear that Poseidon's numerous epiphanies, like those of other Olympians, who took part in the human battle, were a poetic device. Firstly they constituted an alternative way of depicting divine intervention, and secondly they served to account for moments of almost superhuman exertion in the contest when mortal heroes must have been divinely possessed to perform so well. Thus, except when inspiring their favourites from afar, the gods on these occasions were seen and used by the poet as supermen with of course human characteristics. They were not intended to be regarded as religious figures deserving of pious cult. So the poet described the god's physical features as also larger than life. They were poetic inventions, like monstrous Eris, rather than divine figures which came into human vision.

They were taller, bigger, stronger than their human counterparts. The two Ajaxes, for instance easily spotted Poseidon from his large legs and feet[67]. Athena made Diomede's chariot groan with her enormous weight[68], and so on. They often moved about like men on foot or by chariot, although their progress was much faster. Their speed in fact exceeded human powers of sight[69]. Conversely mortal heroes too, could be mistaken for gods because of their striking appearance, their valour or great beauty[70]. In this highly charged atmosphere of epic hyperbole the boundaries between the two worlds overlapped, and we are no longer sure whether to consider the gods as anthropomorphic, or man as *theoeides*[71].

On these occasions the gods were projections of men whom the poet wished to extol as giant heroes of the past. In other words, the

---

[67] *Il.* 13, 71.
[68] *Il.* 5, 838–9.
[69] *Od.* 10. 573–4.
[70] E.g. *Od.* 19, 39–40; 43; 16, 179–83.
[71] See Odysseus' appeal to Nausicaa, *Od.* 6, 149–57; *cf.* Pindar, *Pyth.* 4, 86–8. A collection of instances in Homer, with full discussion, of this type of hero's similarity to the gods, can be found in D. Roloff, *Gottähnlichkeit*, 3–37. "Wie ihre (*viz.* the gods') Leibesgröße das menschliche Maß überragt, so ist auch ihre Schönheit bloß eine dem Menschen . . . gegenüber gesteigerte", p.17.

focus was on man who literally provided the physical model for the
shape of the gods. However, the epic poets were well aware that
divine power also manifested itself in other forms which could be
ill-defined not to say vague. For often the gods in Homer visited this
world, or observed the doings of men, both undetected and visible in
the shape of birds; or they were contained in the elements like fire, or
appeared as a storm at sea, as did Poseidon. Sometimes in simile and
in fact the gods showed themselves as natural phenomena, like
Athena who appeared in the form of a falling star[72]. This rather
impersonal conception of divine power existed beside the more lively
anthropomorphic extensions of heroes, and both were regularly
confused in Homer. How else are we to understand Athena's
metamorphosis in *Iliad* 4 from a meteor to the Trojan hero Laodocus?
Poetic licence seems to reach its peak in the image of Athena during
the killing of the suitors. She is described as first addressing Odysseus
with the voice of Mentor after which she flew up to the roof of the hall
'like a swallow to behold', but then from the rafters she waved aloft
her *aegis* to cast terror in the suitors' hearts[73]. One would like to
know how exactly the sixth century Greek pictured this scene to
himself. It could hardly have been of Athena as a larger-than-life
goddess with *aegis,* helmet and breast-plate like Peisistratus' make-
believe figure on a chariot.

But there are many equally perplexing instances of vaguely
conceived divine epiphanies. Athena intervened physically in *Iliad* 1:
she appeared to Achilles, grasped him by the hair without, however,
becoming visible to anyone else beside him[74]. Perhaps she was a kind
of poetic personification of the hero's own impulse which had been
endowed with a physical or rather superhuman identity[75]. But the
episode is confusing if we are looking for conclusive evidence of
anthropomorphic epiphany. The same uncertainty applies to Thetis'
ascent from the sea like a mist. This image seems irreconcilable with
the ensuing *tête à tête* between mother and son by the sea shore[76].

---

[72] *Il.* 4, 75–8; *cf.* the simile of Ares rising to heaven like a storm cloud, *Il.* 5, 850–61;
864–74.
[73] *Od.* 22, 205–40; 297–8.
[74] *Il.* 1, 194–8.
[75] For a discussion of the passage see *Numen* 26 (1979) 143 and n.77.
[76] *Il.* 1, 359–62.

Also still in the same Book we are presented with a similar contrast between a fully anthropomorphically conceived Apollo bestriding Olympus with bow and arrows and the manner of his descent like Night[77].

Evidently while divine epiphany was an acceptable concept to the Homeric audience, it belonged outside the usual experience of divine power, nor need it always have occurred in anthropomorphic form. Far more common than actual divine *parousia* in Homer was a kind of spiritual communication between god and man. The human character did not see his god but assumed his presence through some outward, or indeed internal, signs. So the Trojan seer Helenus understood the purpose of Athena and Apollo in his *thymos*[78]. Or Odysseus was aware of Athena's support without actually seeing her[79]. Again Nestor divined the goddess' presence in aid of Telemachus because he knew that Athena honoured the father Odysseus[80]. There was no need for Hector to see Athena in order to know that she was responsible for his end[81].

On the face of it the weak credentials of epic epiphany should widen the gulf between Homer and prehistoric Minoan/Mycenaean traditions. This applies to the periodic renewal of kingship, for instance, which continued in various forms into historical times in Greece and Crete[82]. One survival in cult appears to have been the annual ceremony of setting up a throne for Zeus in his cave on Mt. Ida and for the priest to spend three times the normal prescribed period of nine days there as well[83]. He represented his community and received its periodic renewal directly from the god. However, the throne and meeting were symbolic: Zeus presumably communicated with the priest in other than physical form.

Perhaps then one should also revise one's opinion about post-Homeric archaic and classical cult practices. Our knowledge of these is primarily based on literary accounts, and these we know to have

---

[77] *Il.* 1, 44–9.
[78] *Il.* 7, 44–5.
[79] *Od.* 13, 318.
[80] *Od.* 3, 377–9.
[81] *Il.* 22, 296.
[82] Dietrich, *Origins* 61.
[83] Porphyr., *v. Pyth.*

been under the dominant influence of Homeric epic. Foundation myths of cult through divine visitation also generally lay in the legendary past and are suspect. The most likely occasions for direct divine appearances were in fact the many *theoxenia* and *theodaisia* during which major gods were invited to festive banquets and publicly entertained[84]. Historically such festivals were linked with similar divine communions in the Bronze Age and Geometric period. But like Zeus' *theoxenion* on Mt. Ida the occasions were symbolic in nature and probably did not involve actual epiphanies. They lacked the feeling of immediate presence which was suggested by the communal 'Totenschmauss' at which the spirits of the dead dined together with the living in a ceremony of consecration to the powers of the underworld. The Olympian gods did visit their cult centres and enter the houses which their worshippers had built for them. Many of their temples were thrown open once a year for this purpose[85]. But invariably the visit was symbolic, because in archaic times and later the gods became more remote abandoning the friendly *perioche* of the epic world. Not unexpectedly the story was the same in Attic vase painting of the sixth and fifth centuries B.C.[86].

Turning to post-Homeric literature one discovers the same uncertainty regarding presence and physical form of divinity[87]. This even applied to the 'Adventlieder' *par excellence*, that is the Homeric Hymns. In them the Homeric signs of epiphany were developed, refined and passed on to later poets. Gods were distinguished by weight and size, like Poseidon's feet which gave him away in the *Iliad*. Beauty, fragrance and above all shining brightness marked out the

---

[84] For refs. see Pritchett, *Greek State* III, 18.

[85] *E.g.* Paus. 8,47,5.

[86] In the sixth century B.C. Olympians occasionally appeared next to their heroes. Individual gods were shown as attending a sacrifice in their honour. Model and context were heroic epic as a rule. The painters' tableaux recall the special position of privileged heroes in Homer, *cf. Od.* 3, 420; 435. But by the end of the archaic period, on the early red-figure Attic vases, the gods became more remote. They now preferred the company of their peers to that of any mortal. They even poured their own libations. See J. Boardman, *Athenian Black Figures Vases*, London 1974, 216; *Athenian Red Figure Vases. The Archaic Period*, London 1975, 224.

[87] A good survey, with rather different conclusions, can be seen in L. Weniger, "Theophanien, altgriechische Götteradvente", *AfR* 22 (1924) 16–57.

advent of the still only too human Olympian[88]. In the great Hymn to Apollo, for example, the god's appearance is described with extraordinary verve, but without much semblance of reality, from the moment that he leapt aboard the Cretan ship in dolphin shape[89]. His meteor-like arrival at his shrine in Delphi shows the scene up as a poor imitation of Athena's epiphany in *Iliad* 4[90].

Already this cursory examination reveals that, outside some specialized cult of Demeter and Dionysus, epiphanies were quite doubtful events in Greece. In Homer they remained an extraordinary poetic device and consequently were not primarily religious in origin. If this conclusion is correct, it will certainly complicate our understanding of the beginnings and significance of actual iconic representations of the gods.

Homer depicted the gods as human, but as ideal human types rather than as a palpable physical presence which ordinary men must expect to see in their every day lives. The distinction is important if one is not to misunderstand Herodotus' much quoted remark that Homer and Hesiod described the gods' shape or form[91]. The Homeric *eidos* of the gods established the criteria for sculptors of divine images in the archaic age which consequently were equally idealized. But the Homeric Olympians lacked special individual characteristics beyond their superlative strength, size, beauty, etc. Epithets like dark-haired Poseidon, grey-eyed Athena, cow-eyed or white-armed Hera, no doubt reflected survivals from the past when the deity's power manifested itself in theriomorphic or some other form[92]. But for epic purposes such descriptions rarely carried any special significance beyond their poetic adornment[93]. The Homeric poets did, however, in this way create a vocabulary of divine attributes which signalled

---

[88] E. g. *Hymn. Dem.* 275–80; *Aphrod.* 172–5. *Cf.* Hesiod, *Scut.* 7–8; Theognis 9; Aesch., *P. V.* 115; Eur. *Hippol.* 1391. Imitations in Latin poetry are *inter alia* Verg. *Aen.* 1, 403; Ovid, *Fasti* 5, 375. Chapouthier, *Fond. Hardt* (1952) 85; N. J. Richardson, *The Homeric Hymn to Demeter,* Oxford 1974, 206–8; 252.

[89] *H. Hymn Apollo* 400–1.

[90] *Il.* 4, 75–8. See also the comments of Leaf and by Allen & Sikes in *The Homeric Hymns,* London 1904, 119 on 441–2.

[91] 2, 53, εἴδεα αὐτῶν σημήναντες.

[92] Nilsson, *MMR*[2] 501; G. S. Kirk, *The Songs of Homer,* Cambridge 1962, 35; 116; *cf.* Burkert, *Gr. Rel.* 197.

[93] E. Simon, *Die Götter der Griechen*[2], Munich 1980, 7.

areas of special functions for individual gods and also made them
instantly recognizable. The painter gladly accepted this new
convention and depicted Athena with her *aegis*, Hermes with staff
and winged sandals, Apollo with bow and lyre, Zeus brandishing the
thunderbolt, and so on[94]. The sculptor, too, followed the same
precedent when modelling cult statues for sanctuary and temple.
Thus the finished product presented something new and to some
extent artificial in religion along the lines of the mechanics and form
of epiphanies.

The statue then was intended to represent the god but not
incorporate him. Unlike Mesopotamian and Egyptian images[95], it
was lifeless and unable to hear prayer. To speak to such an image, as
Heraclitus put it, would be as senseless as talking to a house[96]. Statues
were no more than part of the temple architecture, both providing a
convenient focal point where prayer might be offered to a god[97]. Not
surprisingly, as the founder of this tradition of divine representation,
Homer had no word for statue. *Agalma* meant beautiful, precious
possession, the god's 'Prunkstück', whose fine workmanship and
beauty brought him pleasure[98]. So archaic sculpture on its own, or as
part of a larger architectural structure like pediment, column and the
like, was primarily a decorative element and designed to please god as
well as man. The archaic cult statue therefore contained no more
intrinsic religious power than the many contemporary dedications
which were put up in order to commemorate an athletic victory, as
grave monuments, to fulfil a vow, or pay a penalty[99].

From the seventh century B.C. the figure of the *kouros* did service
for all these purposes. His youthful form and regular proportions
always remained the same for every function[100]. He also acted as cult
statue, probably in imitation of Egyptian practice. However, unlike

---

[94] Burkert, *Gr. Rel.* 198; *cf.* F. Chapouthier, in *La Notion du Divin depuis Homère
jusqu'à Platon, Fond. Hardt I,* Geneva 1952, 85.
[95] Ringgren, *op.cit.* (see n.23) 105–9.
[96] Heraclitus B5.
[97] Aesch., *Eum.* 242; *cf.* Burkert, *Gr. Rel.* 153.
[98] ἀνδριάς was a later word, J. Boardman, *Greek Sculpture: The Archaic Period,*
Thames & Hudson, London 1978, 26; *cf.* E. Vermeule, *Götterkult,* Göttingen
1974, 121; 158.
[99] Cook, *Grk. Art* 82–3; *cf.* Snodgrass, *Arch. Gr.* 178–80.
[100] Cook, *Grk. Art* 84; Boardman, *Grk. Sculpt.* 22.

any eastern model, the Greek *kouros* and the much less common *kore* recognizably represented a particular divinity only by virtue of his or her special attributes or gesture. The nude male *kouros* set an ideal human standard for all future Greek sculpture both divine and secular[101]. Concept, religious significance and values were thoroughly epic, and these spread throughout the Greek world in proportion to the proliferation of statues and temples after 700 B.C.[102]. In multiple relief and pediment sculpture man, hero and god again freely congregated on the same level. Here myth was the motivating force, epic myth that is, which identified the gods, heroes and others by their particular attributes. But it was the story which was most important beside the decorative purpose of the sculpture, and not any religious message or significance of the divine figures involved, because so many of these scenes were inappropriate to the temple which they adorned from Athens to Zeus' temple at Olympia[103]. One thinks of the pretty but lifeless golden *kouroi* in Alcinous' palace or the golden dogs which guarded it[104]. In a famous anecdote Livy described how the sight of Pheidias' statue of Zeus in Olympia overwhelmed Aemilius Paulus who felt himself to be in the presence of the god[105]. Clearly a hyperbole and a tribute to the artist rather than a statement of faith, because, as we learn from Polybius, the

---

[101] Snodgrass, *Arch. Gr.* 178–9; P. Oliva, *The Birth of Greek Civilization*, London 1981, 156; E. Guralnick, "Profiles of Korai", in *AJA* 86 (1982) 173–82. On the history and significance of *kouros, kore* figures, their common use for secular and religious purposes, see also R. Carpenter, *Greek Sculpture. A Critical Review*, Chicago 1960, 17–26; Chr. Karusos, *Zur Geschichte der spätarchaisch-attischen Plastik und der Grabstatue*, Stuttgart 1961, 26–32; G. Richter, *Kouroi²*, New York 1970. N. M. Kontoleon, *Les écoles de l'art grec antique, Coll. de France*, Paris 1970, 79–87 (*kouros* figure evolved in Cyclades). On Korai as ideal human figures in aristocratic society and projected onto the family of gods see also, L. A. Schneider, *Zur sozialen Bedeutung der archaischen Korenstatuen, Hamburger Beitr. z. Arch. II*, Hamburg 1975, 31–7.

[102] C. G. Starr, *The Economic and Social Growth of Early Greece 800-500 B.C.*, Oxford 1977, 37; 129–30.

[103] Cook, *Grk. Art* 85. On myth in archaic sculpture see K. Schefold, *Myth and Legend in Greek Art*, London 1966; K. Fittschen, *Untersuchungen zum Beginn der Sagendarstellungen bei den Griechen*, Berlin 1969; Snodgrass, *Arch. Gr.* 184.

[104] *Od.* 7, 91–4; 100.

[105] *Iovem velut praesentem intuens*, Livy 45,28,5.

Roman general saw an image of Homer's Zeus[106]. Cicero's assessment of Pheidias' work came closest to the truth. The sculptor, he explained, did not have in mind an exact model, but an ideal type[107].

However, as we have seen, this ideal of beauty ultimately was based on the artist's interpretation of epic data rather than on his notion of the probable form in which divine power manifested itself. Both could in fact be conceived of in anthropomorphic form. But the Greek sculptor was subject to Homeric values and endowed his divine figures with human qualities as well as shape. Homeric epic then imposed human standards and not human form an archaic Greek art. Thus there was a conscious move in Greek divine iconography away from the conceptual towards the observed. To call this process evolution would be begging the question. But this change to the criteria of our own mortal society for measuring the gods never occurred in the east, although there too, the human form provided the model for expressing divine force of presence[108]. At the end of the great Panathenaic procession to the Athenian acropolis the *peplos* was not offered to Pheidias' statue in the Parthenon but to the goddess' image which stood in Erechtheum[109]. But there is no reason to doubt that the latter did not also possess recognizably human features although it actually incorporated the goddess' divine power. In other words the practice of showing gods in iconic form was much older than Homer.

In Book 6 of the *Iliad* the priestess Theano also dedicated the city's offering of a *peplos* to Athena and placed it on the goddess' knees[110]. Are we to agree with the view that the goddess on this occasion had appeared in person and was sitting in her temple in Troy?[111]. Surely not, in the light of what has already been said about Homeric epiphany[112]. There was a statue of Athena which could receive the

---

[106] Polybius 30, 10. Obviously it must also have been 'Homer's Zeus who cast his thunderbolt in approval of Pheidias' work, Paus. 5,11.9.

[107] Cicero, *Or.* 2, 8–9.

[108] Boardman, *Grk. Sc.* 66.

[109] C. J. Herington, *Athena Parthenos and Athena Polias.* 1955; Cook, *Grk. Art* 82.

[110] *Il.* 6, 302.

[111] Vermeule, *Götterkult* 121.

[112] It is unlikely that Athena's image and not the distant listening goddess nodded her refusal to Theano's prayer, *Il.* 6, 311; *cf.* Schol.A: γελοία δὲ καὶ ἡ ἀνανεύουσα Ἀθηνᾶ, although the idea no longer troubled Vergil, *Aen.* 1, 482.

offering. The figure was anthropomorphic. There is certainly no indication to the contrary in the text. And yet the image was no mere representation of an ideal form but in some way was felt to incorporate the goddess herself who received the gift of the *peplos*. Thus the episode concealed other, presumably older, ideas beyond the familiar epic view of divine manifestation. What makes such a conclusion difficult to accept is our thorough conditioning, which we inherited from the nineteenth century, that anthropomorphism in cult statues was a relatively late phenomenon which emerged at the end of a long evolution from a primitive aniconic figure[113].

Textbooks on Greek sculpture still regularly speak of an older pre-Homeric crude *xoanon* which continued to contain the divine power in archaic and classical cult. Since Winckelmann[114], who was one of the founders of the evolutionary theory, we read much about the 'mysteriöse Urzeit der "Xoana"'. But there is little that is particularly mysterious about *xoana* or surprisingly old. Pausanias informed his readers that all ancient statues were called *xoana* especially the Egyptian[115]. The Egyptian were not prehistoric, of course. Also suspicious are Pausanias' instances of old dedications which without exception were made by legendary figures. The truth is that *xoanon* in the sense of statue is not attested before the fifth century B.C., and there is no evidence that its use was confined to aniconic images. Callimachus in fact expressly contrasted Hera's iconic *xoanon* in Samos with her earliest image in the form of an unpolished crude board, *sanis axoos*[116]. *Xoana,* according to Pausanias, were made of wood. That is most likely true and accounts for their poor survival rate. They could be small or life-size and in human shape. They could also be made from other materials, however. Anthropomorphic stone figures were regularly dedicated together with aniconic offerings from Neolithic times[117].

Large anthropomorphic clay statues mostly of goddesses and

---

[113] Still in B. Rutkowski, *Frühgriechische Kultdarstellungen,* Berlin 1981, 114–21, 125.
[114] *Gesch. d. Kunst,* 1, 5 ff.
[115] 2,19,3.
[116] Frg. 100 Pf. On the history and usage of the *xoanon* see W. H. Gross in *PWRE* IX, A2 (1967) 2140–9; Jeanette Papadopoulos, *Xoana e Sphyrelata,* Rome 1980, 1–9; 15–73.
[117] S. Hood, *The Arts in Prehistoric Greece,* Penguin 1978, 89; 91; 15–73.

dating from the fifteenth century B.C. have been found on the island of Keos, and various remains on mainland Greece in Amyclae, Mycenae and Athens[118]. Evidence is extant of large wood and metal statues in Crete at Knossos and Phaistos from Middle Minoan times[119]. All that is left from what must have been a gigantic goddess figure in Knossos are her curls which were cast in bronze. Possibly the casting of monumental bronze figures in the Aegean at the time was subject to eastern influence. Most certainly the tradition was wide-spread in the Bronze Age from Cyprus to Syria, Anatolia and Crete[120]. The highly skilful early sculptors in metal in east and west were believed to possess magic powers. They entered myth as the legendary Daedalus or the Telchines or Corybants[121]. In Homer Hephaestus, too, was a worker of magic for the same reasons. He himself created his maiden attendants from gold. They were robots, however, although the poet described them as life-like with minds, voice, strength and knowledge from the gods[122].

Many examples of anthropomorphic gods worked in bronze and precious metals also remain extant from the Late Bronze Age. A common type was that of an armed figure with helmet, shield and spear or sword protecting the community or the metal which provided its wealth. The figure's realistic features seem eastern-inspired and in fact most examples come from there[123], although identical dedications were made in Cyprus and in the west at Tiryns, Mycenae and in Crete at least at Kato Symi in the south[124]. Spiritually the figure was Aegean. The mixture of styles expressed one common idea as in the splendid twelfth century statue which was found in the Mycenaean built temple in Cypriot Enkomi[125]. Nothing could be

---

[118] Hood, *Arts* 95; 106–7; 109.

[119] A. Evans, *PM* 4, 612; C. Laviosa, *Annuario S. Atene* 45/6 (1967/8) 499–510; D. Levi, *Boll. d'Arte* 1953, 256; Hood, *Arts* 95.

[120] H.-G. Buchholz, "Beobachtungen zum prähistorischen Bronzeguß in Zypern und der Ägäis", in *Cyprus and Crete*, 81–4.

[121] Boardman, *Grk. Sc.* 26; Buchholz, *Acts Nicosia 1979*. 76–86; *cf.* ch. II, p. 85.

[122] *Il.* 18, 417–20.

[123] A good list of examples with discussion and modern bibliography in W. Burkert, "Resep-Figuren, Apollon von Amyklai und die 'Erfindung' des Opfers auf Zypern", in *Grazer Beiträge* 4 (1975) 51–79. See the discussion in ch. IV, pp. 166–173.

[124] Buchholz, *Cyprus and Crete*, 85 n.41.

[125] References in Burkert, *Graz. Beitr.* (1975) 67 n.48; *cf.* Dietrich, "Some Evidence from Cyprus of Apolline Cult in the Bronze Age", in *RM* N.F. 121 (1978) 13;

more true to nature than this anthropomorphic image of the god. It appears that the figure did not obviously represent any theological advance over contemporary aniconic dedications. This juxtaposition continued into historic times. At Amyclae, for example, the tradition of revering the community god in the form of a helmeted and armed warrior survived[126]. The cult then belonged to Apollo whose better known image there was aniconic, however, or at best semi-iconic, consisting of a bronze pillar but with human extremities. His head still wore the helmet, though, and his arms carried spear and bow[127]. An identical figure of armed Apollo stood elsewhere in Laconia at the time, namely on the hill Thornax[128]. These statues were late, of course, but they nevertheless reflected prehistoric, in fact, Neolithic, religious concepts[129].

Aniconic and iconic cult representations were dedicated side by side in Minoan cave and related peak sanctuaries[130]. Quite charming figurines incorporating an Eileithyia-type goddess in the Inatos cave in southern Crete were dedicated next to images of the phallus, one with a face engraved on it[131]. Early aniconic stalagmitic divine images often continued in Bronze Age Aegean cult even after it had been transferred from its original sanctuary in a cave to another shrine within the palace or city. Some stalagmites were partly worked into human figures without, however, losing the unmistakable features of their origins. The practice is still fully documented from the many Neolithic remains in Anatolian Çatal Hüyük, but also in Minoan Crete which preserved semi-human limestone concretions for its palace shrines[132]. There was a link between the Amnisos cave with its stalagmite as the centre of the cult and shaped stalagmitic remains which were deposited in the Little Palace at Knossos. The latter

---

Buchholz, *Cyprus and Crete*, 81–4. According to C. Picard, "Midea a Salamis de Chypre", *Geras Antoniou Keramopoullou*, Athens 1953, 1–16, the statue depicts a Mycenaean warrior.

[126] A terracotta head of such a figure survived from the eighth century B.C. as well as a similar smaller clay statuette, refs. in *Graz. Beitr.* (1975) 63 n.61.

[127] Paus. 3,19,2.

[128] Herod. 1,69; Paus. 3,10,8.

[129] *RM* (1978) 9.

[130] Hood, *Arts* 89; 91; 103; 104; 106.

[131] In Herakleion Museum, unpublished and may not be photographed.

[132] Dietrich, *Origins* 105–7; 124.

betrayed their origins but had the human features of mother and child, because cave cult had always been primarily concerned with birth[133].

Both iconic and aniconic image served the same purpose: they incorporated divine power. The stalagmite at Amnisos and the Amyclaean pillar were literally alive with it like the *lithoi empsychoi* in Semitic cult which at once served as the god's image and his altar[134]. But so were anthropomorphic statues or indeed a mixture of both forms. There is no real tangible sense of chronological evolution from primitive to fully naturalistic form. The 'primitive' always kept its value and power. In fact one could argue for a reverse process of development in the case of the stylized semi-iconic bell-shaped and cylindrical Minoan idols which succeeded the perfectly realistic Middle Bronze Age figurines of the palace or snake goddess at Knossos. Like the countless Mycenaean 'Phi', 'Tau' and 'Psi' figures[135], they are evidence of an artistic decline perhaps but not of any change in divine concept.

In the last chapter the mask and pole as divine image emerged as two striking religious revivals from the Neolithic age, particularly in the cult of Dionysus. The mask on its own served in certain chthonic ritual scenes of *anodos*. As Perikionios Dionysus' image retained the mixture of both life-like mask and aniconic pillar. The mask was fixed to the pillar, sometimes with a capital, or to a tree, and the vase painters were careful to show the green branches sprouting from the figure of the god[136]. The combination illustrates the juxtaposition of iconic and aniconic elements. Both carriers of divine power on their own, they came together into a kind of semi-iconic image of the deity precisely like the historic Amyclaean pillar with hands and feet

---

[133] Dietrich, *Origins* 88; 109–10; 117. On the survival of these traditions in Mycenaean and historic Greek cult see *Historia* 31 (1982) 1–12, above ch. I, 35; 36; ch. II, 77–8.

[134] H. Ringgren, *The Religion of Ancient Syria* in *Historia Religionum*, Leiden 1969, 1, 210.

[135] Hood, *Arts* 110–11. *Cf.* E. French, *The Development of Mycenaean Terracotta Figurines* (*BSA* 66 (1971)) 104; 106.

[136] Ch. II, p. 74, 75; L. Deubner, *Attische Feste*, repr. Berlin 1956, 127; 133; Pl. 20, 1; Nilsson, *Gesch.* I³, 208; 572; 588 and Pl. 37,1. We cannot now enter into the dispute whether the scenes referred to the Lenaea (Deubner) or Anthesteria (Nilsson). See also A. Pickard-Cambridge, *The Dramatic Festivals of Athens²*, Oxford 1968, 32–4.

representing Apollo[137], or Aphrodite's famous statue with 'square feet' in Athens and on Delos[138]. Apollo Epikourios' Corinthian pillar also preserved the same tradition. It stood next to his anthropomorphic votives in Iktinos' classical temple in Arcadian Bassae[139].

Quite regularly the image was completed with a cloak which was hung about the pole or tree. The intention was not to render the figure more realistically anthropomorphic, for that effect could have been better achieved in other ways. But the cloak was an offering to the god, a gift, like that of the *peplos* to Athena or to Hera at Olympia. The classical ritual therefore continued an ancient tradition which remained quite explicit in the Daedala festival during which the cloak was draped about Hera's board-like idols[140]. The nature of the original Neolithic cult was connected with apotropaeic and generative divine powers in all their wide ramifications from healing, warding off sickness to fertility of man and nature in general[141]. There were no doubt exceptions,[142], but by and large we must believe that the shapeless image or stone actively embodied divine power. Despite the massive anthropological and religious literature on the subject, the idea of this power manifesting itself through pillar or tree remains alien to us und very difficult to comprehend. Some partially iconic images came close to expressing individual personality. But they are not epiphanies of particular gods. Rather they must be understood as manifestations of general divine power within a particular sphere[143].

---

[137] Above p. 107; ch. IV p. 167.

[138] Paus. 1,19,2; 9,40,3–4.

[139] *Cf.* ch. IV, 169.

[140] Simon, *Götter*², 59. For a list of divine images which received cloaks *etc.* see F. Willemsen, *Frühe Griechische Kultbilder*, diss. Munich 1939, 36 ff.

[141] On Agyieus and related figures see Yalouris, *Gr & It.*, 100–1; *cf.* my article "Late Bronze Age Troy", in *Historia* 29 (1980) 501–2. Similar aniconic stones, possibly of guardian deities, have also recently come to light in Cyprus at Hala Sultan Tekke, see P. Aström's preface to *Hala Sultan Tekke 5* (U. Öbrink), in *SMA XLV*, 5, IV.

[142] The seventh century B.C. limestone blocks with daedalic masks or heads from a cenotaph in Thera probably were symbolic of sailors lost at sea, Boardman, *Grk. Sc.* 14; fig. 40.

[143] How far the highly individualistic Bronze Age iconic figures like the 15th c. B.C. Kean goddesses or 13th century Mycenaean figures, or even the semi-iconic cylindrical idols from Subminoan Gazi and Karphi, fit into this context is another matter which cannot be decided here. On the 'personality' of the Mycenaean figures see W. Taylour, "New Aspects on Mycenaean Religion", in *Acta 2nd Inter.*

The Neolithic survivals often transcended the bounds of what is possible in human or animal nature, because they represented powers which could not easily be defined by one particular shape. This generalness was responsible for inexplicable features in myth and art like the common sexless or bisexual and hybrid figures. Both sexless and bisexual characteristics emphasized the same idea only in two different ways. Examples of both were common in Neolithic Europe and in the Aegean[144] and had the same significance of giving shape to a universal divine principle. To draw an analogy from another culture, the Indic Aditi figure in the *Rigveda* was an equally all-embracing power: it was called mother, father and son at once[145].

This universal characteristic continued in some isolated instances in the western Aegean during the Bronze Age[146], but, as far as it is possible to judge, did not significantly recur until after its end. There are numerous examples in Neolithic and historic times[147]. The most interesting from the evidence is undoubtedly the so-called Palladion. Whatever the etymology, the Palladion was the armed figure of the community deity with protective apotropaeic properties[148]. In later post-Cyclic tradition it became exclusively associated with Athena but in fact originally had embodied other protecting deities notably from our group with aniconic connections, namely Apollo, Artemis, Hera and Aphrodite[149]. The sex of these protecting city gods became significant only in their fully anthropomorphic representations, that is in the Homeric form. However, the oldest extant examples, like the seventh century bronze figure from Olympia, still show the ancient

---

Coll. Aegean Prehist., Athens 1972, 80. G. Karo some 35 years ago remarked on the personal characteristics of some of the gold masks in the Shaft Graves, in *Greek Personality in Archaic Sculpture, Martin Class. Lect. XI,* Harvard 1948, 7.

[144] Gimbutas, "Pre-Hellenic and Pre-Indo-European Goddesses and Gods: the Old European Pantheon", in *Acta Athens 1972,* 82–97; *cf.* references in previous chapter. See also M. E. Robbins, *Indo-European Female Figures,* thesis, Los Angeles 1978, 15, with many further references.

[145] *R. V.* I, 89, 10; *cf.* Robbins, *Fem. Figs.* 15; 100.

[146] See previous chapter, *e. g.* p. 66; 72.

[147] *Ibid.* and P. J. Ucko, *Anthropomorphic Figurines of Predynastic Egypt and Neolithic Crete,* 1978, 316.

[148] L. Ziehen, "Palladion", in *P. W. R. E.* (1949) 186.

[149] *Historia* 29 (1980) 503.

crude universal shape whose sex at best ist doubtful[150]. Their ancestry was the same as that of the semi-iconic and aniconic images of Apollo Agyieus and Amyklaios[151].

The worshipper tried to show these gods in physical shape. But he had no standard of reference to any realistic iconographic model, and he therefore created many strange and nightmarish aberrations. These have been collected by Marija Gimbutas and need not be cited in detail[152]. Even the grotesque Mother Goddess figurines with their exaggerated emphasis on the procreative function were obviously rather less than realistic images of universal divine power which the artist could not express in any other way. So, too, cultic pillar or stone was of indeterminate sex, because it could be male, female, or even animal. Even the ithyphallic pillars of Hermes were more closely related to aniconic representations of numinous power than to realistic anthropomorphic form. Such figures actually conveyed the same message twice, because pillar and phallus could be identical, both incorporating the power of fertility and protection against enemies and evil[153]. Thus stone herms were immensely strong sources of divine power to guard boundaries of field, road and house and to ensure fruitfulness. But the stone phallus often performed these functions on its own. Herm, Hermes and phallus therefore were really three words for the same thing. In Cyllene in fact the god was revered in the shape of a phallus[154]. Difficulties arose only once the Homeric anthropomorphic Hermes superseded the ancient pillar. Then to portray the youthful attractive Hermes as ithyphallic exceeded the bounds of Greek good taste. Fortunately examples are quite rare and late[155].

Equally puzzling and offensively unnatural would be the close bond between deity and animal in another religious context. From

---

[150] A. Mallwitz, *Olympia und seine Bauten*, Darmstadt 1972, 86, fig. 73; *cf.* Burkert, *Graz. Beitr.* 4 (1975) 66.
[151] *Cf.* E. Kunze, *Berichte über die Ausgrabungen in Olympia VII. Frühjahr 1956 bis 1958*, Berlin 1961, 160 ff.; Vermeule, *Götterkult* 165; *Historia* (1980) 503. See also n. 141.
[152] See previous chapter, *e. g.* p. 65.
[153] H. Herter, "Hermes", in *RM* 119 (1976) 220–1. See also the previous chapter p. 62.
[154] Paus. 6,26,5.
[155] Herter, *RM* (1976) 220.

Anatolia to Cyprus, Greece and Crete votives, glyptic and painted scenes tell the story of the artists' endeavour to express the manifestation and effectiveness of divinity. Bull horns, heads and masks, stags and many other creatures were the instruments and embodiment of the deity. How else could we explain the strange scenes of animal birth from the goddess in ritual scenes like those in Neolithic shrines of Çatal Hüyük[156]? In archaic Greece these beliefs survived to any extent only in the cults of Dionysus and Artemis, and in some strange cults of Demeter in Arcadia and Boeotia. In myth, of course, extravagant beings like Minotaur, Centaur and the like reflect the same ancient tradition. But 'Mischwesen', like Centaurs, continued to play a part in rustic festivals. Geometric and early archaic representations show that human performers disguised themselves with masks and make-up for such ritual[157]. Centuries later classical iconography remembered the intimate relationship of god and animal. Poseidon was associated with horse and bull, Artemis with stag or deer, and so on[158]. Both were closely bound together but no longer interchangeable, a pale echo in fact of the original significance of the combination.

After Homer the images of gods, which became common in large life-like form after the middle of the seventh century B.C., aspired to an ideal human type. They were representative of the god and took their individual personality, no less than their attributes, from epic myth[159]. But also earlier cult images, it turns out, whether aniconic or iconic and anthropomorphic, incorporated divine power rather than served as physical manifestation of a particular god. There is little or no evidence that even the oldest Neolithic idols attracted, or themselves commemmorated, actual epiphanies. In some primitive societies man-made idols were considererd to be the bodily receptacle in which the divine spirit could take up its abode. The worshippers dressed, fed and generally tended such images[160]. Similar cult images underwent certain rituals to inspire them with

---

[156] Dietrich, *Origins* 103.
[157] Burkert, *Gr. Rel.* 170, 269 n.10. On Centaurs see also ch. II, p. 72.
[158] *Ibid.* 114.
[159] See Schefold and Fittschen in n.103 above.
[160] G. Landtman, "The Origins of Images as Objects of Cult", *AfR* (1926) 196–208; especially 196–8.

life. They were fed and otherwise made physically comfortable[161]. Greek idols, too, were ritually washed and dressed but were not thought of as incarnations of the god. It is plain now that, whether iconic or not, they incorporated his numinous power but not the god himself. They were more of a direct link, or point of contact, with him.

Numerous myths record that an idol had fallen from the sky some time in the dim past, or reached its worshippers in some mysterious way like that of the Taurian Artemis[162], or that of Athena Polias[163]. Its mysterious power could hurt and heal like the chthonic hero and daemon[164]. The myth of Orestes' madness after his matricide and cure through the power of the effigy of the Taurian Artemis became popular in the fifth century B.C. The scene of the healing was localised not only in Halae but in places as far apart as Sicilian Tyndaris, Italien Aricia and Commagene in Cilicia. The legend itself was relatively recent. It could not have been made up before the seventh century when the Greeks first came into contact with the Taurian cult on the Black Sea[165]. But the ritual and belief in the power of the image were ancient. So Diomede and Odysseus were obliged to steal the Palladion before Troy could fall[166]. The statue's presence was necessary to the community's well-being. But it could also release uncontrolled strength unless it was tied as well as appeased[167]. There are many examples of such ritual binding in the cults of Hera Tonaia (Rope) in Samos, of Artemis in Erythrae[168], and of Artemis as Lygodesma and Orthia in Sparta[169]. The tradition survives beneath

---

[161] S. H. Hooke, *Babylonian and Assyrian Religion,* repr. Oxford 1962, 48; A. L. Oppenheim, *Ancient Mesopotamia,* Chicago 1964, 186.

[162] Eur., *I. T.* 977–8.

[163] Paus. 1,26,7; *cf.* Apoll. 3,143; *cf.* Dionysus Cadmeius, Paus. 9,12,4.

[164] Dietrich, *Death, Fate and the Gods* 51; 56.

[165] *Cf.* F. Graf, "Das Götterbild aus dem Taurerland", *Antike Welt* 4 (1979) 33–41.

[166] *Zeitschrift für Religions- und Geistesgeschichte* 22 (1970) 356–68; Burkert, *Gr. Rel.* 221; Dietrich, *Historia* 29 (1980) 503.

[167] *Cf.* Burkert, *Gr. Rel.* 153.

[168] Polemon Schol. Pindar, *Ol.* 7,95a.

[169] Paus. 3,16,10–11. The Lygos plant *(vitex agnus-castus)* was said to inhibit the sexual drive, *cf.* C. Kerenyi, *Zeus and Hera,* transl. by C. Holme, London 1975, 157. "Das ist aber spätere Auslegung", Nilsson, *Gesch.* I³, 430, who believes that the Lygos was part of the "Brautbett", in a Sacred Marriage ceremony, *Feste* 48–9. *Cf.* Paus. 3,15,7, Enyalios in Sparta. Further literature in Burkert, *Gr. Rel.* 153

the Christian veneer in Crete and Greece to this day. The miraculous icon of Our Lady in Panagia Kera on Crete was bound to its column by three chains. According to tradition it had left Constantinople three times to return to Kera[170]. The legend exactly recalls the periodic disappearance and restoration of Hera's *xoanon* in Samos[171]. Though her image was tended and even had cakes offered to it[172], the symbol never became the goddess in physical form, merely a watchful divine presence. In the Spartan cult of Artemis Orthia the priestess stood beside the altar during the ritual whipping of the Spartan boys holding the goddess' image in her arms. If the beating was too light, the figure grew heavier expressing the anger of Artemis[173].

Homer did not fundamentally alter this conception of divinity. He built on it. The familiar *perioche* of epic hero and god managed to endow the Olympians with greater humanity and personality. Homer also first defined their separate functions and mythology, for their 'Sagenbild' had largely been created for them by epic[174]. So epic theology combined with Greek and pre-Greek religious traditions to produce the archaic and classical view of the pantheon. The gods had further been exposed to the formative forces of prehistoric European and eastern cults. They had most certainly been influenced by the Minoan and Mycenaean interlude at the end of the Bronze Age. Homer's Olympians, too, shared some basic features with earlier oriental and Aegean cultures. Their family organization, their mountain home, their very origins had been taken from an eastern religious *koine*[175]. However, their individual personality set the Greek gods apart from their models. And the clearest indication of this characteristic quality is signalled by the remarkable etymological obscurity of their names. Helios' and Hestia's significance may always

---

n. 90. The statue of a bound Artemis was found in the Piraeus in 1959, *BCH* 84 (1960) 653, fig. 8 (fourth century B.C.).

[170] The icon was very old, F. Cornelius in *Creta Sacra* I,13,63. For the history and local tradition see S. G. Spanakis, *Crete*, Herakleion 1965, 193.

[171] Kerenyi, *Zeus* 151–2. The cult was originally Argive, or more probably a mixture of Argive and Samian elements, Nilsson, *Feste* 48 (Argos); Kerenyi, *ibid.*, says that Hera's sanctuary came from Argos, but that the legend was much older in Samos.

[172] On the rites of the *Tonaea* see Nilsson, *Feste* 48–9.

[173] Paus. 3,16,11; Nilsson, *Feste* 192; *cf.* Graf, *Antike Welt* (1979) 41.

[174] See Schefold and Fittschen in n. 103 above; Burkert, *Gr. Rel.* 197.

[175] *E. g.* Dietrich, *Origins* 1–68.

have been obvious like the names of other minor figures. But those of the great Olympian gods could not be understood[176]. According to their origins they were not Greek, not even always Indo-European, but their meaning had been lost some time in the dim past. Even the once patently Indo-European figure of Zeus had become a 'person' to the classical Greek and was no longer identified with a Sky-god. As we noticed earlier on, the Greek practice does not fit into the normal, etymologically transparent, categories of divine nomenclature according to function[177], invocatory title[178], locality, or simply the predicative address of 'god'. The Greek went one step further. For him Zeus was a personal experience not the personification of a natural phenomenon. When it rained, he tautologically said, *Zeus hyei*. It is impossible to determine whether the personal evolved from the impersonal concept[179]. This was Usener's principle that personal gods were the result of a quirkish linguistic development[180]. But if, as seems quite certain, the Greeks were unaware of the ancient and widely differing origins of their 'borrowed' gods, they may well have missed out on the first step of this evolutionary ladder.

Greek divine etymologising generally followed the reverse order from personal name to *nomen agentis*. Their ears were sensitive to possible concealed Greek meanings in what were ultimately non-Greek divine names. Cassandra in the *Agamemnon* of Aeschylus called the god Apollo her destroyer, *apollon emos*[181]. The function is familiar enough from Apollo's past as destroyer and bringer of the plague, but to Cassandra the god was a very personal figure[182]. However, Cassandra's theological pun contains a fairly intractable problem. If Homer assigned to the gods their functions[183], when did their names first become known and linked with their cults as we

---

[176] Burkert, *Gr. Rel.* 282–3.
[177] See above p. 88.
[178] Dietrich, *Origins* 189; *RM* 121 (1978) 17.
[179] So Kerenyi, *Zeus* 10.
[180] H. Usener, *Götternamen*, Bonn 1896, 316, "die bedingung für die entstehung persönlicher götter ist ein sprachgeschichtlicher vorgang".
[181] Aesch., *Agam.* 1081. L. R. Palmer suggests that the form of the name (Apollon) arose through the influence of ἀπόλλυμι, "Mycenaean Religion: the theological choices", in *Colloquium Nürnberg* 1981, 361.
[182] All etymologies are unsatisfactory including Burkert's, *Gr. Rel.* 227.
[183] Herod. 2,53.

know them in the Greek world? Chronologically these were two distinct events, because the association of an Olympian name with one particular cult, even his or her oldest Greek cult, was generally much later than the origin of the name itself. In Cyprus, for example, Aphrodite's name had become firmly established by the eighth century B.C., because both Homer and Hesiod connected her with the island. However, her name replaced the older title of *Wanassa,* or Queen, much later in Paphos. The change came perhaps as late as the fifth century B.C. when Cimon's campaign spread Athenian influence in Cyprus[184]. Aphrodite was of eastern descent but had already been subject to Greek epic influence when she lent her name to the cult goddess in Paphos and elsewhere on the island.

The second chief Cypriot deity Apollo had undergone a similar history. His most important cult site at Kourion will be examined in detail in the next chapter. He was still known there as 'the god' in inscriptions of the sixth century B.C. but became identified with Apollo not before classical times[185]. In the aftermath of the conflict with the Persian empire during the Ionian rebellion, the Cypriots felt a strong affinity for the gods of the western Greeks. Hence their important cult figures, which until then had been worshipped simply as 'god' or 'goddess' or Paphos, Golgoi or such and such locality, were identified as major Olympians like Apollo, Aphrodite or Athena[186]. Apollo's name was familiar enough to the Mycenaean immigrants in Cyprus in the thirteenth century B.C. already, though it, too, had originally come from the east[187]. The Cypriot experience, for all its special historic and geographical situation, illustrates in microcosm what happened in Greece. Old, sometimes prehistoric, divine names appeared not only in ancient cult sites but also in more recently instituted precincts to which a cult had been transferred from elsewhere.

In the western Aegean the Minoan/Mycenaean documents still suggest a preference for invocatory titles like Mistress, or Potnia,

---

[184] S. T. Parker, "Cimon's Expedition to Cyprus", *AJP* 97 (1976) 30–8; *Cults* 319. See p. 16 also ch.II, 80; IV, 160.

[185] See ch.IV, p. 153 with references.

[186] See T. B. Mitford, *AJA* 65 (1961) 134 and n. 172; Bennett, *Cults of the Cypriotes* 351–2; 337.

[187] *Kadmos* 14 (1975) 133–42; *cf.* above n. 182 and below ch.IV, n. 364, for a brief discussion of the evidence.

Lord, or King of the Clan, if that is the sense of *anax*[188]. Tradition preserved similar figures like Britomartis, The Sweet Virgin, The Holy One, Ariadne, The Invisible Goddess, Aphaea[189]. However, beside some others and a few obscure functional titles, or epithets, of gods, the Linear B tablets also recorded the names of Olympians such as Zeus, Hera, Poseidon, Hermes, Artemis, Dionysus and Athena. One Pylian tablet (Tn 316) names Zeus together with his Homeric spouse Hera. Poseidon, too, was known as the god of a community at Pylos. There has been much excitement since the discovery of these names in Minoan and Mycenaean worship. Many questions remain, however, regarding their cult and significance at the time. For beside Hera we also meet *diwija*, or Dia, with Zeus on several tablets from Pylos and Knossos (Tn 316; An 607.5; Cn 1287.6). The Pylian tablet contains a similar female counterpart of Poseidon, namely *posidaeja* (Tn 316). Zeus' offspring, presumably with Hera, was Drimios, according to Pylian tablet Tn 319[190]. But Drimios was unknown to Greek divine mythology. Those names, which did become familiar currency in later cult, nevertheless remain unmatched, or at best unrecognizable, in Minoan/Mycenaean art[191]. The picture does not agree with the text.

It seems wise to reserve judgement concerning the functions and standing of these figures at the end of the Bronze Age. Their names form only a part of a far more complex pantheon[192]. Some like Drimios, though evidently associated with our so-called Olympians, fell from use. The same fate was suffered by others, whose significance at present remains totally obscure. Some of those, which unaccountably disappeared, do, however, share one important common feature with the gods with higher survival rate. Their names were very old, easily antedating Mycenaean times. The group included major Olympians no less than figures which were ignored by later mythology like Manasa (PY Tn 316) and Pipituna (Fp 13). A few names, such as Diktynna, did remotely survive but came to be

---

[188] See O. Szemerenyi, "Homerica et Mycenaica", *SMEA* (1979), 217.
[189] Nilsson, *M.M.R.*² 510–512–523–4; *Gesch.* I³, 314–5.
[190] *dirimijo diwo ijewe.*
[191] *Cf.* St. Hiller, "Mykenische Archäologie", *SMEA* (1979), 217.
[192] *E. g.* St. Hiller–O. Panagl, *Die frühgriechischen Texte aus Mykenischer Zeit*, Darmstadt 1976, 289–314, for a good general discussion of cult figures and titles in Linear B; *cf.* J. Chadwick, *The Mycenaean World*, CUP, 1976, 84–101.

superseded in cult. There is no obvious distinction in this group between Bronze Age Crete and Greece. Evidently Minoans and Mycenaeans knew these prehistoric deities and, by the last phases of the Bronze Age, offered them the same kind of worship[193].

No doubt other notable figures lie hidden in this category but have not yet been identified on the Linear documents. Demeter is one likely candidate. A few were not only older than the Bronze Age, but they did not even seem particularly at home in its religion as it is reflected in contemporary iconography. Names and cults of Poseidon, Artemis, Hermes[194], and indeed of Demeter, were rooted in the Stone Age. But the Mycenaeans adopted some of their cults from the earlier inhabitants of Greece and developed them as we can still see in the history of Hermes, for example, and Athena[195]. It is another question, however, whether they also continued the older cults in precisely the same form. The evidence suggests otherwise. At times the link between Stone Age and archaic Greece seems closer than that with the Mycenaean Bronze Age.

Clearly the names of gods were old but not necessarily their association with a particular archaic and classical cult site. Before epic had imposed its Olympian family throughout the Greek world, a few chosen deities dominated universally and spread in proportion with the tremendous growth of sanctuaries and temples. Their cults on the acropolis or community centre formed the heart of the new *polis* from the eighth century B.C.[196]. Some, however, were outside in inconvenient locations or unrelated to a community, because the area had been hallowed by cult since time immemorial[197]. But sites with continuous cult, too, were not often attached to a particular named deity before the eighth century or later. The reasons for this vary. There may simply be a lacuna in our evidence. Occasionally divine names may have changed at older sites, for all we know. Most commonly, however, personalised gods were substituted for titles, local appellative or invocatory forms. This process happened relatively late in Cyprus and has been well documented at the most

---

[193] L. Baumbach, "The Mycenaean Contribution to the Study of Greek Religion in the Bronze Age", *SMEA* (1979), 147.

[194] With still somewhat uncertain credentials for Hermes in Linear B see ch.II p. 76.

[195] On Hermes and Athena, see ch.II, pp. 76–83.

[196] A. Snodgrass, *Archaic Greece*, London 1980, 33; 118.

[197] *Cf.* ch. II, p. 60.

important cult sites. Further west the change began with the archaic age for the same reason. Epic poetry had breathed life into old names. Persons replaced power. The history of the cult at Gortyn in Crete is a perfect example of this process. By the 7th century B.C. Athena had emerged fully armed from the Minoan goddess there. Similar lines of development can be plotted for Dionysus and other gods from Cyprus to the Cyclades and Greece[198].

On the mainland of Greece architecture and tradition suggest that the important cult at Eleusis had also survived from the Bronze Age into historical times. But the date when Demeter took over is less certain. The oldest identifiable votives to her by name belonged to the eighth century[199]. The name was actually as old as the Stone Age, and we do know that the Ionians worshipped the goddess in Attica before they took her with them to Miletus in the eleventh century[200]. At Eleusis, though, Demeter may not have replaced the Mycenaean Potnia, or Lady, until the archaic age. But we can be reasonably certain that the background of the Minoan/Mycenaean cult there in its basic features foreshadowed Demeter's Mysteries[201]. In other words, for all their new personal form at least some major gods of archaic Greece did not entirely break with the past but continued with fundamentally the same significance. At Eleusis the scenes of rebirth and renewal culminated in historical times in Demeter's Mysteries. The path of evolution remained visible even in the last stages of the cult.

It seems likely that the rules, by which a particular deity, or group of deities, became attached to one place, were determined by the community there which would obviously offer its own god for the purpose, provided his background coincided with the nature of the ancient cult. At Symi in southern Crete an extraordinarily well documented cult continued from Minoan to classical Greek and indeed Roman times. It was exposed to eastern and mainland Greek influence through its long history, but such changes as there were came about naturally, and the worshippers continued to use the same implements in the ritual and dedicated identical figurines. But by the

---

[198] Ch. II, p. 47 (Athena at Gortyn); 48; 49.
[199] Coldstream, *Geom. Greece* 332.
[200] Herod. 9,97.
[201] See above ch. I, 33–34.

seventh century B.C. Aphrodite and Hermes owned the cult. From then on their dedications show them to be the familiar personal figures of archaic and classical times. But of course their link with the past was crystal clear[202].

Homer did not reflect the spread and nature of archaic cults with their particular deities. There was little contact in epic with the varied historical past of individual gods. The poet had no regard for history or politics. So his Olympian pantheon, which became common coinage in the *polis,* in a sense existed in an historical vacuum. The nature of these Olympians was governed by literary criteria and revolved about their proximity to man. Their functions arose from myth and from their duties as community deities. The Homeric contribution therefore was intensely personal. In this context the creation of one divine power from another like Athena from the head of Zeus, or Hephaestus and Ares from Hera is unusual and wayward. It was only subsequent to epic, I believe, that the Greek worshipper saw his god as a person in the true anthropomorphic sense as 'man' or 'woman', so to speak, and not as sexless numinous power. Obviously only then could myths like Zeus' seduction by Hera or the adulterous union of Ares and Aphrodite become amusing as well as meaningful.

---

[202] On the site of Symi, history and dedications, see ch. I, pp. 32–33.

An Archaic Sanctuary of Apollo in Cyprus

Kourion was one of the three most important sanctuaries in Cyprus in Roman times. Roman buildings of the first two centuries of our era confused and destroyed earlier structures particularly south of the *temenos* boundaries. However, it is obvious that Roman interest revived and continued the religious traditions which made this sanctuary a significant place of worship in archaic times. Its form and the nature of the finds in the precinct suggest an even longer history of continuity of tradition which began in the Bronze Age if not earlier.

The sanctuary was not associated with any habitation or settlement. Neolithic Sotira Teppes, some three to four miles to the north, and the Chalcolithic settlement of Sotira Kaminoudhia, which lies at the bottom of the eastern slope of the same hill near the modern village and which is being excavated at present, are in no wise connected with the sanctuary[1]. The latter is barely visible from the top of Teppes, or rather the towers of the nearby British radar installation. Physically nearer but equally unrelated is the Late Bronze Age settlement on the hill of Episkopi Bamboula some two miles west of the sanctuary. Bamboula was an important city judging by the architecture of the buildings, fortifications, by the necropolis and finds there[2]. It replaced the earlier settlement at Phaneromeni which is visible from the acropolis of Bamboula directly to the west on the

---

[1] On Sotira Teppes (Neolithic II, 5th mill. B.C.) see P. Dikaios, *Sotira*, Philadelphia 1961; 'The Stone Age of Cyprus', *SCE*, IV, IA, Lund 1962; E.J. Peltenburg, 'The Sotira Culture: Regional Diversity and Cultural Unity in Late Neolithic Cyprus' in *Levant* X (1978) 55–74; N.P. Stanley Price in *Levant* XI (1979) 46–83; V. Karageorghis, *Cyprus. From The Stone Age to the Romans*, London 1982, 29.

[2] Excavation reports on Bamboula by J.F. Daniel in the *University Museum Bulletin*, Philadelphia, in 1937; 1938; 1939; 1940; 1948; *AJA* 42 (1938); 43 (1939); 45 (1941); J.L. Benson, 'Bamboula at Kourion: The Stratification of the Settlement', Parts 1 and 2, in *RDAC* (1969 and 1970); *Bamboula at Kourion: The Necropolis and Finds*, Univ. Mus. Philadelphia 1972; S.S. Weinberg, 'Kourion – Bamboula: The Late Bronze Age Architecture', in *AJA* 56 (1952) 178 ff.

sweltering western banks of the Kouris river about two miles from its mouth[3].

Bamboula, however, was only one of numerous settlements in the area which was loosely referred to as Kourion in classical times. One succeeded another and temporarily rose to prominence for a period until it too was left abandoned for a new site. Many tombs have been discovered with burials ranging over long spans of time without always being related to a particular known settlement. A large cemetery at Kaloriziki below and eastward of the bluff of Kourion contained burials over some six hundred years from the end of the Bronze Age (Late Cypriot IIIB) until the beginning of the classical period (475 B.C.)[4]. It too served several unidentifiable cities which may have been contiguous to the necropolis, as in the case of Bamboula and Phaneromeni in the Bronze Age, or nearer to the sanctuary area on the bluff itself.

Possibly a shift to the latter site in Cypro-Geometric I coincided with the arrival of a large number of new Mycenaean settlers during the eleventh century B.C. One of the tombs in Kaloriziki contained gold and the magnificent gold and enamel sceptre of a Mycenaean born king of that age[5]. However, the name of the city may have been known in Egypt a century earlier if the word Kir, which was inscribed on the walls of the temple at Medinet Habu during the reign of Ramses III (1198/1167 B.C.), can be identified with Kourion[6].

The story was the same in archaic times (700 – 475 B.C.) when the sanctuary received its wall and altars. Numerous cemeteries in the · surrounding district from the Yerokarka region to 'At Meydan' to the west and Kaloriziki south of the modern road to Limassol and nearer the sea testify to the density of contemporary settlement without revealing its exact whereabouts. Perhaps there were several, and the earlier practice of frequent moves to new sites continued without, however, affecting the common bound of cultural tradition which had united the entire area near the sanctuary since the Bronze

---

[3] S.S. Weinberg, 'Exploring the Early Bronze Age in Cyprus', in *Archaeology* 9 (1956) 112–21; J.R. Carpenter, 'Episkopi-Phaneromeni' Kourion 29–37; 'Excavations at Phaneromeni', *SCA*, 59–78.

[4] J.L. Benson, 'The Necropolis of Kaloriziki', *SIMA* 36 (1973); *Kourion* 50–55.

[5] Karageorghis, *Cyprus* fig. 86.

[6] *Kourion* 89; G. Rachet, *Dictionnaire de l'Archéologie*, Paris 1983, 516.

Age[7]. Remarkably no settlement seems ever to have covered the actual site of the sanctuary.

In the middle, between the Kourion bluff, one mile west of the village of Episkopi, and the sanctuary a mile further west, lies the Roman stadium[8]. If you walk up there from the Kourion bluff and continue to the sanctuary you can detect parts of the ancient way which by the second century of our era connected all three elements: city, stadium and sanctuary of Apollo. East of the stadium and slightly above it the small Christian Basilica arose around a large ancient warer cistern. It was constructed from purloined materials some of which came from the theatre in Kourion city[9]. Amongst the remains there was a fourth century B.C. marble statue base with a dedicatory inscription to Demeter and Kore[10] whose cult in the area appears to be confirmed by the find of a number of terracotta votives of women[11]. There are other indications, albeit slight, that a mystery cult may have been celebrated in some proximity to, or association with, the sanctuary in Hellenistic times[11a].

In any event the religious-tradition at Kourion was a continuing one which preserved the old but was also receptive to new influence through the ages. Predominant amongst them were the ideas from Mycenaean archaic and classical Greece whence came the Greek Apollo. But the ties with ancient Cyprus always remained evident and were subtly reflected in the legend attached to the foundation of Kourion.

Literary tradition records that Kourion was an *Argeion ktisma*[12]. Herodotus also spoke of the Kourians as Argive settlers[13]. These, however, came in the second wave of Mycenaean or Achaean arrivals, that is some two or three hundred years after the main body of the colonists bringing with them the practice of cremating their dead[14].

---

[7] *Kourion* 40; 57.
[8] Built in the 2nd century A.D., V. Karageorghis, in *BCH* 88 (1964) 366; 369–71.
[9] V. Karageorghis, 'Chroniques des Fouilles et Découvertes Archéologiques á Chypre'. in *BCH* 96 to 99 (1972 to 1975); D. Whittingham, in *Kourion* 80–85.
[10] *IKourion*, 62.
[11] *Terrac.*, 224.
[11a] See n. 397.
[12] Strabo 14, 683.
[13] *Argeion apoikoi*, Herod. 5,113,1.
[14] G. McFadden in *AJA* 58 (1954) 131–42; Karageorghis, *Cyprus* 118.

The immigrants were primarily Laconians and Argives who are said to have given way under the pressure of north/west Greeks at home. In fact contemporary burials at Kaloriziki (LCIIIB and later) bear out the traditional evidence[15].

The name of the town's founding hero, beyond its Greek credentials, conceals a pre-Mycenaean Cypriot association. Koureus was connected with Kinyras[16], the legendary king of Cyprus[17]. In Homer[18] Kinyras presented Agamemnon with a breast-plate as a *xeineïon* and was generally involved in the Trojan Expedition on the Greek side[19]. But another tradition appears in the account of the usually reliable Theopompus[20], according to which, perhaps during the *Nostoï*[21], Agamemnon and his followers captured Cyprus and expelled Kinyras. Thus the historical legend testifies to earlier contact with Achaeans in the thirteenth century B.C. on home ground in Cyprus[22].

Kinyras' name was Semitic, possibly Phoenician[23], and helps to join Cypriot, Phoenician and Greek tradition. Kinyras' Apollodoran genealogy, if nothing else, illustrates this union of the three elements. The combination was seen through Greek eyes: the family has been Grecised, explaining Cypriot and Phoenician connections through the various members of the Greek 'Stammbaum'[24]. This latter was therefore devised late, but for all that it reflected contacts between each group not only in Cyprus, and not only after the Phoenician settlement on the island in the 9th century B.C., but also in earlier periods at the end of the Bronze Age in Cyprus and further to the east. Kinyras was connected with other important Greek families,

---

[15] F. Schachermeyr, *Die Ägäische Frühzeit 5. Die Levante im Zeitalter der Wanderungen vom 13. bis zum 11. Jahrhundert v. Chr.*, Vienna 1982, 271.

[16] Steph. Byz. *s. v.* Κούριον

[17] On Kinyras see C. Picard, 'De Midéa à Salamine de Chypre', in *Geras Antoniou Keramopolou*, Athens 1953, 1–16; C. Baurain, 'Kinyras de Chypre', in *Mélanges de l'Université Saint Joseph* 48 (1973); H. v. Gärtringen, 'Kinyras', in *Kleine Pauly* III (1979) 216–7; *Cults*, 283–8.

[18] *Il.* 11, 20.

[19] Cf. schol. on Hom. *ad loc.*; Apollod. *ep.* 3,9.

[20] In *Fr. Gr. Hist.* 115, Fr. 103; cf. Schachermeyr, *Äg. Frühz.* 30.

[21] Earlier, according to Schachermeyr, *op. cit.* 131.

[22] Cf. M. P. Nilsson, *The Mycenaean Origin of Greek Mythology*, Berkeley 1932, 62.

[23] Schol. Hom. *Il.* 11, 20; Apollod. 2,1,3; 3,1,1; 3,14,3.

[24] See the discussion in Bennett, *Cults* 284–8.

notably with Teucer, the founder of Cypriot Salamis[25]. But the tradition, which knew of Kinyras as the father of Koureus[26], stressed not only the Greek connection but equally firmly the older roots of the settlement of Kourion.

At least as interesting as the historical background for the religious historian is Kinyras' connection with the cult of Aphrodite in Paphos which he is said to have instituted and which his descendants the Kinyradae administered there. The Arcadian Agapenor, whom Strabo recorded as founding New Paphos[27] and Pausanias as establishing a sanctuary – presumably to Aphrodite – in Ancient Paphos[28] came later, like Koureus, also in the second wave of settlers in the 11th century B.C.[29]. Even stronger was Kinyras' connection with Apollo in Cyprus as favourite, and indeed son, of the god[30]. Therefore Kinyras' myth remembered the pre-Mycenaean date of Apollo's and Aphrodite's cults in Cyprus and their probable relationship in some form. On grounds of geographical proximity, and for other reasons, one suspects that in pre-Greek times there existed a bond between the Paphian and Kourian worship. In any case the Koureus-Kinyras connection vouches for the significance of Kourion prior to Greek influence.

Perhaps it is for this reason that Koureus was no longer thought respectable as a genuine Greek founding hero in later generations. Some 4th and 3rd century B.C. inscriptions refer to the worship of a hero Perseutes at Kourion[31]. The name, of course, derived from another, but far better known, Argive hero Perseus whose eastern connections would have made him particularly suitable for the office of Greek patron in Cyprus[32]. His claim to the status of ancestral founder hero grew strong in Roman times, and Kourion could be

---

[25] *Marm. Par.*, cited by Schachermeyr, *op. cit.* 108.

[26] See n. 16.

[27] See n. 12.

[28] Paus. 8,5,2.

[29] Contemporary tombs have recently been found in Paphos, 'Fouilles à l'ancienne Paphos de Chypre: les premiers colons Achéens', V. Karageorghis in *CRAI* (1980), 122–36.

[30] Pind. *Pyth.* 2,15; *Nem.* 8,18; schol. Theocritus 1,109. For Kinyras' many associations see also *Cults* 436.

[31] *IKourion* No. 25; 65; 66; pp. 60–62; pp. 128–9.

[32] *Cf. Cults* 447–8.

referred to as 'City of Perseus' or 'Blood of Perseus'[33]. But precisely why and when the Kourians amended their legendary past remains unknown.

Thus from present evidence the sanctuary of Apollo at Kourion was an archaic institution. The precinct, which was partly or wholly preserved by the Romans, is devoid of any architectural remains prior to the seventh or eighth century B.C. The large limestone blocks of the archaic boundary wall, which were excavated in the summer of 1983 at the northern end of the *temenos,* lie on bedrock and beneath the later Roman wall. But the sanctuary occupies a majestic and commanding site. If cult occurred there in earlier times it must surely have centred on a natural feature like a grove of trees which has long since disappeared. Inscriptions of the fifth century B.C. identify the god receiving worship in the sanctuary as Apollo[34]. His commonest epithet there was that of Hylates, god of the woods or grove, a title which is epigraphically attested in the Kourion sanctuary from Hellenistic times only[35]. But inscriptions merely provide a *terminus ante quem* of Apollo's association with the sanctuary. His name was in all probability known in Cyprus as early as the 13th century B.C. What then is the evidence of Apollo's first appearance in the sanctuary, and what does it reveal about the god, the history and nature of his cult? Such and related questions are of great interest not only with reference to the sanctuary at Kourion but also in the wider context of archaic religious belief in Cyprus as a whole. Autopsy of contemporary sites shows that the sanctuary at Kourion fits into the context of other archaic cults, but also preserved a number of confusing and possibly unique features of is own. Cyprus lies somewhere between Apollo's eastern beginnings and his western destiny as a major Olympian god who became representative of the values of Greek civilization.

The sanctuary at Kourion has been methodically excavated in a number of archaelogical campaigns which began in 1935 and were

---

[33] Inscription on statue of Priscus Publicola, proconsul, erected by Kourion city in 3rd cent. A.D.; and reference to *haima Perseos* in 2nd cent. A.D. Hymn to Antinous, *IKourion* 89; 104.

[34] *IKourion* 18; 19.

[35] *IKourion* 50.

annually renewed until 1953[36]. After a gap of some twenty-five years excavation resumed in 1978 until 1984[37]. The rewards of this work, as seen through the eyes of the religious historian, have not been particularly rich regarding the site of the *temenos* itself, that is the heart of the entire complex. What does emerge as certain after all the work up to date is the total absence of pre-archaic monumental remains in the sanctuary area. It may be that the site was sacred since time immemorial[38], but no visible hint survives of this nor evidence of previous worship with the exception of one single Middle Cypriot (2000 B.C.) jug, the fragments of which were found stuck in the Circular Altar. The vase may have come from one of the many prehistoric tombs nearby and been dedicated on the altar by a devout worshipper centuries later[39].

Only a recent campaign in 1983 uncovered the solid limestone blocks, on bedrock, of the first archaic *peribolos* wall at the northern end of the *temenos*. Thus this boundary, and perhaps the original eastern limit near, but west of, the later Roman water pipes[40], seem clearly defined. To the west the wide Roman street leading to the temple of Apollo effectively obliterated any trace of the archaic *peribolos*[41]. The same applies south of the *temenos* where the later so-called East Complex may well have covered over a part of the archaic precinct. The structures of this complex comprise the East Building, a house and stoa. According to the excavators, these were erected in the late fourth or third century B.C. and therefore constituted the oldest extant post-archaic buildings[42]. The form and

---

[36] G. McFadden in the *Bulletin of the University Museum* (Pennsylvania) (1938) 10–17; (1940) 22–28; (1950) 14–26; (1951) 167–8; *AJA* 56 (1951) 128–9. See also the discussion with bibliography by R. S. Bagnall – T. Drew-Bear, 'Documents from Kourion', *Phoenix* 27 (1973) 103–5 and notes. For brief history of early visits to the site and excavation see further D. Soren – D. Buitron, 'Sanctuary of Apollo Hylates', in *Kourion* 58–9.

[37] Reports in *RDAC* 1979, 316–20; 1981, 157–9; 1982, 144–7; 1983; D. Buitron – D. Soren, 'Excavations in the Sanctuary of Apollo Hylates at Kourion', in *SCA* 99–116; *cf. Archaeology* 33 (1980) 55–7.

[38] So *TAPS*, 71.

[39] *RDAC* 1981, 158.

[40] Wall D, *RDAC* 1979, 320 and Fig. 2.

[41] *TAPS* 74.

[42] *TAPS* 20–1; *cf.* the excellent *resumé* by Buitron and Soren in *Kourion* 58–67.

function of the East Complex have been much debated. Perhaps it included the house of the priest who administered the cult and the sacred treasury. The impressive buildings no doubt reflect an upsurge of interest in the cult at the time[43]. At the southern end of the East Complex and adjoining the 'Kitchen' McFadden discovered a semi-circular pit filled with hundreds of 'discarded' earlier terracotta votives which came from the *temenos* during the 8th and 7th centuries B.C. Such pits with 'deconsecrated' votives can also be paralleled in most other sanctuaries. Frequently they were placed just within or outside the *peribolos* wall. In this case, however, the pit was apparently made at the end of the first century A.D.[44], that is much later than the Hellenistic buildings of the East Complex, and therefore need not have been connected with the boundary of the archaic precinct. Countless pilgrimages to the latter, visits and continual building programmes nearby, no less than the many successive excavations, have successfully confused and confounded its contents for all time.

The modern visitor sees the sanctuary as it might have appeared in its last phase in the 4th century A.D. The remains of major Roman buildings to the east, south and south-west dominate the site which hinges on the street as its central axis leading to the temple. The Roman temple of Apollo itself stands out as the most prominent focal point of the sanctuary[45]. It was probably built under Augustus, although the extant remains, which are being used in the modern reconstruction, came from a second temple half a century later during the principate of Nero[46]. An earlier classical temple (late 5th century B.C.) had stood on the same site which also preserved remains from the archaic age[46a].

The full site made up an impressive unit which, however, creates a misleading picture of what the place might have looked like in archaic times. Apollo's temple, which provides the most conspicuous feature of the sanctuary, is not only outside the archaic precinct but, from the

---

[43] *TAPS* 73.

[44] *Ibid.*

[45] The dedicatory inscription to Apollo Hylates was found in front of the temple, *TAPS* 21; *IKourion* No. 105. Also *pithos* with legend Apollo Hylates, fragments of which were found inside the temple, No. 123.

[46] *TAPS* 74, and now *SCA* 101–2.

[46a] *RDAC* 1983, 232–44.

point of view of cultic history, unrelated to it as not having formed an
integral part of the ancient sacred area[47]. Nevertheless deity and cult
continued without interruption at Kourion. The Romans manifestly
preserved and respected past sacred traditions by keeping the archaic
precinct as a major feature of their own planning design and redefining
its dimension by building a new *peribolos* wall on top of the old in the
north and possibly east, and partly by constructing new walls at the
eastern edge of the street. Even the conduits for water of the early
second century A.D., which supplied the Trajanic Baths east of the
East Complex, were carefully laid to run outside the *temenos* to east
and north[48].

But by the end of the 1st and early 2nd century A.D., if not earlier,
the cult had expanded from that of the protecting city-god to involve
the figure of the Roman emperor[49]. Then Apollo was worshipped
not only as Hylates but also as Kaisar[50]. No doubt the Kourion
sanctuary had reached its most resplendent period as an important
cult centre in Cyprus under Trajan[51]. But the reasons were mostly
political and even more mundane, because with its *palaistra* and
stadium Kourion had become an important venue for sports and
chariot racing in honour of city-god and emperor[52]. Evidence of this
pastime survives in an uncommon number of lead *defixiones* from the
3rd century A.D. which were discovered in a well at Kourion. The
curses inscribed on them and directed against unpopular competitors
record the lively partisanship of the many sports supporters who
came to watch the races[53]. Perhaps by then the Kourion sanctuary
had turned into a place of entertainment rather than of worship[54].

Such secular practices evolved from a few salient aspects of the
earlier cult. They were not gratuitously imposed from outside in

---

[47] For this reason Scranton's comparison of Kourion with Apolline cult sites in
Greece is not really valid, *TAPS* 68; 73.

[48] *RDAC* 1982, Fig. 1; *RDAC* 1983, Fig. 1.

[49] *Cf. IKourion* p. 210.

[50] *IKourion* No. 108; 111; 120; 123–4; 144.

[51] *TAPS* 74; *cf.* S. Glover, 'The Cult of Apollo at Kourion', in *Kourion* 73.

[52] *Cf.* the statue of an athlete in the *palaistra*, *Kourion* 59; fig. 61.

[53] Now in the British Museum, *IKourion* No. 127–42; *cf.* the critique by Drew-Bear in
BASP 9 (1972) 85–107. For the common use of such curse tablets to influence race
horses and their riders see K. Preisendanz, in *Kleine Pauly* I (1979), 1424.

[54] *Cf. TAPS* 74; Bennett, *Cults* 348.

Roman times but reflected cultic features which must have been present in some form already very early in its history. The archaic *temenos* somehow retained its importance throughout the history of the sanctuary. It is a pity therefore that the sparse monumental remains within the confines of the *temenos* reveal so little about the early form of cult. The area in question has been much examined and discussed without establishing its precise dimensions beyond reasonable doubt except to the north and possibly east. The northern boundary in particular seems certain, as we noticed above, and has been confirmed by the most recent discovery of another major votive pit just north of the *peribolos* and containing some 10,000 fragments of offerings. All of these, with few exceptions, can be dated between the 5th and 3rd centuries B.C.[55]. The rectangular pit lies adjacent to the wall just outside the precinct and was placed there for 'discarded' votives sometime in the 3rd century B.C. or very shortly after[56]. The great number of votive figurines reflects the cult's popularity in classical times. Elsewhere we can only guess at the size of the precinct. It might well have been considerably more extensive in the west for example. A remarkable circular structure, which was recently discovered west of the Roman street, could conceivably have come within the original sanctuary boundaries[57]. This so-called West Enclosure or *tholos* consists of a large, circular paved walk with a diameter of some 18 metres. It was surrounded and sheltered from outside view by a low wall. The interior of the circle was lower than the surrounding ring-walk and open to the sky. It had no floor but was made up of bare rock into which seven round or square shallow pits had been cut[58]. The excavators suggest that the pits contained sacred trees about which ritual dances were performed[59].

The oriental custom of planting sacred trees was known in Cyprus from the Late Bronze Age. There was a sacred garden for example in Kition in the Late Cypriot II/III sanctuary complex in Area II (Floor IV, 1300–1200 B.C.)[60]. But the form and shape of the Kourion

---

[55] *RDAC* 1983.
[56] *Ibid.* Fig. 1.
[57] Buitron – Soren in *SCA* 102–3; *cf. Kourion* 63–4; *BCH* 106 (1981) 727–30.
[58] *SCA* 114–5.
[59] See above n. 57; 58 and Appendix below; Karageorghis, *Cyprus* 185.
[60] Karageorghis, *Cyprus* 69; 94; Fig. 72, with references to excavation reports and discussions.

enclosure differed from the more usual open type of sacred garden. Sjöquist identified two walled but unroofed square 'rooms' as an enclosure for two sacred trees in the archaic *temenos* of the sanctuary at Ayia Irini[61]. His explanation was founded on scenes of apparent tree cult on Minoan sealings of the Late Bronze Age[62] and needs retesting in the light of up-to-date knowledge of Minoan cultural ties with Cyprus. In any case the two *cella*-like structures at Ayia Irini bear no resemblance to the circular *tholos* and pits of the building at Kourion. Most disappointing of all is the late date of the West Enclosure which was probably contemporary with the Augustan temple. Judging by the sherds, which were found on the terrace of the Enclosure, the surviving remains could not have been erected prior to the Julio-Claudian period[63] and no trace endures of any earlier structure. Thus the sole extant feature, that links the archaic *temenos* with the *tholos*, is its east/west alignment with the circular altar of the former. The Romans built this monument in a conspicuous position on a terrace. It seems likely therefore that it and *temenos* were somehow intended to be related through a conscious piece of archaising. No doubt the ritual within the *tholos* recalled that of earlier ages.

The Central Court, which is the starting point of the Roman street to the temple, lies below, that is south and west of the circular altar[64]. Although not included in the innermost holy *temenos*, it was part of the actual sanctuary area. Some structures on the Central Court certainly were pre-Roman[65]. But a more significant indication of the court's true function may be that as many as 8 of the 23 pre-Augustan Greek inscriptions, which were found in the sanctuary, came from the Central Court and five from the Altar Precinct[66]. Both areas were obviously closely involved in cultic ritual throughout the ages, although the Central Court appears to have been separated from the large circular altar by a foundation wall and fence of some sort. A mysterious large rectangular stone with a hole cut through the top

---

[61] E. Sjöquist, 'Die Kultgeschichte eines Cyprischen Temenos', in *AfR* 30 (1933) 338–40; *cf.* E. Gjerstad, *SCE* IV, 2 (1948) 3–4.
[62] *AfR* 30 (1933) 350–6.
[63] *SCA* 103.
[64] *TAPS* 6–8; 63; *RDAC* 1982, 317 and Fig. 1.
[65] See above n. 42.
[66] *TAPS* 8; 12; 73–4.

was found lying north of the altar[67]. It has now been set upright again beside the altar. Its function is unknown, as is the date when it was first erected there. But Scranton's suggestion that the stone acted as a fencing post for a railing about the altar is unconvincing[68]. Many similar old and more recent stones have been found in Cyprus with symbolic or religious significance[69]. Furthermore one solitary fence post seems inadequate for a railing.

The sanctuary was destroyed by an earthquake late in the 4th century B.C.[70]. It began in the 7th, or possibly 8th, century B.C. about the two altars within the archaic *temenos*. A few large stones from the semi-circular altar survive lying against the Roman boundary wall in the west[71]. Bones and ash were found with it as well as fragments of pottery and figurines some of which had been scattered over a wide area. Two scarabs date the altar to the 7th, or slightly later to the early 6th, century B.C.[72]. The much larger circular altar a few metres to the south belongs to the same period. Its outlines were reconstructed by the excavators from the preserved portion on the west side, in part up to three courses high. Many stones, which lay loosely scattered in the immediate vicinity to the east, probably came from this altar[73]. Much evidence of ash and almost countless fragments from votives and offerings testify to centuries of continuous use. Two splendid bulls, one of silver and one of gold, which were discovered stuck in the lower stones of the altar, belonged to the 7th century B.C. as did the bulk of other gifts[74]. Only one item falls seriously out of context and that is a piece of Red Polished Ware from the Middle Bronze Age[75].

The majority of archaic votives of bulls, chariots, horsemen and the like duplicate those of other Cypriot sanctuaries in which deities were worshipped who protected the community's welfare and the

---

[67] *SCA* Fig. 6–4.
[68] *TAPS* 6–8. See below p. 172 and n. 377.
[69] *E.g.* S. Swiny, 'Standing Stones: Perforated Monoliths', in *Kourion* 151–2 with further references.
[70] *TAPS* 74; D. Soren, 'Earthquake: The Last Days of Kourion', in *SCA* 117–33.
[71] *RDAC* 1982, 144; *SCA* Fig. 6–2.
[72] *RDAC* 1982, 146; Fig. 2.
[73] *RDAC* 1979, 317; 1981, 158.
[74] *RDAC* 1981, 158; 1982, 144.
[75] See n. 39 above.

fertility of field and home. The sacrificial victims were mostly young sheep and goats and quite suitable for such a divinity. The god at Kourion specially favoured the right hind leg of goats as an offering[76]. Other archaic dedications show strong eastern influence. Apart from the two scarabs already mentioned, these include a 7th century B.C. bronze belt with lions fighting a griffin[77] and a six-sided steatite stamp seal of the 6th century B.C.[78]. The shape of the seal and the iconographical designs on its various sides show a mixture of eastern, Cypriot as well as Greek elements including the xenophile Egyptian Bes. One side has an armed warrior, another a figure with trees[79]. The cultic tree is matched by the scene on the 7th century scarab of rock crystal which came from the semi-circular altar[80]. Perhaps the tree belonged to the cult of Hylates or to his grove of which, however, no trace remains.

Both altars are in a poor state of preservation. Without the copious deposits of ash, bones and the left-overs of other offerings, they might never have been identified with certainty. Indeed the circular altar went undetected by the first excavator who dug his exploratory trench directly through its eastern segment[81]. The stones of the altar themselves, which were found *in situ* or which have been replaced to complete the large circle of some 6 m diameter, show no trace of burning. They clearly belonged to the foundation of the altar whose shape therefore and original height it would be difficult to imagine from the remains. More mysterious still is a line of stones like those of the circular altar but running beneath it from just south of the altar towards the north and abutting against the northern *peribolos* wall. It

---

[76] *RDAC* 1981, 159. The hindquarters of sheep and goats were most commonly burnt on the altars of the temples at Kommos in Crete (1000 B.C. – 150 A.D.), D.S. Reese, 'Faunal Remains from the Kommos Temples, Crete', in *AJA* 88 (1984) 257. Goats remained the favoured sacrifice for Apollo in Roman times (G. Wissowa, *Religion und Kultus der Römer²*, repr. Munich 1971, 296). Curiously at Apollo's circular temple in Nettleton, Wiltshire, the god favoured the right forelimb of a lamb, W.J. Wedlake, *The Excavation of the Shrine of Apollo at Nettleton, Wilts., 1956–1971*, London 1982, 178.

[77] Fragmentary: H. Browne, 'A Bronze Belt from the Sanctuary of Apollo at Kourion', in *SCA* 135–40.

[78] M. Arwe, 'A Cypriote Cubical Stamp Seal', in *SCA* 141–4. Below n.353.

[79] *Ibid.* fig. 9–1; 9–2.

[80] *RDAC* 1982, 146, Fig. 2a.

[81] *RDAC* 1981, 157–8; *SCA* Fig. 6–4.

seems the altar had been built across, or possibly formed a part of, this marginally earlier wall[82]. Such an explanation is probable rather than certain, however.

Alongside this wall many broken offerings were found including bronze and iron knives which may have been used for sacrifice and then dedicated to the god. South of the altar small votive jugs have also come to light and fragments of other archaic ware. The excavators speak of a low platform rather than a wall from which these many offerings had fallen or been swept away to make room for the dedications of new generations of worshippers[83]. But interior dividing walls were quite common features of other Cypriot sanctuaries. Perhaps then these few stones are all that remains of a wall which subdivided the earliest sanctuary court or precinct into two parts. One of these would be easily accessible to all but the other more sacred and reserved for the priest and a few 'initiates'[84].

Exact parallels of the Kourion sanctuary there are none. The closest comparable arrangement appears to be in the sanctuary at Ayios Iakovos which has a similar large circular altar, a wide wall/platform which runs southward, however, and nowhere near the *peribolos* wall[85]. The wall separated the outer from the inner sanctuary precinct. The altar and another smaller circular platform lay within the latter but there was no evidence of ash or votive gifts in that immediate area. Ayios Iakovos was much earlier than Kourion. The former sanctuary probably came into use in Late Cypriot II, that is about the 14th century B.C., but it followed even older traditions which had been established from the Early Bronze Age[86] as witness the terracotta model of a sanctuary at Vounous[87]. These traditions of walled open court with one or two altars and usually a *cella* stayed alive in the archaic rural sanctuaries which flourished in Cyprus during the 7th and 6th centuries B.C.[88]. The Kourion sanctuary, which was founded then, was no exception regardless of differences in architectural detail.

---

[82] *TAPS* 6–8; 63; *RDAC* 1979, 317; 1981, 159; 1982, 146; 1983, Fig. 1.
[83] *RDAC* 1983.
[84] *TAPS* 6–8; cf. *RDAC* 1979, 317; 1982, 146.
[85] *SCE* I (1934) 356–70 and Plan XIII.
[86] Karageorghis, *Cyprus* 69.
[87] *Op. cit.* fig. 31.
[88] Karageorghis, *The Ancient Civilization of Cyprus*, London 1969, 168–9; *Cyprus* 106–7.

This continuity of form is less obvious in the city temples like those of Kition where elaborate building methods of Mycenaean and Phoenician settlers concealed the same basic ingredients of court, altars *etc.*[89]. In the case of country sanctuaries their Bronze Age ancestry is quite evident. The best instance of uniterrupted cultic use survived in the *temenos* at Ayia Irini which endured continuously from the Late Bronze Age until the 5th century B.C. In fact the place remained sacred in people's memory beyond that date into Roman times. The precinct was refurbished, changed or added to several times in the Geometric and archaic periods without substantially altering the nature of the cult[90]. Some thirty-five years ago Gjerstad classified the sanctuaries, which were known at the time to have been in use between Cypro-Geometric and Cypro-Classical, in five categories[91]. There is no need to rehearse the finely observed distinctions between the different types of the many examples. In the light of what is known today Gjerstad's division seems overly subtle[92]. They range from the 'primitive' open court of irregular shape to a detached *cella* or chapel and Greek-type temple. Kourion had not yet been excavated but it clearly belongs to the first type. Thus the Cypriots followed no diachronic pattern of development in the construction of their sanctuaries from simple rustic to elaborate city form. All types seem to have been broadly related and possessed a common ancestry.

Far more significant, and this point was recognized by the early Swedish excavators too, is the manifest architectural link with the east particularly Syria and Palestine. Again the complex city temples more immediately betray their dependence on eastern styles. Gjerstad identified the liwan-type arrangement of one or several, but usually tripartite, cult rooms opening onto a court in the Cypro-Geometric III *temenos* of Athena at Idalion[93]. The sanctuary of the 'Horned God' at Enkomi, which was constructed of ashlar blocks by the Mycenaean settlers at the end of the 13th century B.C., reproduced the common tripartite form of three *cellae*. The famous statue was

---

[89] Karageorghis, *Cyprus* 98; 'The Sacred Area of Kition', *Temples*, 85–9.
[90] Sjöquist *AfR* 30 (1933) 308–55; *cf. SCE* IV, 2 (1948) 1; Karageorghis, *Cyprus* 141–2.
[91] *SCE* IV, 2 (1948) 1–23.
[92] Type 2: detached chapel without *temenos* no longer seems a viable category, *SCE* IV, 2, 17 and 19.
[93] *SCE* IV, 2 (1948) 2.

found in the centre room[94]. The roughly contemporary Temple I in
Kition had a similar tripartite set of *cellae* west of the court[95], and so
did the sanctuary at Palaipaphos of the same period[96]. The style had
affinities with Aegean architecture[97] but ultimately derived from the
east especially from Ugaritic models[98].

Gjerstad's Type IV sanctuary is architecturally related. It consists
of one or two rectangular courts with altars *etc.* and a hall or *cella* at
one end forming one coherent unit. Cypriot examples are the archaic
sanctuaries of of Aphrodite and Apollo at Idalion and the somewhat
later classical one of Athena on top of Vouni rock[99]. The style of
Type IV had direct eastern antecedents in Anatolia, Syria and
Palestine. It recalls a humble Hittite cult place of open court
surrounded by walls with a *naiskos* at the rear wall which was used
between 1800 and 1200 B.C.[100]. More directly the type is linked with
the architecture of temples at Megiddo and Agad[101] and quite
generally with ancient Canaanite temples in a tradition which
continued without break from Chalcolithic to the Bronze Age[102].
The Kition temples in Late Cypriot II and III in the north of the city
are also Type IV sanctuaries. They recall eastern sites like Lachish,
Tell Farah and particularly the Philistine temple at Quasile[103]. The
link continued well into the Iron Age and was clearly reinforced by
the later Phoenician occupants[104]. The Cypriots also used Type IV in
the country sanctuaries outside city limits, however, as in the case of
Aphrodite's archaic precinct near Idalion. Everywhere it seems they
conservatively retained the open court arrangement when the eastern

---

[94] Karageorghis, *Anc. Civ. Cyprus* 141.

[95] Karageorghis, *Cyprus* 94.

[96] Tripartite shape on Roman coins, F. G. Maier, 'The Paphian Shrine of Aphrodite and Crete', in *Cyprus and Crete*, 228–34.

[97] Karageorghis, *Cyprus* fig. 70.

[98] P. Dikaios, *Enkomi*, Mainz 1969/71, 514; N. K. Sandars, *The Sea Peoples*, 1978, 145–6; 151–2; Karageorghis, *Cyprus* 92.

[99] *Cf.* the similar plan of the Vouni Palace, *SCE* IV, 2 (1948) 6–8; 13–6; Fig. 4, 2 & 3.

[100] K. Bittel, 'Hittite Temples and High Places', in *Temples* 65.

[101] Z. Herzog, 'Israelite Sanctuaries at Arad and Beer-Sheba', in *Temples* 120.

[102] R. Amiran, 'Some Observations on Chalcolithis and Early Bronze Age Sanctuaries and Religion', in *Temples* 47; 49.

[103] V. Karageorghis, 'Kition, Mycenaean and Phoenician' *(Mortimer Wheeler Archaeological Lecture, British Academy 1973) Proc. Br. Ac.* (1973) 27.

[104] Karageorghis, *Cyprus* 123–7.

models had already been furnished with a roof[105]. This arrested development reflects the same kind of stubborn clinging on to past traditions as in the use of the syllabic script. Accordingly not much is to be learnt from individual architectural styles about the cult which preserved Eteo-Cypriot mixed with imported religious beliefs. All modern authorities agree that these were concerned with a general deity of nature and fertility who became a community god and protector of its source of prosperity. A few sanctuaries apparently 'specialised' or arrested their development at an early stage. A phallus and other symbols of procreation among the dedications at the late archaic sanctuary of Kommissariato in Limassol, for example, suggest the continuation of a narrow fertility cult[106].

It is understandable that the name of the community deity could change with the nationality of the worshippers. Thus Temple I in Kition was rebuilt by the Phoenician newcomers in the 9th century B.C. to become the home of Astarte[107]. In the late archaic sanctuary at Meniko, to the west of Nicosia, the Phoenicians installed the Syrian/Phoenician god Baal[108]. But the cult remained basically unaltered: πολλῶν ὀνομάτων μορφὴ μία[109]. Hence common offerings not only connected Meniko with Kition but with many other Cypriot sanctuaries of all types including of course that of Apollo at Kourion. The finds in Meniko of terracotta figurines of men, bulls, horses and riders and of a model chariot are familiar from Kourion and indeed most archaic sanctuaries[110]. Horse riders and chariots were dedicated in the later phases of the cult. Such figurines have in fact also turned up in the higher levels of Temple 5 in Kition[111].

But other offerings show that cults and sanctuaries, regardless of the date of their foundation, retained links with the past and directly

---

[105] A. Mazar in *Temples* 88 & 89.

[106] V. Karageorghis, *Two Cypriote Sanctuaries of the End of the Cypro-Archaic Period*, Rome 1977, 49–65.

[107] V. Karageorghis – M.G. Guzzo-Amadasi, *Fouilles de Kition III. Les Inscriptions Pheniciénnes*, 1977, 149; *Cyprus* 123–4.

[108] Baal-Hamman, *cf.* note 106, 17–45.

[109] Aesch. *P. V.* 212.

[110] Karageorghis, *Cyprus* 148. On the chariot see M.A. Littauer – J. Crouwel in Karageorghis, *Two Sanct.* App. I, 67–73.

[111] Karageorghis, in *Temples* 90.

or indirectly with the east. Evidence survives in the continuing popularity of votive figurines of bovids. Bulls, bull masks and skulls, which were worn as masks, recall those of the Early Bronze Age as at Vounous[112] but endured at Enkomi and Kirion to the end of the Bronze Age[113]. The Cypriot types remained fashionable with the Phoenicians in the Geometric period at Kition in Astarte's temple and in Temple 5[114], and later still in archaic sanctuaries including Kourion with its terracotta figurines of masked priests or worshippers. Some are human masks[115] which had a similar ancestry in the Bronze Age in Kition, where they had been deposited in an 11th century B.C. *bothros* near Temples 4 and 5[116], in Enkomi[117] and in Palestine at sites like Gezer, Hazor and Tell Qasile[118].

Cyprus was renowned for its resources of metal. Its wealth lay in the copper mines which naturally were guarded by the gods of the community[119]. Thus the metal industry fell into the province of divine administration at least from the Later Bronze Age. Accordingly workshops, as in Kition and Palaipaphos, were built as part of the sanctuary or temple complex[120]. It is worth emphasizing then that, apart from its exceptional fondness for syncretising, due no doubt to the island's geographical situation, Cypriot religious development was not unique. Others, including Mycenaeans and Greeks, went along the same route. Even the association of metallurgy with cult was not confined to Cyprus but had parallels elsewhere in east and west, in Timna in Palestine and on Kea in the Aegean, for example[121].

With the overwhelmingly rich evidence from the east it is not surprising that other similarities in outward form and in cult and cult offerings have been overlooked. For example, the Philistine temple of Qasile was not only similar to those of Enkomi and Kition,

---

112 Karageorghis, *Cyprus* 49.
113 *Op. cit.* 101; 105.
114 *Op. cit.* 105; 126.
115 *Terrac.* 39.
116 Karageorghis in *Temples* 85; *Cyprus* 105.
117 *BCH* 86 (1962) 395–6; A. Caubet – J. C. Courtois, 'masques chypriotes en terre cuite d'Enkomi', *RDAC* 1982, 69–71.
118 Philistine period; *RDAC* 1982, 71, with reference to excavation reports.
119 B. C. Dietrich, 'Some Evidence from Cyprus of Apolline Cult in the Bronze Age', in *RM* 121 (1978) 15–6; Karageorghis, *Cyprus* 106.
120 Karageorghis, *Cyprus* 70; 84; 98; 104; 109.
121 Karageorghis, *op. cit.* 104.

particularly Temple 5, but also to the recently discovered temple at Mycenae[122]. Unlike other Philistine sites, Qasile had no direct contact with the Mycenaeans[123]. There must have been a common prototype. The sanctuary area near the so-called House of Tsountas in Mycenae originally lay outside the citadel. A processional street led to this sanctuary complex from the palace[124]. Central to the earliest phase of the sanctuary in LH IIB was an open court with a large circular altar. The court was surrounded by walls and sacred rooms all of which opened onto it. An interior subdividing wall from the altar to the corner of one of these *cellae*[125] in remarkable fashion reproduced salient features of the sanctuary at Ayios Iakovos in Cyprus and of course the form and relationship of altar and wall at archaic Kourion. There is no need to press the analogy too closely but the principles of lay-out and arrangement are manifestly the same.

If consequently we widen our focus in the light of recent discoveries, looking beyond Cyprus and its immediate neighbours to the east, it becomes possible to see other models and parallels in the western Aegean. It would be surprising if Minoan visitors and Mycenaean settlers at the end of the Bronze Age had left no mark of their own corresponding customs aside of a few horns of consecration and goddess figurines with upraised arms. In fact the Mycenaean remains beneath the sanctuary of Apollo Maleatas on Mt. Kynortion in Epidaurus also reveal an open air sanctuary terrace with altar and associated cult buildings[126]. The Mycenaean and Epidaurian sanctuaries have other similar examples on the mainland. One of these can probably be identified in Tiryns in the 'Unterburg'. Cult there in LHIIIC occurred in the open about a horseshoe-shaped altar with the remains of animal sacrifice and included separate *cellae* structures[127].

---

[122] A. Mazar, 'The Philistine Sanctuary at Tell Qasile', in *Temples* 105.

[123] *Ibid.*

[124] Reports of excavations conducted by Mylonas and Iakovidis in 1972 and 1973 in *Ergon* 1972, 59 ff.; 1974, 66 ff.; *Prakt.* 1972, 114 ff.; *BCH* 97 (1973) 296. See also G. Mylonas, 'The Cult Centre of Mycenae', *Proc. Brit. Acad.* 67 (1981) 307–20. *Cf.* Schachermeyr's account in *Die Ägäische Frühzeit*, II, Vienna 1976, 106–14; E. French, 'Cult Places at Mycenae', *SCABA*, 41–8.

[125] *Ergon* 1974, 67, Fig. 55.

[126] V. Lambrinoudakis, 'Remains of the Mycenaean Period in the Sanctuary of Apollo Maleatas', *SCABA* 59–65.

[127] K. Kilian, 'Zeugnisse Mykenischer Kultausübung in Tiryns', *SCABA* 48–58.

Various finds on the Mycenaean cult site on Mt. Kynortion, including a number of bronze double axes, show strong Minoan influence in this Late Helladic cult. It has rightly been compared with Middle Minoan peak cult[128]. A good example is the MM open air sanctuary on Mt. Jouktas near Knossos[129]. But the later sanctuaries on the mainland, like Mycenae, Epidaurus and others, despite the obvious cultic links with Minoan Crete, were not imitations of an earlier Cretan model. Quite to the contrary, the typical arrangement of one or more altars in an open *temenos,* which was associated with separate cult rooms as in Mycenae, should be identified as essentially un-Cretan. Ultimately, as we noticed earlier on, the model came from the east[130].

On the northern slopes of Mt. Jouktas, some way below the summit but manifestly related to the sacred peak shrine, another important Middle Minoan sanctuary has recently been discovered at a prominent site which is called Anemosphilia. In many respects the architecture of this temple and the type of sacrifice, which appears to have been performed in it, seem unique. The temple structure, as far as it is possible to judge from the remains, was far more impressively monumental than the buildings on the peak. Both sanctuary areas, however, retained the basic features of open area and separate *cellae.* In Anemosphilia these were tripartite in form as in Cypriot Paphos, Kition and Enkomi, and the open area was surrounded by a vaguely circular *peribolos* wall[131]. The occurrence in the west of the original type of open air sanctuary illustrates common religious traditions which Cyprus continued more conservatively than her partners into historical times.

---

[128] See above n. 126.

[129] A. Karetsou, 'The Peak Sanctuary of Mt. Juktas', *SCABA* 137–53.

[130] *Cf.* B. Rutkowski, 'Religious Architecture in Cyprus and in Crete in the LBA', in *Cyprus and Crete* 223–7; *cf.* Karageorghis in *Cyprus and Crete* 317.

[131] G. & E. Sakellarakis, 'Anaskaphe Arkhanon' (in Greek), in *Praktika* 1979, 347–92. Despite the gap of centuries there is a strikingly similar scene of a bull surrounded by, and smelling, flowers on vases from Anemospilia and archaic Cyprus which could have been used for the same purpose of holding the sacrificial blood of the bull. One large amphora with bull and flowers in relief was found inside the door of the central *cella* at Arkhanes, *Praktika* 1979, 369–72, Figs. 4 & 5; Pl. 181. Compare this with the 7th century B.C. jug from a grave at Arnadi, Karageorghis, *Cyprus Museum*, Athens 1981, Fig. 41.

Pretty well contemporary with the large temples of Enkomi and Kition is a more modest rustic type of sanctuary in Phylakopi on the island of Melos. The votives show mixed outside influence from Minoan and Mycenaean as well as eastern cultures superimposed on native Cycladic forms. The cult site itself, however, although considerable architectural changes occurred over two and a half centuries, unmistakably recalled the familiar arrangement of open court with *cellae*. Two cult rooms or shrines flanked and opened onto a court. The West Shrine was unusual in that it had two further inner chambers beyond the west wall with features somewhat reminiscent of the temple discovered by Taylour at Mycenae[132]. Although the West Shrine was constructed in LH IIIA, that is before the East Shrine (LH IIIB), both continued in use from the end of the 13th century B.C. until the sanctuary was abandoned in IIIC some one hundred and fifty or more years later.

Unlike the Geometric and archaic Cypriot rustic sanctuaries, altars and votives were not in the open but inside the West room which appears to have been where the cult was performed. The main feature of the court consisted of a round stone *baetyl* in front of the southern door leading to the West Shrine[133]. The excavator looked to Greece and to the Delphic *omphalos* for comparison[134]. This is undoubtedly correct, for the *omphalos* shared the same ancestry with older *baetyls* as the seat of divine power[135]. However, closer contemporary parallels existed in the east and in Cyprus like the conical stone of the Paphian golddess known later as Aphrodite. Roman coins of the Flavian period show the *baetyl* in the central *cella* facing the sanctuary court[136]. No archaeological evidence remains of this arrangement[137], but there is no reason to doubt that the stone stood in the temple of

---

[132] Dietrich, 'Evidence of Minoan Religious Traditions and their Survival in the Mycenaean and Greek World', *Historia* 31 (1982) 9. On the Phylakopi sanctuary see C. Renfrew, 'The Mycenaean Sanctuary at Phylakopi', in *Antiquity* 52 (1978) 7–15; cf. *AR 1977/78* in *JHS* (1978) 52–4.

[133] *AR* (1978) Fig. 91.

[134] *Antiquity* (1978) 10.

[135] Cf. Dietrich, *Origins*, 52; 308–9.

[136] Reproduced by M. Ohnefalsch-Richter, *Kypros. The Bible and Homer*, London 1893, Pl. LXXXII, 8; LXXXIII, 19; 22, who also shows similar examples on coins from Byblos, LXXXII, 7, and Emesa, LXXXIII, 3.

[137] Maier, 'The Paphian Shrine of Aphrodite and Crete', in *Cyprus and Crete* 233.

the Late Bronze Age or that it is the same as the famous black stone which was discovered on the site and now stands on display in the Cyprus Museum in Nicosia[138].

The Paphian temple precinct was within the city limits. It was considerably more elaborate than the Melian sanctuary, although again the format of *cellae* about a court corresponded in principle in both places. Closer in scale is the simpler rustic sanctuary of Ayia Irini which also illustrates, as we noticed above, all stages of the typical development of Cypriot sanctuaries. In Ayia Irini, too, the cult occurred inside the *cella* in the Late Bronze Age, that is within the important east shrine which contained table of offerings, altar, votives and the like[139]. The performance of the cult ritual only moved outside in Geometric and archaic times with the remodelling of the precinct area[140]. Not much survived from the earliest stages of the *temenos*. But one feature of signal interest, because of its parallel at Phylakopi, is the round black stone which the worshippers preserved from the Bronze Age sanctuary and placed beside their new altar in the open court. It remained central to the cult throughout the archaic period and no doubt continued to incorporate the divine power of the same godhead as in prehistoric times[141].

These are exciting analogies and quite vital to the comparison of Minoan, Mycenaean and Cycladic cult with Cypriot practices. Both West and East Shrines at Phylakopi contained a number of terracotta bull figurines[142] which played a part in the cult ceremonial. The bull was and remained important in Aegean cult in the Bronze Age and in historic times[143]. But the discovery of bull votives in the context of this type of sanctuary[144] recalls the similar gifts in the contemporary cult rooms at Ayia Irini and also in Dali in Cyprus[145]. The bull figurines in the archaic Cypriot sanctuaries, including Kourion, were direct descendants of the Bronze Age tradition. There were no double axes, horns of consecration or other obviously Minoan/

---

[138] Room 4. G. Hill, *A History of Cyprus* I, Cambridge 1940, 71–2; Pl. Ib.
[139] Sjöquist in *AfR* (1933) 309–11; figs. 1 and 2.
[140] *Op. cit.* 323–30; *cf. SCE* IV, 2 (1948) 3–4.
[141] *AfR* (1933) 317; 324; 347–8.
[142] *Antiquity* (1978) 13–4.
[143] Dietrich, *Origins* 111; 114–7; 150; 210.
[144] See n. 142.
[145] *AfR* (1933) 310; 314–6.

Mycenaean cult symbols at Phylakopi[146]. But one 'psi' figurine and another female female figure from the West Shrine show Mycenaean influence on the cult. The most impressive witness of this is the famous Lady of Phylakopi. This wheel-made terracotta figure, which was found in the inner chamber of the West Shrine, has been identified as 'a mainland piece of the Late Helladic IIIA2 period'[147]. The arms were broken off but had probably been upraised in the familiar gesture. This latter, as well as the figure's cylindrical shape, betray their Minoan/Mycenaean connection.

Other votives from Phylakopi are decidedly un-Mycenaean, however. They include a gold head or mask[148] and a series of five remarkable male figures which were found near the n./w. altar in the West Shrine[149]. These have been described as 'exceptional, indeed without parallel' in the Aegean during the Late Bronze Age[150]. That is true for Greece and Crete where male idols are uncommon in the L.B.A.[151]. Even the figures from Mycenae, which Taylour identified as male[152], would have been more appropriately described as sexless or semi-iconic[153]. If one now takes a closer look at our Lady of Phylakopi it appears that her sex, too, is far from unambiguous. The shape of the figure is cylindrical. She has breasts but a prominent beard as well. Is it man, woman or both?[154]. One of the male figures seems even more emphatically hybrid being endowed with male genitals and breasts[155].

Hermaphrodites of this kind are not entirely unknown in the Minoan/Mycenaean world as witness the group of dancers from Kamilari[156]. But they, and male figures in general, were more at home

---

[146] *Antiquity* (1978) 14.

[147] *AR* (1978) Fig. 93; *Antiquity* (1978) 10; 12–13.

[148] *Antiquity* (1978) 13; Pl. VIa.

[149] *Antiquity* (1978) 10; 13; Pl. V; VIb.

[150] *Op. cit.* 13.

[151] E. French, *The Development of Mycenaean Terracotta Figurines BSA* LXVI (1971) 148.

[152] W. Taylour in *Antiquity* 43 (1969) 91–7; 44 (1970) 270–80.

[153] *Cf. Antiquity* 52 (1978) 13.

[154] 'But we unhesitatingly claim the Lady of Phylakopi as female', Renfrew, *ibid.*

[155] *Ibid.* and Pl. VIb. Male statuettes from Syria were often shown with breasts, *e. g.* *Syria* 29 (1952), Pl. I; T.J. Dunbabin, *The Greeks and their Eastern Neighbours*, London 1957, Pl. 8,1.

[156] 15th/14th century B.C., Herakleion Museum Case 71, No. 15073.

in the east and in Cyprus in particular. No examples survive from the Bronze Age, but figures from the beginning of the archaic period continued earlier traditions. This is manifestly true at the model sanctuary of Ayia Irini with its history of uninterrupted cult from the Late Bronze Age. Among its vast number of votive human figurines only two were obviously female[157]. Some also were sexless and one bisexual with breasts and beard[158]. In appearance the last is similar to the Lady of Phylakopi although a snake winds its coils along the back of the Cypriot figure. The arms were preserved, however, in the 'Segnungsgestus' and emphasize the link with the western Aegean. Most bisexual figures at Ayia Irini are partly human partly bull centaurs. Such strange 'Mischwesen' of men with male genitals, female breasts and the body of a bull were frequently offered up in the sanctuary in its archaic period[159].

Curiously this type of figure in some manner also related to the Minoan idol with upraised arms[160]. But the connection may have been one of artistic style rather than of religious content. There is no means of statisfactorily testing any theory. It seems clear, however, that the figurines of men, hybrids and Minotaurs represented adorants and not a deity. The majority were modelled in the attitude of worshippers, some including centaurs clutching sacrifical victims under one arm[161]. Male votaries were extremely common in other archaic Cypriot sanctuaries. They were offered up at Kourion from the very beginning in the 8th or 7th century B.C.[162] At least one example of a bronze hybrid centaur has also turned up there in the sanctuary[163].

The sanctuary at Phylakopi disappeared with the Bronze Age. However, the strong eastern and Cypriot elements in the Cycladic cult make it possible to form a reasonable opinion about some of its

---

[157] *AfR* (1933) 342.

[158] No. 2316, see Gjerstad in *Medelhavsmuseet Bulletin* 3 (1963) 27; 39, fig. 42; *RDAC* 1971, 34, fig. 4.

[159] *AfR* (1933) 333–4; 343.

[160] V. Karageorghis, 'The goddess with uplifted arms in Cyprus', *Scripta Minora 1977–8*, London 1977, 27; *cf.* J. Karageorghis, *La Grande Déesse de Chypre et son Culte*, Lyon 1977, *e. g.* 123–4; 135–7.

[161] *Cf. AfR* (1933) 333.

[162] *Terrac.* 218–9.

[163] Seen in the *theke* in the Kourion Museum.

aspects. Particularly useful in this respect is the evident similarity with Ayia Irini because of its long history. There the *baetyl*, bull, male and warrior figures have been interpreted as representing an evolution of the central cult figure from an aniconic and theriomorphic to a fully anthropomorphic deity[164]. If correct this would mean that the stages of development, which at Ayia Irini extended roughly from the 13th or 12th to the 7th century B.C., had been completed before the end of the Bronze Age at Phylakopi. But at Kourion, as at other similar archaic sanctuaries, this evolutionary process, or at least its last two stages judging from the votives, were telescoped into the first two centuries of usage. It seems far more likely that all types of images from aniconic to anthropomorphic existed side by side from very early times. Both in Phylakopi and Ayia Irini the *baetyl* always incorporated the numinous power of the deity. It is likely that visual conception of divinity was not precisely defined but could assume practically any form. In the same spirit the monstrous figures of bisexual centaurs, which surrounded the altar at Ayia Irini in respectful poses of adoration, symbolically expressed the notion that all parts of nature offered worship to the god.

The predominance of male votaries at Phylakopi echoed an almost exclusive male presence in archaic times at Ayia Irini and at Kourion. Towards the end of the period bull figures gradually grew less while mixed and bisexual creatures disappeared altogether from the votive dedications at Ayia Irini[165]. By then the community god and protector was imagined as male and anthropomorphic. The two bronze statuettes of the so-called 'Smiting God' are therefore the most exciting discoveries in the sanctuary at Phylakopi, because they show that the concept of anthropomorphic divinity was well established already prior to the end of the Bronze Age. Both figures, which were found east of the East Shrine and the other above Wall 661 in the sanctuary court area[166], were of gods as opposed to the other human male votaries. The 'Smiting God' with threateningly raised right arm and with helmet is identical with the many bronzes of an armed Warrior

---

[164] This is Sjöquist's thesis, although his notion of the relationship between bull and anthropomorphic god is not entirely clear, *AfR* (1933) 316–7; 319–22; 327; 336 etc.

[165] Cf. *AfR* (1933) 342–3.

[166] *Antiquity* (1978) 11, figs. 2 & 3; Pl. IVa & b.

God, also with raised spear and usually a shield on the left arm. He wears the same type of conical helmet as the Phylakopi figures but often with horns.

The archaeological evidence seems convincing enough regarding correspondances in sanctuary type, offerings, even cult figure over a wide area in the Aegean. But on its own it can not explain some quite fundamental questions, such as the date of Apollo's first arrival in Cyprus. The suggestion that Mycenaean settlers brought the god with them in the 13th century B.C. conflicts with the clear message from important sanctuaries like Kourion that Apollo's name was a relatively late intrusion into the cult. And yet the archaic sanctuary still preserved the same type of cult which had been celebrated on the island from the days of the Bronze Age. What aspects then of Apollo's nature are identifiable in Kourion from the varied evidence of cult, and what light do they throw on archaic Apolline cult in Cyprus in general?

By far the majority of archaic and classical shrines of Apollo also lay outside the *polis*[167]. And many of them were hypaethral in the beginning like Delos, Corinth or Klaros. Some like Didyma actually retained cult in the open until the end of their history[168]. The Kourion sanctuary therefore conformed with general Greek practice[169]. The central open space at Kourion, perhaps a grove of trees originally, reflected the features of a typical Cypriot rustic sanctuary, although it now seems that the sanctuary had its own temple before the end of archaic in the 5th century B.C.[170]. This mixture of foreign and native elements was characteristic of Cypriot cults and should not cause surprise at Apollo's most important site.

The god was popular in Cyprus no less than the 'Cyprus-born' Aprodite. Their cults surpassed all others. Both the Paphian Aphrodite and Apollo at Kourion had several common bonds which cast light on their nature and history in Cyprus. The connection

---

[167] J.N. Coldstream, *Geometric Greece*, London 1977, 328.

[168] G. Roux, 'Le vrai temple d'Apollon à Délos', *BCH* 103 (1979) 129; 130; 133. The archaic Pythion in Cretan Gortyn had the typical Cypriot form of *temenos* and *peribolos* wall.

[169] Scranton's contrast between Cypriot and Greek custom is wrong, *TAPS* 68.

[170] Remains of such a temple have turned up in the foundations of the Roman structure, D. Soren, 'Some New Ideas on Dating and Rebuilding the Temple of Apollo Hylates at Kourion', in *RDAC* 1983, 232–44.

survived in the form of dedications in Kourion of votive Aphrodite figurines from neighbouring Amathus[171]. A few mostly late statues of Aphrodite, including the marble head of the goddess from a 4th century A.D. villa in Kourion, have also turned up[172]. Apollo himself was worshipped at Aphrodite's most important shrine in Palaipaphos[173] and had his own cult in New Paphos. To this we shall return presently. However, an interesting indication not only of the link between the two but of the antiquity of the substance of their cult consists in the aniconic idol[174] in the shape of a stone *baetyl* from south of the *temenos* at Kourion. It was discovered many years ago by McFadden but has only recently been published after languishing in the Episkopi Museum for almost half a century. A second similar example also came to light some distance further south[175]. Both cones directly recall those from Aphrodite's sanctuary in Palaipaphos (Kouklia) and of course the black stone *baetyl* from her temple[176]. West of the sanctuary nearer the sea and on the west of the Diarrhizos river two large limestone blocks of Aphrodite can still be seen. They stand forlorn and abused in the middle of a modern factory unlike the rocks of *Petra tou Romiou* on the beach further east near Pissouri where the goddess even today is said to have come ashore.

The traditional link between both cities was equally close, as was the history of their foundation from neighbouring kingdoms in Laconia[177]. However, while the early origins of Paphos have been startlingly confirmed by the discovery there of an 11th century B.C. inscription in the Arcadian dialect[178], the Kourion sanctuary lacks any pre-archaic history[179]. The few extant literary references to

---

[171] Young, *Terrac.* 224f.
[172] *Annual Report of the Director of the Dept. of Antiquities* 1968, 16f.; A.S. Murray, A.H. Smith, H.B. Walter, *Excavations in Cyprus* 1900, 84; Bennett, *Cults* 155f.
[173] References in *Terrac.* 225.
[174] Cap, hair, ears, curious round bosses in lieu of facial features.
[175] See now D. Buitron – D. Soren, 'Missouri in Cyprus: The Kourion Expedition', *Muse* 13 (1980) 26–8 and fig. 5a.
[176] Above pp. 140 and 141 and n. 136. See also F.G. Maier, *A Brief History and Description of Old Paphos (Kouklia)*, Cyprus Ant. dept., 16; Karageorghis, *Cyprus* fig. 127.
[177] See above pp. 123–126.
[178] Bronze *obelos* from Tomb 49, no. 16 at Palaipaphos-Skales with five signs in the Cypriot syllabary: *o-pe-la-ta-u* (Opheltes), V. Karageorghis, *CRAI* 1980, 134–6, fig. 12; *cf. Cyprus* 120.
[179] See above p. 126; 127.

Apollo's sanctuary at Kourion hardly do justice to the importance of the cult. As late as the end of the 2nd century A.D., when the fame of Apollo at Kourion had reached its peak, Aelian merely mentioned the god's grove as a refuge for deer[180]. Strabo recorded that those who touched Apollo's altar were thrown from the cliff[181]. The first notice remembered the earliest tradition of an open area with sacred grove as original cult centre. The arrangement was more typical of archaic rural shrines in Cyprus than of the nature of Apolline cult in Greece. The altar, which Strabo referred to, was next to the cliff (εὐθύς ἐστιν ἄκρα) and need not have been within the *temenos* at all but in the city. Only the city stood on the steep bluff overlooking the sea. Nilsson had probably never seen the site because he called the bluff a 'Vorgebirge'[182]. Nevertheless the penalty for desecrating Apollo's altar was notorious and may well have been associated with Apollo's best known sanctuary on Cyprus. The ritual itself, however, reveals an apotropaeic cult of which the 'sacrificial victim' was a 'Sühneopfer' very much like the annually chosen unfortunate who was 'sacrificed' to Apollo on Leucas and cast into the sea from the rocks on which stood the god's temple[183]. Neither case involved real human sacrifice, as Hill supposes[184], merely an act of expiation or atonement. In Leucas the priests tied wings to the *pharmakos* to break his fall, while men waited below in boats to pick him out of the sea[185]. It seems that both Strabo and Aelian referred to peripheral practices in Apollo's cult at Kourion.

The remains and votives of the sanctuary show that, despite its relatively late institution in archaic times, the cult clearly reflected Cypriot traditions from the Bronze Age on one hand and was typical of the many other contemporary rural cult places on the island on the other. The offerings from Kourion for example exactly reproduced those of Ayia Irini whose history of cult, however, had been continuous from the Bronze Age[186]. A kind of basic vegetation cult provided the common ground, as witness the ubiquitous bull votives

---

[180] *N.A.* XI, 7.
[181] XIV, 6, 3.
[182] M.P. Nilsson, *Griechische Feste mit Ausschluss der Attischen*, Leipzig 1906, 111.
[183] Strabo X, 452.
[184] G. Hill, *A History of Cyprus*, Cambridge 1940, I, 66.
[185] Nilsson, *Feste* 111, with further refs. in n. 1.
[186] See above p. 135.

and, to a far lesser extrent, the associated figure of the snake. Both were of course well known dedications throughout the Aegean in the Bronze Age. The Cypriot bull no doubt possessed its own special significance in the wider context of a general fertility cult, as did the use of mask and horned bucrania. These first occurred in the Early Bronze Age sanctuaries like Vounous. But they also preserved close links with the east which were continually reinforced as appears from the history of Temple V at Kition and elsewhere[187].

The thousands of votive offerings, which survived from the area of the *temenos* and the so-called McFadden deposit to the south of it[188], have been studied and exhaustively discussed in an exemplary publication some thirty years ago[189]. Subsequent discoveries, like the *bothros* north of the boundary wall, where many classical and later discarded figurines had been deposited, add little new to the picture[190]. The earliest types of votives of the 8th and 7th centuries B.C. were predominantly terracottas of bulls some with snakes crawling up their forelegs or appearing between the horns. Standing votaries, usually male and often carrying gifts under one arm, were also dedicated during this period[191]. From the last quarter of the 7th century gifts of horsemen, riders and chariot groups became more frequent[192]. By the 5th century few bulls remain. Other animals have disappeared altogether, and so have the standing single votaries. Riders, charioteers, warriors *etc.* have virtually displaced most other forms in the 5th and following century when all votives were practically identical. By now they were mass produced in types which continue down to 200 B.C. After a decline of about one hundred and fifty years, interest in the sanctuary revived under Roman rule from 50 B.C. Some types long lost, like standing votaries, reappear once more. Other offerings are new in this period, including terracottas of a dog and cock, lamps *etc.* They show, like contemporary dedications of doves and other birds, a less rigorous

---

[187] See *e. g.* Karageorghis, *Cyprus* 49–50; 94–8; *cf. Muse* (1980) 31 n. 30 for references to further modern discussions of the topic.

[188] Above p. 128.

[189] *Terrac.*

[190] Above p. 130.

[191] *Terrac.* 219.

[192] *Ibid.*

discipline in the specific type of votives which had been prescibed in previous centuries[193].

Thus from the archaeological point of view the greatest change in votive practices occurred at the end of the 7th century at about 600 B.C. At this time apparently a more overt vegetation ritual gave way to the worship of a kind of military warrior god[194]. In cultic terms, however, the division signals a change in fashion of votive dedication rather than novel cult forms. Just how misleading archaeological evidence can be in the absence of literary records appears from the paucity of votives of deer which were virtually confined to the 6th century B.C.[195]. Without Aelian's reference to Apollo's concern for deer there would be little indication of their importance at Kourion together with sacred groves. Bulls and masks survived at least into Hellenistic times, while conversely figurines of horsemen were offered to the divinity from the beginning of the sanctuary. In fact the earliest example came from a 9th century tomb at Kaloriziki[196] near the sanctuary. Horsemen may have been dedicated elsewhere in Cyprus as early as the Early Bronze Age[197], but there is no doubt that figurines of men riding, on carts, leading bulls, even models of chariots have been found in both tombs and sanctuaries from the Late Bronze Age at Enkomi, Idalion and Ayia Irini[198]. They continued to be dedicated together in most rustic sanctuaries of the archaic period[199]. Evidently the bull from quite early on symbolised more than animal fertility. The animal also in some way incorporated the god who fought for and protected his community[200]. Thus figures of warrior and horsemen could be offered up together with the bull because there was no conflict in religious concept. Consequently the cult at Kourion did not dramatically change its nature at any one

---

[193] *Op. cit.* 221 f.
[194] *Op. cit.* 220; *cf.* Karageorghis in *CAH*[3] III, 3, Cambridge 1982, 61.
[195] *Terrac.* 2.
[196] Found by Daniel in 1934, *Terrac.* 10.
[197] *Cf.* the horse man vase from Vounous, Cyprus Museum R. III.
[198] Karageorghis, *Cyprus* 101; *cf.* V. Tatton-Brown, *RDAC* 1982, 177f. Perhaps the chariots were Mycenaean imports in IIIB or even earlier, *cf.* the famous 14th century B.C. crater from Enkomi, Karageorghis, *Cyprus Museum*, Athens 1981, No. 28; and a IIIB crater from Pyla, Cyprus Museum R. XII.
[199] Karageorghis, *Cyprus* 139 ff.
[200] *Cf.* M. Yon, 'Du Taureau à l'Aigle', in *CNRS*, Paris 1981, 92.

particular point in its history, although in the course of time the emphasis shifted to more political and indeed sporting aims. Judging from the votives, which repeated those of far older sanctuaries like Ayia Irini and Ayios Iakovos, it appears that at Kourion Bronze Age and archaic customs were telescoped into one. Conservatism in Cypriot cult, particularly in the more rural shrines, was such that this kind of anachronism of 12th and 13th century B.C. offerings in the 7th century raised no eyebrows. This applies not only to horsemen, bulls and masks but to the other aspects of cult which are represented by numerous votives.

A sacred grove held a central place in the cult at Kourion. Models of sacred trees were dedicated in the sanctuary quite early on and at least from the 7th century B.C. They were free-standing or often in the centre of a ritual group as object of cult[201]. One tree perhaps symbolised the entire grove at Kourion. There are signs that trees were worshipped within a sacred enclosure at Ayia Irini. Perhaps the *tholos* west of the *temenos* at Kourion was constructed in memory of earlier sacred gardens[202]. However, trees were common features of simple rustic shrines everywhere[203].

Models and fragments of many other ritual groups of priests or worshippers have turned up in the fill of the archaic precinct. They were most popular in the 7th and 6th centuries B.C.[204]. In addition to sacred trees the figures also surround other cult objects like column, well or spring. Two examples have a human figure in the middle[205]. The groups are splendid testimony of actual ritual performance or procession. Occasionally a worshipper hopes to identify with the deity by donning the mask of a bull[206] or of the god in human form[207]. The famous E.B.A. clay models from Vounous and Kotchati demonstrate the Cypriots' predilection for showing cult and funerary

---

[201] *Terrac.* 39; 41 No. 840; 841; *cf. Muse* 13 (1980) fig. 3.
[202] See above p. 130.
[203] *E. g.* Nilsson, *GGR³* I, 210.
[204] *Terrac.* 39f.; 220.
[205] *Terrac.* 40f. No. 809; 816.
[206] *E. g. Terrac.* Nos. 825–8; 834–9.
[207] No. 823; 824. On masked figures and their significance in Cyprus see Sjöquist, *AfR* 30 (1933) 344–7; V. Karageorghis, *Harv. Theol. Rev.* 64 (1971) 261–70. Hermary, *BCH* 103 (1979) 734–41.

ceremonial in progress[208]. The much later archaic examples from Kourion also have many parallels from other sanctuaries notably again from Ayios Iakovos of the 10th century[209] and contemporary archaic votives (650–580 B.C.) from Ayia Irini[210]. Generally the ritual involved dancing and music. The participants moved about the cult object either from right to left or counter clockwise[211] often swaying in wild abandon while one strikes the beat on his drum[212] or another clashes the cymbals in accompaniment[213]. The scene recalls the so-called tympanon players from Paphos[214]. But ritual dancing was not uncommon. Many representations of 'ring-dancers' in Cyprus survive[215], but the best again from Aphrodite's sanctuaries at Chytroi and Soloi[216].

Music and dancing were close to Apollo's nature as healing and purifying deity. It is therefore of great interest that terracottas of lyre-players began to appear in Kourion from the 7th century B.C. that is early in the history of the sanctuary[217]. They are votives, that is human players and not figures of the god Apollo. There is a sculpture of Apollo holding his lyre in his sanctuary in Potamia which saw cult from archaic times to the 3rd century B.C.[218]. In a roughly contemporary sanctuary outside the city wall at Salamis and close to the Monastery of St. Barnabas another statue was discovered of

---

[208] *E. g.* Karageorghis, *Cyprus* figs. 31; 32.

[209] *SCE* 1, 364, No. 13; 16.

[210] *SCE* II, 679 ff., No. 123; 1169; 1693. Compare similar (fragm.) examples from Vouni but slightly later from the 5th century B.C., *SCE* III, 235, Nos. 122; 124. See also *Terrac.* 39 f.

[211] *Terrac.* 801; 808; 810–16.

[212] No. 807 (?).

[213] One as yet unpublished terracotta from the most recently discovered *bothros* and now in the Episkopi *theke*.

[214] *E. g.* one terracotta figure (Cypro-Arch. II, 600-475 B.C.) from Aphrodite's sanctuary at Yeroskipos, in the Paphos Museum.

[215] See A. N. Stillwell, *Corinth XV*, 2, 42, *plus* examples from outside Cyprus, *Terrac.* 220. A famous group was found in the neopalatial tomb at Kamilari, Herakleion Museum No. 15073, *cf.* the LM IIIA example from Palaikastro, Gesell, *Minoan House Cult* 129.

[216] J. L. Myres – M. Ohnefalsch-Richter, *A Catalogue of the Cyprus Museum*, Oxford 1899, Nos. 528 ff.; 5401 ff.; *cf. Terrac.* 39.

[217] *Terrac.* 219.

[218] V. Karageorghis, in *RDAC* 1979, 289–315; *CNRS* No. 593 (1981) 83.

Apollo also with his lyre. The shrine belonged to Aphrodite[219] whose equally deep concern for music and dance had early on brought her close to Apollo in this rustic precinct[220]. Hill suggests that Apollo's lyre was responsible for the god's connection with the figure of Kinyras[221] and through him with Aphrodite. The word *kinyra* (Hebr. *kinnôr*) described a ten-stringed lyre. But the traditional links between the two figures are too strong and Kinyras' background too substantial to have grown out of such a simple etymological coincidence.

Apollo's name first occurs in the sanctuary in the 5th century B.C. It was inscribed on the figure of a 'temple boy'[222]. Two earlier dedicatory inscriptions simply refer to 'the deity'[223] who may already have been Apollo[224] or more probably was still nameless at the time. Later epithets at Kourion are sometimes badly documented like Pythios[225], Polykteanos and Lakeutes[226], of uncertain meaning[227], or altogether doubtful like Lenaios[228]. Only Hylates and Kaisar are indisputable and important. Both were generally invoked together in Roman dedications of the late 1st or early 2nd century A.D.[229]. They show that by the time of Trajan's principate the community god had become identified with the Roman emperor[230].

---

[219] Early discoveries of heads of Aphrodite are reported in *BCH* 87 (1963) 354, fig. 45; 88 (1964) 332, fig. 65.

[220] M. Yon, *Salamine de Chypre V. Un dépôt de sculpture archaiques*, Paris 1974, *cf.* the review by V. Watson in *JHS* 96 (1976) 244.

[221] Hill, *Hist. of Cyprus* I, 68 f. *Cf.* above pp. 124–125.

[222] *IKourion* 46, no. 18; *cf.* 49, no. 19 (4th cent.); *ICS* 198, no. 185; no. 184.

[223] τῶ θεῶ, probably genitives, *i.e.* (the property) of the god, 6th century Corinthian oenochoe and a slightly earlier Egyptian bronze situla of the Saite Dynasty, *IKourion* 38, no. 14; 40 no. 15; *ICS* 199, no. 189; no. 188.

[224] *ICS ibid.*, 'Dédicace "au dieu" (no. 188), c'est à-dire Apollon'.

[225] *IKourion* 89, no. 41.

[226] See refs. in *Terrac.* 223 n. 1. Hill, *Hist. Cyprus* 89 accepts the epithet without discussion.

[227] For the derivation of *Lakeutes* from *lasko* = the crackling of the sacrificial meat in the fire, see O. Masson, *Glotta* (1960) 112–14; L. Robert, *CRAI* (1978) 338–44.

[228] *IKourion* 52, no. 21; *ICS* 198, no. 184; no. 186. Scranton proposed Linos, but that seems far fetched, *TAPS* 72 f.

[229] *IKourion* 207, no. 108; 215, no. 111; 233, no. 120; 237, no. 122; 238, no. 123; 241, no. 124.

[230] *Cf.* Mitford in *IKourion* 210.

The Hylates was the god of the woodland or grove. The epithet defines the central feature at Kourion and in many Apolline cults both in east and west. In Boeotian Tilphossion there was a sacred grove in his honour together with a sacred spring[231]. At Achaean Patrae Apollo shared a grove with Aphrodite[232], with his sister Artemis at Daphne on the Orontes in northern Syria[233]. The *temenos* within the large grove (80 stades in circumference) and springs offered a safe refuge like the Kourion sanctuary. In Epirus the grove contained snakes, offspring of the Delphic Python, and it was also enclosed by a *peribolos* like Kourion. The snakes were fed by a young priestess who consulted them as a kind of oracle[234]. Tradition records that the trees from Apollo Karneios' grove in the Troad were used in the construction of the Wooden Horse to end the siege of Troy[235]. Other Apolline groves, usually with springs of water and an oracle, were on Chios[236], in Phrygia[237], at Oichalia in the Messenian plain[238], in Achaea at Pagasae and in Thessaly[239]. Augustus hung up the spoils from his victory at Actium in the grove of the Aktian Apollo[240]. At the grove and oracle at Gruneion near Myrina in Asia Minor[241] former prisoners in a strange custom fixed their chains to the trees of the grove[242].

The Kourion *hyle* also had a spring about which worshippers performed sacred rituals and which was later exploited to build the Roman baths at the south-eastern boundary of the sanctuary[243]. The spring and precinct conceivably witnessed some oracular activity judging from a 3rd century B.C. dedicatory inscription to Apollo

---

[231] Homeric *Hymn to Apollo* 384; Strabo 411.
[232] Paus. 7,21,4.
[233] Strabo 750.
[234] Aelian, *nat. an.* 11,2.
[235] Paus. 3,13,5.
[236] Grove of palm trees, Strabo 645.
[237] Naculeia (?), *IG add.* 3847[b].
[238] Karnasian grove of cypresses, Paus. 4,33,4.
[239] Apollo Pagasites, Pagasaeus, Hesych. *s. v.* Παγασίτης; Hesiod, *Scut.* 70, πᾶν δ' ἄλσος καὶ βωμὸς Ἀπόλλωνος Παφασαίου λάμπεν.
[240] Strabo 325. On the sanctuary of Apollo Aktius see also *IG* VII, 513; 515; 517; Thuc. I, 29.
[241] Paus. 1,21,9.
[242] Serv. on Verg., *Ecl.* 672; *Aen.* 4, 345.
[243] *Kourion* 62.

Pythios[244]. The testimony is weak, however, as if the peculiarly Apolline combination of grove, spring and oracle had been specially created at Kourion in imitation of older traditions at other cult sites. In any event, none of the three elements directly involved vegetation cult. Nor was Apollo particularly concerned with tree cult[245]. The palm beneath which he was born, and which stood beside his famous *keratinos bomos* on Delos[246], belonged to Leto who was arguably a goddess of nature[247]. Apollo's tree was the laurel which had no primary connection with birth or fertility[248]. Its main property, which linked the laurel with Apollo, was its power of purification at the god's important festival in Delphi, Tempe and Delos. So the cleansing branches of a laurel tree were ritually swung at the foundation of Apollo's sanctuary at Didyma[249]. The god himself was Daphnephoros carrying the laurel at the Daphnephoria in his honour in Attica and Boeotian Thebes[250]. His oldest temple in Eretria was

---

[244] Dedication of statues by the priests of Apollo Pythios, Hylates and Hera, *IKourion* 89f., no. 41. Mitford's identification of a mantiarch in a 6th century B.C. funerary inscription from Meidan at Episkopi is too uncertain, 27-9, no. 9.

[245] The different fruit trees and other species of trees, which were cultivated in the Gruneion (Paus. 1,21,9), however, more directly recall the type of oriental gardens which had early on found favour in Cyprus at Kition *etc.*, Karageorghis, *Cyprus* 69; 94.

[246] Homer, *Od.* 6, 162f.; Ovid, *Her.* XXI, 101f.

[247] *Hom. Hymn Apollo* 16-18; 117-19. Nilsson *GGR³* I, 249; 562.

[248] Eur., *Hec.* 458ff.; *Ion* 919ff., in a natural piece of poetic licence joined Apollo's famous laurel with the palm in Delos, *cf.* the cypresses in Messenia, Paus. 4,33,4. The identification of Karneios in the Troad with *kraneia*, the wild cherry-tree, though assigned to Praxilla of Sicyon, Paus. 3,13,5, is a much later etymology. On trees and Apollo's birth myth see Ch. LeRoy, 'La Naissance d'Apollon et les Palmiers Deliens', *Études Déliennes*, *BCH* Suppl. I (1973) 263-86. The myrtle appears to have possessed similar purificatory properties to the laurel and was also connected with oracles, *cf.* Apollo Myrikaios at Korope in Thessaly, Nikand., *Ther.* 612 and schol. *ad loc.*; *cf.* a 1st cent. B.C. inscription in *AM* (1882) 71. Apollo once has the epithet Myrtates in Cyprus at Marathounda, *BCH* 89 (1965) 250; *REG* 80 (1967) 558f., No. 658 (*cf.* the epithet Myrtoos in Cyrene, *IG* III, 5138); *cf.* Bennett, *Cults* 355. Apollo Platanistios had a temple on the road from Troezen to Hermione, Paus. 2,34,6. The epithet does not occur elsewhere.

[249] Callim. Frag. 194, 28-31; Clem. Strom. 5,48,4.

[250] Paus. 9,10,4. His temple at Phlya was the Daphnephoreion, Athen. 10, 424F. *Cf.* Nilsson, *Feste* 164f.; W. Burkert, *Griechische Religion* 161; 165 and n. 12. On the Boeotian Daphnephoreion see also A. Schachter, *BICS* Suppl. 38.1 (1981) 83-5.

built of wood in the 8th century B.C.[251]. In Cyprus the Daphnephoros was known in the dialectal form of *Daukhnaphorios* in a rustic shrine at Lefkoniko near Salamis[252]. The connection of the laurel tree with Apollo's oracle at Delphi and then on Delos was secondary *via* purificatory ritual[253], although it enjoyed great popular success[254] giving rise much later to the tradition of the Pythia chewing laurel leaves to become divinely inspired[255].

Apollo's grove was revered for its power to protect. He was the *Alexikakos, Apotropaios,* the healer and purifyer from contamination. The two allied elements of water and oracle were connected with the same basic concept of purification[256]. The *temenos* within the grove represented the divine *perfugium* in Kourion and elsewhere as at Daphnae[257], in the sanctuary of the Ptoian Apollo at Akraiphia in Boeotia and of course in Delphi. The refuge had a *peribolos* in Kourion and at Epirus[259], or stones around its boundary as in Delos, Chios, Naxos and Paros[260]. In Akraiphia *stelai* served as markers. The sacred precinct within was taboo to ordinary men[261] and transgressors were severely punished. They were arraigned in court[262], or cast from rock or cliff in Kourion, Leucas and in a strange ceremony in Ionian Magnesia near Miletus[263]. Protection, penalty

---

[251] *Antike Kunst* 17 (1974) 60–68; Burkert, *Gr. Rel.* 150.

[252] *ICS* 311 ff., no. 309.

[253] P. Amandry, *La mantique apollinienne à Délphes, essai sur le functionnement de l'oracle* (Bibl. des ecoles francaises d'Athènes et de Rome), fasc. 170 (1950) 129 f.; H. W. Parke and D. E. W. Wormell, *The Delphic Oracle*, Oxford 1956, I, 26; Dietrich, 'Reflections on the Origins of Oracular Apollo', *BICS* 25 (1978) 8.

[254] *E. g.* Aristoph., *Plutus* 213; *cf.* 'tremere omnia visa repente / limina laurusque dei' (Delos), Verg., *Aen.* 3, 90 f.; Ovid, *Met.* 15, 634 f., *etc.*

[255] The tradition may have started as late as the 2nd cent. A.D., Oenom. in Eus., *PE* 5, 224 a; Luc., *Bis Accusatus* 1. However, earlier prophets might have indulged in the same practice, Parke – Wormell, *ibid.*

[256] See n. 253.

[257] Strabo 750.

[258] *IG* VII, 4135.

[259] Aelian, *nat. an.* 11, 2.

[260] *IG add.* 2384ᵉ (3 rd cent. B. C.) ὅρος χωρίου ἱεροῦ Ἀπόλλωνος Δηλίου. (Paros), *cf.* the Delion in Naxos, Plut. 254 F; *BCH* (1879) 231, inscriptions mentioning boundaries of the Delion on Chios.

[261] 2nd cent. B. C. inscr., see n. 258 above.

[262] Before the Amphictyons in Akraiphia, n. 258.

[263] Sacred men leaped down from rocks near Apollo's cave and pulled up trees by their roots and carried them, Paus. 10, 32, 4.

and purification through a *pharmakos* were part of one and the same range of functions of Apollo.

Outside Cyprus Apollo was almost invariably named after the locality of his grove like Ptoios (hero and place), Karnasios, Gruneios, Telphousios, Pagasaios, Pagasites and so on. But the island was known as the land of Hylates[264]. The name was confined to Cyprus. It was not a toponym but a translation into Greek of the function or quality of the native cult figure[265]. The original Cypriot term is obscure. Perhaps it was something like Opanon Melanthios a rural fertility god near Amargetti who also became identified with Apollo in Hellenistic times[266]. More likely he was simply addressed as 'the god'. Hylates on his own is read in two 5th century B.C. inscriptions at Drimou about halfway between Paphos and Marion[267] and later twice in Chytroi near Nicosia[268]. As an epithet of Apollo Hylates first appears in two or three inscriptions of the 4th century B.C. at Nea Paphos[269]. They are above the entrance and within a 'cave' which had been converted from a rock-cut tomb in the necropolis of Alonia tou Episkopou. The 'adyton' stood inside a larger precinct whose cult was first instituted during the last quarter of the 4th century B.C. possibly by Nikokles, king of Paphos, at the time when Nea Paphos was founded to settle the former inhabitants of Marion[270]. Now the *temenos* stands in the private garden of an abandoned villa. Put the impressive remains still show the importance of the cult. An opening in the roof of the 'cave' suggested to Mitford that the ritual of Apollo Hylates involved some oracular activity[271]. This seems a reasonable

[264] Lycophron 448. *P-W* R.E. 'Hylates' (1914) 116; Glover in *SCA*, 147.

[265] Messenian Hylae may be an exception, Paus. 10,32,4, but Jessen argues, *P-W* R.E. 'Hylates' 116f., that the place was really called Aulai and Apollo Aulaites not Hylates. The god appears as Aulaites on Magnesian coins.

[266] Ἀπόλωνι Μελαθίῳ, Hill, *Hist. Cyprus* 80 n.3; Mitford, *JHS* 66 (1948) 36–9; *Cultes*, 136; Karageorghis, *CNRS* no. 593, Paris 1981, 83.

[267] τῷ θεῷ τῷ Ὑλάτᾳ; τῷ Ὑλάτᾳ , *ICS* 141f., nos. 85 and 86; Mitford, 'Paphian Inscriptions Hoffmann Nos. 98 & 99', *BICS* 7 (1960) 6.

[268] About 300 B.C., *ICS* 264f., nos. 250 and 250a; Mitford, 'Further Contribution to the Epigraphy of Cyprus', *AJA* 65 (1961) 129 n.153.

[269] *ICS* 96–8, nos. 2 & 3; *BICS* 7 (1960) 1–10; Mitford, 'Unpublished Inscriptions of the Cyprus Museum', *Op Ath* 3 (1960) 204.

[270] *ICS* 93; *BICS* 7 (1960) 1–10; *Op Ath* (1960) 200–5; J. Mlynarzak, 'The Paphian Sanctuary of Apollo Hylates', *RDAC* 1980, 239–42, with further references.

[271] *BICS* 7 (1960) 6–8.

proposal. Many Apolline oracles traditionally issued from caves or actually survived in that form like the famous Klarian oracle. The link was late, however, and probably did not come about before the end of the archaic period[272].

In his Boeotian sanctuary and asylum the Ptoian Apollo also had an oracular cave which provided the central feature of the *temenos*[273]. Like Nikokles' converted cave it was a 'Spruchorakel'[274]. Apollo had taken over from the hero Ptoios but not before the 7th century B.C. or possibly even later. This kind of new cult practice, which evolved in the archaic/classical period, supplied the model for the Paphian institution. An important Greek national god was deliberately joined to a popular native figure for political propaganda purposes. The god, who came to be known as Hylates, possessed firm roots in Cypriot tradition. Stephanus and Nonnus cite cults in his honour in Erystheia, Amamassos, Tembros, Tamassos, even Hyle[275]. None of them, however, beside Drimou and Chytroi is reliably documented. In Kourion dedicatory references to Hylates together with Apollo do not begin before the second half of the 3rd century B.C.[276]. The inscriptional evidence shows, as has already been pointed out[277], that Apollo Hylates moved to Kourion relatively late, although that sanctuary was destined to grow into his most important cult centre in Roman times[278]. The Paphian model, particularly in view of that city's close links with Kourion, proved attractive to Kourion. However, the grove, spring and sacred asylum in the latter sanctuary were bound to invite Apollo's patronage.

The time gap between Apollo Hylates in Paphos and Kourion was relatively small. It need not be stretched much further to include the notices of Hylates in Drimou and Chytroi. The 6th and 5th centuries mark the beginning of the proliferation of Greek divine names and

---

[272] *BICS* 25 (1978) 5–7.
[273] Paus. 4,32,5; Herod. 8, 135; Plut. *de def. or.* 412.
[274] Nilsson, *Feste* 163; *GGR*³ I, 626. For a detailed discussion, with sources, of the sanctuary and oracle see Schachter in *BICS* Suppl. 38.1 (1981) 52–70.
[275] Invented from Lycophron's Ὑλάτου γῆ. *s. v.* Ἐρύσθεια, *Dion.* XIII, 444. Refs. with text in *P-W* R.E. 'Hylates' 116.
[276] *IKourion* nos. 60; 61; 62; 64.
[277] Mlynarzyk, *RDAC* 1980, 243.
[278] *Cf.* Glover in *SCA* 147.

titles[279]. But Cypriots had already been travelling west to pay homage to Apollo in Greece. For example a certain Hermaeus dedicated a bronze tripod to Apollo in Delphi at the end of the 7th century B.C.[280]. In the following century a textile maker from Salamis offered the god a *peplos* in his temple at Delphi[281]. Links with the Greek world grew intense under Egyptian domination of the island in the 6th century[282] and peaked in the following century under pro-Athenian and anti-Persian administrations like that of Evagoras I of Salamis[283]. The impact on the religious life in town and country shrines of this archaic/classical Greek import was considerable. But it was not the first time of course that western Aegean gods had come to Cyprus. The new classical wave of Olympians met with the gods of the Mycenaean settlers of some five or six hundred years previously[284]. Among them in some form or other were the two most prominent Cypriot divinities Apollo and Aphrodite. Continuous contact with the east, especially through settlements at Al Mina and Tarsus, constantly renewed such old ties with Mycenaean culture and religion[285].

Their roots went deep in Cyprus[286] with cults which flourished in the Late Bronze Age at the time of Mycenaean settlement[287]. Demodocus' reference in the *Odyssey* to Aphrodite's sanctuary and altar at Paphos[288] shows that the Cyprian-born goddess was established in the Olympian family of Homer long before archaic and classical Greek contacts with the island. Both Apollo's and Aphrodite's common Mycenaean past is also reflected in the pre-Agapenor tradition of Kinyras founder of Paphos and ancestor of the

---

[279] Karageorghis, *Cyprus* 144, suggests that Eteocypriot gods were anonymous.

[280] *BCH* 95 (1971) 295–304; *cf.* Karageorghis, *Cyprus* 136.

[281] *CAH*² (1982) III, 3, 67.

[282] *CAH*² (1982) III, 3, 61; 66.

[283] *Cf.* Glover, *SCA* 149.

[284] *E.g.* Karageorghis, *Cyprus* 143; *Cultes* 129–42; K. Hadjiioannou, *I archaia Kypros eis tas ellinikas pigas*, 4 (i), (ii), 1980, 27 ff.

[285] *CAH*² (1982) III, 3, 66.

[286] *Cultes* 132 f.; 135; 137.

[287] See already Hill, *Hist. Cyprus* I, 70; *Op Ath* 5 (1964) 43, for this view of Aphrodite's past history. *Cf.* Bennett, *Cults* 275; 497 n. 71; 72 *etc.* for further modern literature.

[288] *Od.* 8, 363.

Kinyradae[289]. The venerable association of the two gods could still be exploited in the 4th century B. C. by Nikokles who founded the cult of Apollo as Hylates along the route of the procession of Aphrodite's mysteries from Old to New Paphos[290]. The Paphian goddess was known under the Mycenaean title of *Wanassa*[291]. Her priest was the king of Paphos and descendant of Kinyras still in Ptolemaic times[292]. Perhaps Apollo, too, had been worshipped as *Wanax* although no recorded instance survives[293]. But their close bond is evident and the Mycenaean ancestry of their cult impeccable. Mythological and cultic ties with the west were strongest in Laconia and Arcadia, both centres of Mycenaean emigration to Cyprus[294]. Once the link had been established the exchange of religious practices worked both ways. The Mycenaean *Wanassa* returned to Arcadian Tegea as Paphia before the end of the Bronze Age had been rung out[295].

It was the same with the cult of Apollo who found his way back to Sparta from Cyprus as Amyklaios[296]. The epithet, like the name of the place Amyclae, arose from contact with the Semitic Mikal, or 'Lord' like *Wanax*, in Cyprus prior to the collapse of the Mycenaean world[297]. The evidence in the main consists of two inscriptions of the 4th and 3rd centuries B. C. from Idalion. One is a bilingual dedication in which the Phoenician Reshef Mikal is translated into syllabic Cypriot as Apollo Amyklos[298]. The other is in Greek to Apollo Amyklos[299]. The inscriptions are late but reflect a process which took

---

[289] See above pp. 124–125.
[290] Strabo XIV, 6, 3, p. 683; Hill, *Hist. Cyprus* 71; Mlynarzyk, *RDAC* 1980, 245.
[291] *Cultes* 135; Dietrich, 'Some Evidence from Cyprus of Apolline Cult in the Bronze Age', *RM* 121 (1978) 6.
[292] *RDAC* 1980, 243.
[293] It is stretching the evidence, however, to call Apollo the male associate of *Wanassa*, *RDAC* 1980, 244.
[294] For a list of cults and cult epithets see *Cults* 740.
[295] Laodice, daughter of Agapenor (or of Kinyras, according to another tradition) founded a temple to Aphrodite Paphia in Tegea, Paus. 8,5,3; 53,7; Hill, *Hist. Cyprus* 68.
[296] See *RM* (1978) 1–18.
[297] See previous note and *ICS* 248. *Cf.* Apollo Mikal in a 3rd cent. B. C. inscription from Kition, I. Nicolau, 'Inscriptiones Cypriae alphabeticae VIII, 1968', *RDAC* 1969, no. 16, 87–90.
[298] *CIS* I, 89; *ICS* no. 220, 246–8.
[299] *Cultes* 138; *ICS* 235 n. 2; Mitford, *CQ* (1950) 99.

place some centuries previously. The link between the early Apollo and Mikal and the much larger associated figure of Reshef had been their common nature as apotropaeic and protecting deities. Both Apollo and Reshef could inflict sickness and also heal. Apollo's bow and arrows, which carried plague and death to the Achaean army in *Iliad* 1, may have been borrowed from the Semitic Reshef who was shown with these attributes in Syrian iconography of the 17th century B.C.[300]. The extreme Cypriot conservatism in religious practices preserved the tradition of Bronze Age cults into the 4th century and beyond. The many dedications from later ages similarly kept the evidence of the two-way traffic in cultic exchange.

If the impulse towards Apollo Amyklaios originated in the east, other epithets provide evidence of a move in the opposite direction. For example, a 4th century B.C. bilingual inscription on a statuette from Apollo's sanctuary near Tamassos equates Apollo Heleitas with Reshef *'lyyt*[301]. The Greek version reads *Apeilon* which was a Cypriot formation of the Laconian *Apellon*[302]. In this case the model was Greek, while *'lyyt* represents the transcription of Heleitas into Phoenician. Perhaps the cult of Heleitas was an import from a Laconian town with the name of Helos[303]. But the form Heleitas was unique and only occurred in Cyprus. Evidently the cult figure had long established itself in Cyprus before coming into contact with the east. Heleitas most likely described a localised cult of Apollo 'In The Marsh' *en helei*[304]. Another contemporary inscription from the same sanctuary at Frangissa near Tamassos more obviously preserved the memory of a prehistoric Cypriot Apolline cult which was eventually taken over by the Phoenicians when they annexed Tamassos to their kingdom of Kition in the middle of the 4th century B.C.[305]. In the dedication to Apollo Alasiotas god and title were rendered into the Phoenician equivalent Reshef *'lhyts*[306]. Alasiotas like Heleitas is a

---

[300] *RM* (1978) 2; 11; 18.
[301] *Cultes* 139; *ICS* no. 215, 224–6.
[302] *ICS* 226; W. Burkert, 'Apellai und Apollon', *RM* 118 (1975) 6, with a discussion of the etymology.
[303] References in *Cultes* 139 n. 2; *ICS* 226.
[304] *Cf. e. g.* Hera Heleia in Cyprus, Hill, *Hist. Cyprus* 48 n. 2; *Cultes* 139 and n. 4; *ICS* 226.
[305] E. Gjerstad in *SCE* IV, 2, 497; *cf.* Glover, *SCA* 148.
[306] *Cultes* 139 n. 1; *ICS* no. 216, 226–8.

hapax but is best explained as an adjectival formation from Alasia which was the ancient name for Cyprus. Alasia has not survived in the Greek sources but was common currency with this significance in the Late Bronze Age in eastern texts such as the Amarna letters[307]. Alasiotas was not a toponym in the narrow sense but described the national god who had received worship since the Bronze Age. The late Phoenician dedication proves that god and cult continued even under the new owners of Apollo's sanctuary in Tamassos[308].

Alasiotas falls into the first of three groups of Apolline epithets in Cyprus. It was a special title like Amyklos, Amyklaios, Heleitas and Hylates describing a cult locality or particular characteristics and qualities which the god possessed in Cyprus. The people could look upon them as 'their gods'[309]. In the second group are adaptations of Greek or wider Aegean aspects of Apollo like Daukhnaphorios[310], Agyates[311] and Myrtates[312]. The local dialectal forms betray the early date of their arrival in Cyprus[313]. This second group is clearly distinct from more familiar Greek epithets like Pythios[314] or Lykeios[315]

---

[307] Literature and discussion of the topic are vast; see *Cultes* 139; 140 and notes; *ICS* 228, for refs. to modern theories regarding the localisation of Alasia and equation with Alasiotas. Attempts to identify a Laconian Alesion, on analogy with Amyklaios and Amyklai, have long been abandoned, *ICS, ibid.* See also K. Hadjiioannou in *Alasia I* (C.F.A. Schaeffer *et al.* eds.), Paris 1971, 33–42; L. Hellbing, *Alasia Problems* (*SIMA* 57), Göteborg 1979.

[308] *Cultes* 140f.; Glover, *SCA* 148; Karageorghis, *Cyprus* 144. The epithet Kyprios from Soloi (3rd cent. B.C. inscr. *SEG* 20.292; *AJA* 65 (1961) 134 no. 34) is evidently a later coinage. But for a different view see Mitford in *AJA* (1961) 134 and n. 172.

[309] ἡμέτερος (Hylates, Kerynetes) in an imperial oath of allegiance to Tiberius from Nicoclia, Mitford, *JRS* 50 (1960) 75–9; Glover, *SCA* 147; 149.

[310] *ICS* 309, p. 311–2; Meister, 'Dauchnaphorios', *K. Sächs. Gesellsch. d. Wissensch. Leipz. Ber. Ph.-hist. Kl.* 60 (1908) 6–7.

[311] *SEG* 20, 309; *AJA* 65 (1961) 129 and n. 155.

[312] *SEG* 23, 655; *BCH* 89 (1965) 250; *RDAC* 1965, 120f.; *REG* 80 (1967) 558f. no. 658.

[313] This point is made by Bennett, *Cults* 745, who also compiles a list of other examples of this type.

[314] *IKourion* no. 41; cf. Kyprios above n. 308.

[315] Mersinaki. Apollo had a *temenos* there together with Athena. The epithet on an alphabetical dedication is cited by Masson in *ICS* 216 – Ἀπόλλωνι Λυκίῳ, cf. *SCE* II, 354–78; 623 nos. 3–6; 637f. no. 9. Also 3rd century B.C. dedication to Apollo Lykios in Soloi, *SCE* III, 622, no. 4; *AJA* 65 (1961) 116. On the cult and origins of

which were direct imports from the west in the classical age or even later. In the west Apollo's predilection for topographical epithets shows that he came as a fully formed god and a kind of missionary figure that absorbed others in spreading his universal influence[316]. The process was similar in Cyprus but more complex. Like Aphrodite at Paphos, Golgoi *etc.* he was sometimes nameless at first as the Lord of Alasia, In The Marsh, Of The Grove and so on. Nevertheless the evidence suggests that the actual name Apollo was already familiar to the Mycenaeans before they came to Cyprus. But whether they brought the 'finished' god with them in the 12th century B.C. is another question which may never be answered. There is no doubt, however, that Apollo came to Cyprus twice from the west: once in the Bronze Age and again in the classical age of the 5th century.

The fortuitous discovery of a Hellenistic inscription from the region of Pyla preserved the evidence of another survival from the Bronze Age. It is a dedication to Apollo Keraiates[317]. Like the other epithets from our Group II, Keraiates is the Cypriot dialectal variant of a Greek form Kereates. Pausanias recorded a cult of Apollo Kereates near Aegys in southern Arcadia[318]. The close link of the region with Cyprus in the Bronze Age shows once more that we are dealing with an ancient cult of Apollo[319] which was brought to the island by the Achaeans[320]. The nature of the Arcadian cult is less clear. Kereatas is generally understood to refer to the 'Horned God' on analogy of the figure of the Dorian Karneios, a ram-shaped 'Hirtengott' whose cult was absorbed by Apollo[321]. However, nothing certain is known of a cult of Apollo as a ram or as a special god of shepherds. The apotropaeic protecting rites of the famous

---

the Greek Apollo Lykios see Nilsson, *GGR*³ I, 536–8: 'Der λύκειος scheint fest im Mutterland zu wurzeln'; Burkert, *Gr. Rel.* 108.

[316] 'Apollo (kam) als fertiger Gott an die verschiedenen Kultstätten an', Nilsson, *Feste* 103.

[317] On a Hellenistic limestone pithos, *AJA* 65 (1961) no. 16, 116; *SEG* 20, 138; *BCH* 90 (1966) 7–9.

[318] Paus. 8,34,5. Glover, *SCA* 149; *Cults* 350; Karageorghis, *Cyprus* 101.

[319] Contrast the view of U. v. Willamowitz-Möllendorff in *Der Glaube der Hellenen*, Darmstadt 1959, I³, 321.

[320] Karageorghis in n. 318 above.

[321] Sources in S. Wide, *Lakonische Kulte, repr. Darmstadt* 1973, 63–6; 73–87; S. Eitrem, *Der Vordorische Widdergott*, Christiania Vid. Selsk. Forth. 1910, 4.

Karneia festival, in which Apollo was involved, suggest his characteristic function of Alexikakos or purifying protecting deity[322]. Pausanias' brief notice gives nothing away. Kereatas could have been a local Arcadian title after a place Kerea near by[323]. Such uncertainty regarding the Arcadian Kereatas undoubtedly weakens the popular modern etymology and identification with a god who was represented as endowed with rams' or any other animal horns. The link between Arcadian Kereatas and Cypriot Keraiates is eminently reasonable, but not that with the so-called 'Horned God' of Enkomi and especially not on etymological grounds.

The famous 12th century statue from the Achaean temple at Enkomi and its identity have been much discussed[324]. Mycenaean influence is apparent in the style of the statuette but so are its oriental elements[325]. The figure combined the characteristics of both Reshef and Apollo although its name remains a mystery[326]. An extreme view, which explains the statuette as representing a Mycenaean warrior[327], is unlikely to be right mainly because of the position where it was found. The comparison is apt, however, because the god's horns are not part of his body but adorn his helmet[328]. It was in

---

[322] Nilsson, *GGR*³ I, 536; *cf.* Burkert, *Gr. Rel.* 354–8; and Nilsson, *Feste* 118–29 on the Carneia.

[323] This was first suggested one hundred years ago by I. Pantazides, in AE 1895, 58 ff. and has been cited with approval by Nilsson, *GGR*³ I, 536, n. 8.

[324] P. Dikaios, 'The Bronze Statue of a Horned God from Enkomi', *AA* 1962, 1–39; *Enkomi. Excavations 1948–58*, vols. I-III, Mainz 1961 & 1971, 527–30; K. Hadjiioannou, *Alasia I*, 32–42; 'Apollon Kereatas' in *eis mnem. K. I. Amantou*, Athens 1960, 91–9; H. W. Catling, *Cypriote Bronzework in the Mycenaean World*, Oxford 1964, 255 f.; E. Vermeule, *Götterkult*, Göttingen 1974, 159 and refs. in n. 293; V. Karageorghis, 'The Mycenaean Origin of the Cypriote Culture', in *XII Congr. Intern. des Sciences Hist. Rapports* (1965) IV, 77–80; V, 591–4; *Cyprus* 101; O. Masson, 'Remarques sur les cultes chypriotes à l'époque de bronze récent', *East Med* 114 f.

[325] Dikaios, *Enkomi* III, 2 (1969) Pl. 138–44; H.-G. Buchholz – V. Karageorghis, *Altägäis und Altkypros*, Tübingen 1971, no. 1740, 163. On the mixture of styles see also Dikaios, *AA* (1962) 29 f.; C.F.A. Schaeffer, *AfO* 21 (1965) 68; F. Schachermeyr, *AAlt* 25 (1972) 156; Vermeule, *Götterkult* 159.

[326] Variously named as Reshef, Apollo, Nergal, El, Baal or even Kinyras. For discussion and references see particularly Schaeffer, Catling and Dikaios in n. 324 above.

[327] C. Picard, 'Midea a Salamis de Chypre', *Geras Antonious Keramopoullou*, Athens 1953, 1–16.

[328] *Cf.* Vermeule, *ibid.*

fact a divine warrior not a humanised ram or bull. There is no
evidence that Apollo was ever shown with the horns of either creature
as Nomios or indeed under any other guise[329]. His connection with
livestock and shepherds was as their protector. This, too, was the
significance of the statue which Pausanias saw in Achaean Patrae of
Apollo standing with one foot on the skull of an ox[330]. The helmet
with horns on the head of the Enkomi god was that of a warrior, and
it is in this capacity of fighter and protector of his community that the
god can be identified with the eastern Reshef and the Greek god
Apollo who performed the same function. The equation fits perfectly
judging from another 12th century B.C. example of a 'Horned' god
which was discovered in the *cella* of the same sanctuary[331]. It is a
smaller and cruder figure of solid bronze, more fully armed and
belligerent than the first with shield and spear in addition to the
horned helmet. This figure stands on a base in the form of a copper
ingot. The threatening pose of the 'Ingot God' is that of protector of
the copper mines which provided the community's wealth[332].

    'Horned God' and 'Ingot God' of Cypriot Enkomi might well
have been the same deity. That is of course impossible to decide on
topographical grounds alone. However, both represented the same
concept or principle which united Cyprus with the east, with Greece
and in fact the Aegean in general. The 'Warrior God' was an
astonishingly common figure in the Late Bronze Age, if not even
slightly earlier, and survived little altered in form and function in
archaic times. The type is represented in many votives of armed
figures or as warrior leading a horse, the 'Pferdeführer', and so on.
Votaries appear like their god in the archaic sanctuaries of Cyprus
including Kourion but also in Greece in numerous bronze plaques
and figures either free-standing or as part of tripods which were
offered up in Delphi and Olympia[333]. An illuminating link of this

---

[329] Apollo Nomios in Arcadia, Cicero, *de nat. deorum* 3,57; Epirote Orikos *IG* IV, I²,
    447; *cf.* Ap. Rhod. 4, 1215; Serv. Verg. *Ecl. Proem.*
[330] Paus. 7,20,2; *cf.* Nilsson, *GGR³* I, 536.
[331] *BCH* 88 (1964) 353–5; Pl. 16; Schaeffer, *AfO* 21 (1966) 59–69; Buchholz –
    Karageorghis, *Altäg.* No. 1741.
[332] *Cf.* a similar figure of a goddess standing on a copper ingot of the same date and of
    Cypriot origin. Now in the Ashmolean Museum in Oxford, H.W. Catling in
    Alasia I, 15–32; Karageorghis, *Cyprus* 103 f.
[333] Burkert, 'Resep-Figuren, Apollon von Amyklai und die „Erfindung" des Opfers
    auf Zypern', *Grazer Beiträge* 4 (1975) 60 f.

type with Apollo consists in votive armaments and iron figurines in battledress which were presented to Apollo Epikourios the 'Helper' in his 7th century B.C. temple in Arcadian Bassae[334]. The 'Warrior God' was not only identified with Apollo and Reshef, with whom he had a particularly close affinity, but also with other major gods because the type was fairly universal from the beginning.

In other words, not every 'Smiting God' was an Apollo. Name and title have differed with the cult site in order to reflect the deity of a particular locality. The two fine bronzes from the Mycenaean shrine at Phylakopi must therefore also remain nameless[335]. The iconography of the 'Warrior God' and his probable origins have been much discussed and are agreed to be oriental[336]. The oldest examples are Hittite in character and come from the region near Sivals in the first half of the second millennium B.C., that is before the Empire period[337].

A few bronze figures of the type have turned up in the west and are roughly contemporary with the Phylakopi god. They were found in Tiryns, Mycenae, even Attica, Thessaly and on the island of Crete in the Patsos cave[338]. All of these, however, are strikingly un-Minoan or un-Mycenaean in appearance[339]. In fact the greatest number have turned up in Syria and Palestine from sites like Ugarit, Lachish, Megiddo, Beth Shan, Gezer, that is precisely those places whose religious links with western sanctuaries were established above[340].

---

[334] F. A. Cooper, 'Arkadian Epikouroi and the date of the temple at Bassae', *Gr. and It.*, 210. The author's connection of the epithet with the Arcadian *epikouroi* or mercenary figures is wayward. The cult at Bassae was not strictly speaking a military one. On the temple and meaning of Epikourios = Alexikakos, see Paus. 8,41,7–9; Nilsson, *GGR³* I, 540; Burkert, *Gr. Rel.* 231, 401.

[335] See above pp. 143–4.

[336] A survey of modern literature and discussions in V. J. Canby, 'Some Hittite Figurines in the Aegean', in *Hesperia* 38 (1969) 141–9. More recent and fuller in Burkert, *Graz. Beitr.* (1975) 51–79, especially n.1, with full references to modern literature to which one might add Catling, *Cypr. Bronzework* for the LBA, J. Bouzek, 'Syrian and Anatolian Figurines in Europe', *Proc. Prehist. Soc.* 38 (1972) 156–64, H. Seeden, *The Standing Armed Figurines in the Levant* (Inst. f. Vorgeschichte, Univ. Frankfurt a. Main, Prähistorische Bronzefunde I, 1), Munich 1980.

[337] References in Burkert, *Graz. Beitr.* (1975) 53, n.3.

[338] For references see Canby, Bouzek, Burkert in n. 336 above.

[339] This was obvious to A. Evans already, *P.M.* III, 477; 480.

[340] Above pp. 134–141.

Therefore it is not surprising that the 'Horned God' and the 'Ingot God' of Enkomi fit into the same tradition of the 'Warrior God' regardless of his name[341]. Not only the artistic form of the 'Kriegertyp' was eastern inspired but no doubt also its clearly defined anthropomorphic shape. In Cyprus unambiguous anthropomorphism of such figurines was relatively late in archaic times. Numerous sanctuaries continued to cherish some odd shapes and strange aberrations. Similar conservatisms survive of protecting, apotropaeic figures further west, like the semi-iconic figure of the Amyclaean Apollo[342].

Evidently the oriental iconographic form of the god as human warrior was extremely successful in the Mediterranean world. The figure of the threatening fighter god still with his eastern conical helmet provided the principal model for the earliest Greek divine sculptures. Even the most important gods of the pantheon like Zeus, Poseidon and Apollo were represented in this eastern style of 'Warrior God' during the Homeric age of the 8th century[343]. In Cyprus the familiar type of statuette, with some stylistic variations but still recognizably the same, continued to be dedicated in sanctuaries of Apollo in archaic and classical times. Notable examples are in Tamassos and in Limniti[344]. It may be that a similar figure from Ayia Irini represented Apollo, too[345], but that is no more than an inspired guess.

It is certain, however, that Cypriot conservatism once more preserved a style which, together with the mixture of oriental features, had begun to go out of fashion in the west from the early 7th century. The Mantiklos Apollo from Thebes, for example, was well on the way to the kouros-type sculpture, although he still carried a

---

[341] Karageorghis thinks of the 'Ingot God' as a 'Smith God' on analogy of similar protective figures on the island of Keos and in Timna in Palestine, *Cyprus* 104. The god may have had a female counterpart in the form of an 'Ingot Goddess' like the Oxford figure, above n.332, and the pair survived in Greek tradition as Hephaestus and Aphrodite. *Cf.* Dietrich, 'Tradition in Greek Religion', *Renaissance*, 89.

[342] See ch. III, 107; 109.

[343] *Cf.* Burkert, *Graz. Beitr.* (1975), 52; 64. The bronze figure of the Syrian 'Smiting God' of Mycenaean date was still used in the cult at Thermon in the 8th or 7th century B.C., C. Rolley, 'Un Dieu Syrien à Thermon', *BCH* 108 (1984) 669–70.

[344] O. Masson, 'Kypriaka', *BCH* 92 (1968) 403–9; H.-G. Buchholz, *AA* 1978, 210–3, figs. 55a–c.

[345] *BCH* 92 (1968) 408, figs. 32–3.

bow and wore a helmet on his head[346]. The transition from one type to another seems equally well expressed by the bronze statuette of Apollo from his temple in Dreros on Crete of the last quarter of the same century[347]. Such development is in stark contrast with the continuation of the 'Warrior God' as Apollo in two of his archaic rustic sanctuaries near Tamassos which have been excavated by Ohnefalsch-Richter at Frangissa and near the modern town of Politiko in the bed of the Pediaeus river[348]. Among the sparse finds is the head and helmet of a youthful warrior from Frangissa which is all that remains of a large terracotta statue[349]. However, a fine small bronze statuette of a warrior god with conical helmet and another cruder figure, which had originally been fastened to a bronze base, both from the Pediaeus sanctuary, brilliantly capture the pose and spirit of the ancient 'Kriegertyp'[350]. The same sanctuary contained a magnificent classical bronze statue of Apollo of which only the head, the famous Chatsworth Head, survives[351]. The change from the archaic bronzes is all but total. Both iconographically illustrate Apollo's two epiphanies in Cyprus[352]. The former, the old warrior figure, had slipped into the background. It is astonishing, however, that both forms, though they represent two stages of the same developmental process, existed side by side in a sanctuary which only began in the archaic age.

Apart from the innumerable votives, little obvious evidence of the 'Warrior God' endured in Kourion[353]. The community god's

---

[346] Both lost, E. Simon, *Die Götter der Griechen*³, Munich 1980, figs. 117/118, 123f.

[347] The weapons, which the figure carried, have also been lost, but the helmet, though not conical, still survives on Apollo's head, Simon, *Gött.* figs. 119; 125. J. Boardman, *BSA* 62 (1967) 61, proposes an earlier date for the Dreros bronzes on stylistic grounds.

[348] Full references in Buchholz, *AA* 1973, 340 and notes; *AA* 1978, 209f. and notes.

[349] Brit. Mus. Inv. No. 1910/VI–20,4; *AA* 1978, fig. 53.

[350] Masson, *BCH* 92 (1968) 402ff., figs. 27/28; Hadjiioannou in *Alasia I* (1971) 33ff., fig. 4; *cf. AA* 1978, 210 and fig. 53, (Frangissa head), 213 and figs. 55b and c.

[351] Brit. Mus. Inv. No. 1958/4 – 18,1, 460 B.C.; Masson, *BCH* 88 (1964) 212f.; Pl.9; *AA* 1973, 340; 1978, 212 and fig. 54a.

[352] *Cf.* R. Meiggs, *The Athenian Empire,* 1972, Appendix, where the head is cited as a representative example of Attic influence on Cyprus. See also *AA* 1978, 212 n.107, with further modern literature.

[353] A curious six-sided cubical stamp seal, which was found within the sanctuary and is now in the Episkopi Museum, shows a fully armed warrior on one side. The other panels with god and tree, horned Bes figure *etc.,* show a mixture of Syrian,

belligerent nature always remained dear to the Cypriots. In Kourion it manifested itself in the continued dedications of armed fighters and of chariots which no doubt took part in cultic ceremonies somewhere near the sanctuary like the chariot contests on the second day of the Hyacinthia[354]. The Romans instituted athletic competitions in honour of the community god whom they linked to their emperor through the epithet of Kaisar[355]. A full programme of foot races, wrestling *etc.* was staged in the stadium which they built in the 2nd century A.D. between sanctuary and town[356]. However, aside from two mysterious small stone *baetyls*[357] the sanctuary concealed few if any remnants of an aniconic 'Warrior God' like Apollo's statue in Laconian Amyclae[358]. No clear bond survived in Kourion of aniconic figures like the *baetyls* in Ayia Irini and Phylakopi beside anthropomorphic images[359]. And yet the persistence of aniconic forms in Apolline cult into classical times and beyond is remarkable testimony of the tenacious hold of ancient practice. Outside Amyclae the Delphic *omphalos* is a good example of this kind of continuity[360]. Perhaps the most striking instance survived in Arcadia. The cult statue of Apollo Epikourios there was in the form of a Corinthian column. It stood in the *cella* of Iktinos' classical temple as an expression of Apollo's power beside the many contemporary and older archaic votives or representations of the god in the sanctuary area in anthropomorphic shape[361].

Stones, *baetyls* and pillars were common in Apolline cult usually in his nature as Agyieus but also as Alexikakos, Apotropaios,

---

Egyptian and Phoenician elements beside the 'striding Greek warrior with characteristic shield and crested helmet', Arwe in *SCA* 1981, 141–3, figs. 9–1 and 2. Above p. 133.

[354] See below p. 174.

[355] Cass. Dio 51,1,2; *IG* IV 591; VII 49; XIV 739; 746; 747. See also below p. 176 and n. 398.

[356] *BCH* 88 (1964) 366; 369–71. D. Whittingham, 'Kourion: the Roman Stadium', *Kourion* 1982, 75–9.

[357] Above p. 147.

[358] P. 167, ch. III, p. 107; 109.

[359] pp. 141; 145.

[360] Nilsson, *GGR*[3] I, 204f.; Dietrich, *Origins* 55; 92; 308f.

[361] N. Yalouris, 'Problems Relating to the Temple of Apollo Epikourios at Bassae', in *Gr. & It.* 89–104. Above ch. III, 109.

Prostaterios, Thyraios and Propylaios[362]. Apollo Agyieus' protective powers, which he shared with the 'Warrior God', resided in his nature as apotropaeic god of purification. The innate divine strength in his image kept away evil and blight from his subjects. A manifestation of this aspect of Apollo was his cult as Smintheus which crops up in many centres[363]. The cone-shaped *baetyls* of Agyieus were virtually ubiquitous on roads, at public buildings and in front of houses guarding them against ill[364]. The cult was common both in the east and in Greece, particularly in Arcadia[365]. Achaean migrants to Cyprus would have been familiar with the same kind of figure which had also come to the island from the eastern Mediterranean.

Both Apollo as 'Warrior God' and Agyieus met in the oriental god Reshef. Apollo Agyieus was related to Reshef Mikal through the figure of Amyklaios in Sparta and in Cyprus in Idalion[366]. Mikal's pillar had been worshipped in Beth Shan from the 14th century B.C.[367]. His function seems to have been identical with that of Agyieus. In Kition his pillar is mentioned in a Phoenician inscription of the 5th century B.C.[368]. The Cypriot documentary evidence is

---

[362] In Acarnania, Laconia, Megara, Attica *etc.* Evidence in Reisch, 'Agyieus', *P.W.R.E.* (1894) 909–13; A. B. Cook, *Zeus,* Cambridge 1925, II, 160ff.; L. R. Farnell, *Cults of the Greek States,* Oxford 1907, IV, 371ff.; S. Solders, 'Der ursprüngliche Apollo', *AfR* 32 (1935) 142–55; Dietrich, *RM* 121 (1978) 10 and notes; Yalouris, *Gr. and It.* 100f. Solder's etymology of Apollo from *pella* = 'stone', is as plausible as any that have been proposed. *Cf.* the ever popular Dorian *apellai* = 'popular assembly', in Burkert, *RM* 118 (1975) 1–21. The gloss in Hesych. ἀπέλλαι· σηκοί, has produced an etymology from *apella* = 'fenced enclosure (usually of cattle)', or 'stone (*peribolos*) wall', Nilsson, *GGR³* I, 556. This recalls the type of sanctuary we have discussed. But scholars who favour this derivation connect it with the doubtful identification of Apollo with a 'Hirtengott', see Burkert, *RM* (1975) 12, for refs. and discussion. Most interesting and pertinent is the etymology from Hitt. hierogl. *apulunas,* a god of the city gates of Bogazköy, Nilsson, *GGR³* I, 558f. But that, too, is plagued by linguistic doubts, see Burkert, *op. cit.* 3 and n.13.

[363] Dietrich, 'Late Bronze Age Troy: Religious Contacts with the West', *Historia* 29 (1980) 501 with notes.

[364] Refs. in *RM* (1978) 10; Yalouris, *Gr. and It.* 100f.

[365] *E. g.* Paus. 8,48,6.

[366] 4th century B.C. inscription *CIS* I, 89, above p. 160.

[367] Conrad, *Reschef* 164.

[368] *CIS* I, 86, 1, 14. J. B. Peckham in *Orientalia* 37 (1968) 304–24; J. Teixidor, in *Syria* 46 (1969) 339; see *Historia* 29 (1980) 501.

admittedly late, but it reflects much older tradition. In Kition, for example, the Phoenicians took over the Mycenaean Temple I in the 9th century B.C. The central entrance to the holy of holies was flanked by two free-standing pillars[369]. These were *agyiai, baetyls* or pillars which embodied the power of the god who guarded temple, home or entire city[370]. Six such Apolline stones probably guarded the entrance to Troy VI, performing the same function as the *baetyls* at the gates of the Hittite capital Bogazköy[371].

In Cyprus Agyieus occurs at least once in an inscription near Kythrea[372]. The dialectal form of Agy(i)ates puts it into our Group II[373], but otherwise the cult context remains obscure. The name is not attested in inscriptions from the Kourion sanctuary, but an interesting descendant of this guardian stone survived. This is a capped *stele* of the 3rd century A.D. which now stands in the garden of the Episkopi Museum but once guarded the entrance to the sanctuary welcoming the visitor on his arrival[374] and sending him on his way again with a blessing[375]. The ancestry of the friendly stone is clear, but more enigmatic are the two small stone *baetyls* from the sanctuary and the

---

[369] V. Karageorghis, *BCH* 94 (1970) 252; 'The Sacred Area of Kition', in *Temples* 86.

[370] On the meaning of the *agyia* see D. B. Thompson, *Ptolemaic Oenochoai and Portraits in Fayence*, Oxford 1973, 63–9. The word is probably non-Greek or rather pre-Greek, O. Szemerenyi, *Syncope in Greek and Indo-European and the nature of the Indo-European accent*, Naples 1964, 206–8; *cf.* F. Frisk, *Etym. Wörterb.* III (1972) 18.

[371] *Historia* 29 (1980) 500f. Possibly this 'Torgott' was identical with, or related to, the Syrian and Anatolian god of the city gates who was represented from as early as the 14th century B.C. (Alaça Hüyük) in crude iconic or semi- and aniconic form near the city entrance, R. D. Barnett, 'Bringing the God into the Temple', *Temples*, 10–20, with discussion. Occasionally the gates by themselves seem to have been endowed with divine power, *cf.* 24th Psalm, 'Lift up your heads, o gates . . . that the King of glory may come in.'

[372] S. Menardos in *Athena* 18 (1905) 334f.; *cf. SEG* 20, 309; *AJA* 65 (1961) 129 and n.155. A. Heubeck detects the name in a 6th or 5th century B.C. syllabic inscription of uncertain origin but now in the British Museum (Inv. No. 1950. 5–25.1), *ICS* no. 327, p.324. See Heubeck's review of *ICS* in *BiOr* 20 (1963) 171 and n.5, cited by Bennett, *Cults* 327. See also G. Neumann in *Kadmos* 2 (1963) 53–67.

[373] Above p. 162.

[374] καλῶς ἔρχη, on left face, presumably looking outward.

[375] καλῶς ὑπάγεις, on right face. [Εἴλε] ως ὑμεῖν ὁ [Ἀπ] όλλων, on front of *stele* above a wreath, I. Nicolau, 'Epigraphy', in *Kourion* 96 and fig. 71.

large *stele* which was found near the circular altar[376]. Neither type is related to the Agyieus. In the case of the monolith there is also some doubt regarding its age[377].

Better evidence in support of our god has turned up outside Kourion. Prominent sites of Achaean settlement in Cyprus and others, which also enjoyed cultural links with the east, preserved aniconic stone images with similar function to that of Agyieus' *baetyls*. They are rectangular and square stepped stones either standing on their own or serving as bases for pillar or *stele*. The most interesting are two blocks from the sanctuary of Myrtou Pigadhes because in shape they reproduce the grand Mycenaean stepped altar with horns of consecration[378]. Stone and altar were both God's House and Altar in Semitic and particularly Phoenician belief[379], and the Mycenaeans evidently believed in the same tradition. Other similar stones of this period have been discovered near the Mycenaean Temple I at Kition[380], in Enkomi[381], in Aphrodite's sanctuary in Palaipaphos[382], and in Hala Sultan Tekke. Karageorghis suggests[383] that many of them may have been the capitals of free-standing cultic pillars which the Mycenaeans imported. This is possible, although no Mycenaean examples are extant, but does not affect the religious

---

[376] Above pp. 131; 132.

[377] S. Swiny has made a study of over twenty such stones throughout the island and will publish his findings. He kindly told me that in practically all cases the archaeological finds, if any, associated with the stones are late ranging from Roman to Christian. There are tethering stones amongst them, locking stones *etc.*, although most of them had superhuman properties and in popular belief to this day serve some ritual purpose involving health and fertility, *cf.* Swiny, 'Standing Stones: Perforated Monoliths', *Kourion* 151 f. The two large stones near Kouklia, however, are undoubtedly ancient, above p. 147.

[378] J. du Plat Taylor, *Myrtou-Pigadhes,* Oxford 1957, 12–25. The bases are most recently discussed, with reference to those from Hala Sultan Tekke, by I. Jacobsson, 'Stepped "Bases" from Hala Sultan Tekke', forthcoming in *Acts of the 2nd Intern. Congr. of Cypriot Studies, 20–25th April 1982 (Cyprus 82), cf.* P. Åström, 'Stepped Blocks from Hala Sultan Tekke', also forthcoming in *RDAC* 1984. Prof. Åström generously allowed me to see both articles ahead of publication.

[379] H. Ringgren, 'The Religion of Ancient Syria', in *Historia Religionum,* Leiden 1969, I, 210, *cf. RM* (1978) 11.

[380] V. Karageorghis, *AAA* (1971) 106.

[381] *AAA* (1971) 102f.

[382] F. Maier, *RDAC* 1974, 137; *Cyprus and Crete* 233.

[383] *AAA* 4 (1971) 101ff.; *cf. Cyprus* 94.

significance of these stones. However, the closest parallels in Greece are the column bases on either side of the entrance to the Treasury of Atreus in Mycenae[384]. These are also rectangular and have three steps on three of their sides. At Hala Sultan Tekke no sanctuary has yet been identified by the excavators. But a salient feature of the eight stepped bases and stones, which have so far come to light on the site, is their original position near the entrance to a passage, room *etc.*[385]. This does suggest that they most probably shared the same function as pillar, stone or *baetyl* of the Agyieus figure. No doubt their form, including that of the pillar bases in Mycenae, owed much to eastern influence without affecting their essential protecting powers from Attica to Anatolia. In Megara, along the road from the *agora*, there was a sanctuary of Apollo Prostaterios with an interesting image of Apollo[386]. Near by, and at the Gates of the Nymphs, in the ancient gymnasium Apollo Karinos was shown in the form of a small stone which was shaped like a pyramid[387]. The unusual title (the Carian) conceals the same nature of Apollo as Agyieus and coincides with that of Reshef and Mikal in Cyprus.

The apotropaeic Agyieus and armed 'Warrior God' make up two important and related aspects of Apollo as community god and protector. Both came together in the Laconian Apollo Amyklaios whose cult closely depended on Cypriot models. The famous bronze cone with weapon-carrying arms and helmet on head[388] successfully combined the two main concepts which were similarly reflected in the Hyacinthia festival. The first day of this 'Sühnefest'[389] was spent in a solemn 'Totenopfer' and ceremonial purification. More joyful celebrations with singing and dancing followed in the course of the other two days[390]. An aetiological myth explains the purificatory

---

[384] Jacobsson, *Cyprus* 82.

[385] Åström, *RDAC* 1984.

[386] Paus. 1,44,2.

[387] Paus. 1,44,3. The stone is probably reproduced on Megarian coins, *Syll. Numm. Graec. Copenhagen, Attica – Aegina* nos. 477–9; *cf.* Yalouris, *Gr. and It.* 100.

[388] Above p. 167.

[389] Dietrich, 'The Dorian Hyacinthia', *Kadmos* 14 (1975) 141.

[390] Polycrates fully describes the festival in Athen. 4, 139D. Perhaps the immediately preceding report by Polemon (4, 138E) also belonged to the same festival, Nilsson, *Feste* 131–40; *cf. Kadmos* 14 (1975) 134f. I wrongly believed that the sad and joyful aspects of the Hyacinthia were incompatible elements of the same festival.

ritual as an act of atonement for the killing of Hyacinthus. That side belonged to the apotropaeic Agyieus figure for it recurs in the festival of Apollo Agyieus in Tegea which knew of a similar story of mourning for the dead Skephros[391]. The joyful part of the festival is more recognizably Apolline containing procession, dancing contests and the singing of the paean. Polycrates' report, however, also mentions contests and parades of decorated chariots which more closely recall the many votives of this type in Cypriot sanctuaries and an aspect of Apollo that had faded in his classical figure[392].

But how much of this pomp and pageantry actually passed through the rustic sanctuaries of Cyprus is another question which is not likely to be answered in the absence of literary evidence. That the ceremonies at Kourion also included a sombre element can be gathered from the tradition which attached to the altar of Apollo there. Still more positively the terracotta models of groups of dancers and ritual processions preserve the memory at least of celebrations like those on the two final days of the Hyacinthia. It is of great interest in this context that the votives of the lyre players, which began to appear in the sanctuary of Kourion in the 7th century B.C., were of children[393] because it was children who played the same instrument during the festivities in Amyclae while engaged in rhythmic dancing[394]. Otherwise the finds of the *temenos* in Kourion suggest a popular but relatively humble cult activity before Roman interest in Apollo elevated it to a state occasion.

There is no doubt, however, that the history and nature of the cult continued the traditions of the Bronze Age in Cyprus and shared its main features with other and better known cult centres on the island. I have tried to explore the links of this cult and its cult figure with the outside world and with Greece in particular. Such a study is possible because of the full comparative material and the remarkable conservatism of the islanders coupled with a willingness to accept religious concepts from abroad. The problem of the naming of the god at Kourion remains unsolved. At present we are bound by the

---

[391] Paus. 8,53,3; *cf.* Nilsson, *Feste* 166.
[392] Athen. 139F only mentions girls, but others presumably also participated, *cf.* Nilsson, *Feste* 136.
[393] Young, *Terrac.* 219, above p. 152.
[394] Athen. 4, 139E.

dates of the extant inscriptional sources, according to which Hylates' cult did not begin in Kourion but was introduced from other centres namely Chytroi and Drimou possibly as late as the 3rd century B.C.[395]. Regarding the identification with Apollo in Kourion, the first mention of the name in the 5th century inscription[396] suggests a date during the god's second, classical epiphany in Cyprus. However, the descendants of prehistoric inhabitants in and about Kourion would have been aware of the earlier figure particularly through their knowledge of, and close contact with, the Achaean settlers in Paphos and their goddess Aphrodite. Their strong adherence to past traditions also ensured that prehistoric traits of the community figure were preserved in the archaic cult, although there is absolutely no evidence that the actual site of the Kourion precinct had been hallowed ground in the Bronze Age.

The 'cave' and oracle of Apollo Hylates in neighbouring Paphos, together with local features of grove and spring, the epithet Pythios (3rd century B.C.) at Kourion, suggest that by the Hellenistic age some form of divination connected with chthonic aspects of Apollo may well have been practised in the sanctuary area[397]. If true it would, however, have remained peripheral in Kourion. Its precinct, altar and archaic votives, which had been offered to the old protector and community god, retained little more than antiquarian interest after the Roman renaissance of Apollo's cult in Kourion. Politics, and sport in support of politics, concealed its simple origins. Therefore dark areas remain concerning details of the cult and the question whether renewed Roman interest in the worship of Apollo reinforced genuinely ancient traditions or exploited the people's faith in the god

---

[395] *IKourion* no. 60, 119; above p. 158.

[396] *IKourion* no. 18, 46.

[397] *IKourion* no. 41, 89, above 154–5; 157. Certain indications suggest that Kourion witnessed mystery rites in honour of Demeter and not unlike those of Aphrodite which included an annual procession by initiates from New to Old Paphos (Strabo XIV, 6, 3 p.683). The Basilica at Meydan lies on a convenient route between precinct and city of Kourion. The site may have held a shrine of Demeter and Kore because a 4th century B.C. syllabic dedication to the goddess was found there, D. Whittingham, 'The Small Basilica: "At Meydan"', *Kourion* 80–85. One of the curators of the Episkopi Museum, Christophis, showed me a terracotta Demeter / Baubo figure which was found in a burial near Episkopi. The statuette resembles those in the Paphos Museum, presumably from the Paphian Mysteries.

for personal and dynastic purposes. An example of the latter in Greece is Augustus' revival of an old cult of Apollo near Actium and the institution of games in his honour[398]. This kind of calculated use of the 'church' in the service of the state, at which the Romans excelled, had incidentally been anticipated in Kourion in Hellenistic times. Many Alexander-type votives are witness to that and an occasional dedication of a figure in the likeness of Alexander himself[399].

The same doubts persist concerning the purpose of one of the most impressive structures which was obviously related to the sanctuary. This is the splendid ring-shaped walkway which lies directly to the west of the large circular altar. Perhaps it was used for ritual dances about a sacred grove, as has been suggested[400]. But the building was erected in imperial Roman times, because the associated finds date from then[401], and there is at present no way of telling what ceremonies occurred within the *tholos* and whether these had been newly devised or whether they resurrected older ritual which had fallen into disuse during the one and a half centuries of the sanctuary's decline[402]. Perhaps further work will throw some light on these problems. But our ignorance concerning this important part of the sanctuary complex is a reminder that there is still much to be learned about Kourion.

Appendix on the tholos

Round buildings within or associated with, a sanctuary are notoriously difficult to explain on religious and not aesthetic or

---

[398] Cass. Dio 51,1,2. Scenic performances were also often included in the celebrations in suitable theatres like the splendid one at Kourion. On the part played by Apollo in Augustus' dynastic ambitions and 'Religionspolitik' see G. Wissowa, *Religion und Kultus der Römer*, repr. of 2nd ed. Munich 1971, 296–7; K. Latte, *Römische Religionsgeschichte*, Munich 1960, 223–4; 303–4.

[399] Young, *Terrac.* 221.

[400] Above p. 130 and notes 57–9. See also the Appendix.

[401] 1st century A.D., *SCA* 103.

[402] From about 200–50 B.C., Young, *Terrac.* 221.

purely architectural grounds. When and why was that shape required by cult as opposed to the orthodox rectangular temple?[1]

A puzzling feature of the Kourion *tholos* is the seven pits inside the circular enclosure. They were cut into the rock in a circle except for the seventh which breaks the line lying in the entrance area to the north[2]. The excavators believe the pits held sacred trees or bushes. But the cavities are relatively shallow and not suitable for the purpose[3]. They also lack means of drainage or watering like the *bothroi* of the sacred garden in the courtyard between Temple 1 and 3 in Kition. These latter are interconnected by irrigation channels leading to wells[4].

If the *tholos* had been built to revive older cult, then closer parallels of *tholos* and pit, which spring to mind, are the 4th century B.C. round building at Marmaria in Delphi and the contemporary *tholos* with 'snake pit' in Asclepius' Epidaurian sanctuary. Their function, too, has never been fully explained[5], or that of the pits. Who can say what special rite or sacrifice revolved about them except that it was chthonic in nature? The labyrinthine arrangement beneath the *tholos* in Epidaurus[6] might well have been part of chthonic divinatory procedure. The several pits in Kourion could have served a similar purpose. But in any case it is not too far-fetched to suggest that the Kourion structure reproduced Hylates' 'cave' oracle in Paphos in 'modern' form as a conscious piece of archaising not unlike Peisistratus' *Ploutonion* in the cave at Eleusis. The *tholos* was obviously linked to the old sanctuary and in no wise conflicted with Apollo's temple in the north. The circle about a central feature within the

---

[1] See P. G. Themelis 'Early Helladic Monumental Architecture', *AM* 99 (1984) 335 on the common Cypriot Neolithic circular dwellings and for examples of EH *tholoi* in Greece. The LBA *tholos* tomb and its origins are discussed by E. Vermeule, *Greece in the Bronze Age*, Chicago 1964, 120–36. H. Tzavella-Evjen considers some notable *tholoi* in a paper on 'Circular Buildings and the Sanctuary of Apollo Hylates at Paphos and Kourion', which is due to appear in *Cyprus 82*, and which she kindly allowed me to read in advance.

[2] Buitron and Soren in *SCA* 102–3.

[3] Not even for palms, *SCA* 102.

[4] Jennifer Webb, *A Short Guide to the Excavations at Kition*, Print. Off. Rep. Cyprus, 4.

[5] G. Gruben, *Die Tempel der Griechen*[3], Munich 1980, 99, points to the *tholos* in Olympia and suggests hero cult.

[6] Gruben, *op. cit.* 141.

second chamber in the Paphos 'cave' is not too far removed in lay-out from our circular walk, albeit on a far less grand scale than in Kourion.

Circular structures, pits and even free-standing pillars occur in other expatriate cults of Apollo and as far afield as Roman Britain. A splendid example has been excavated recently in Nettleton, Wiltshire. The temple and sanctuary were an important cult centre from the 1st to the 4th century A.D. It is not surprising therefore that the British precinct reproduced some features of the cult in Kourion[7].

---

[7] W. J. Wedlake, *The Excavation of the Shrine of Apollo at Nettleton, Wiltshire, 1956–1971,* London 1982, *passim* and *e.g.* 65: pits (but wrongly compares the southern votive deposit in Kourion); 190, fig. 81, Pl.XXXVIa: limestone pillar and base; 178: remains of sacrifices including many right forelimbs of sheep; *etc.*

Conclusion

Archaeological remains turn out to be an unreliable witness of old or new in the history of Greek religion. Continuity of cult site is no guarantee of continuity of cult. The same sacred precinct might have served one divinity over generations of worshippers, but it could also have provided a home for two or more gods. Perhaps a new arrival heralded novel beliefs and practices. Did Dionysus at Ayia Irini, Apollo and Artemis in Dreros or Aphrodite and Hermes at Symi continue essentially Minoan cult? Did even those Olympians, whose names occur on the Linear B documents, remain unaltered into classical times? The tablets certainly do not provide the text for the archaeological picture. However, more often than not old cults did not disappear but developed in response to new attitudes which came about through changes in the political and social climate. Tradition was strong in matters of faith. Conservative Cyprus preserved many examples of the gradual evolution, the constant adaptation of inherited religious beliefs to changing social requirements. At Kourion a general *theos* figure became Hylates, Apollo and eventually under Roman government was worshipped as Apollo Kaisar with largely secular pomp and sporting contests.

The Cypriot evidence is full and quite explicit. It helps to draw a comparable map for events in western cults. Evidently changes in divine nomenclature, new foundations of sites and sanctuaries say little about the history of cult content. It follows inversely to our first premise that discontinuity of cult site did not necessarily mean the end of a cult tradition. Minoan peak and cave cults, for example, moved to new homes at the end of Middle Minoan and later, crossed over to the mainland at the end of the Bronze Age and in some related form, into which it had developed, ultimately survived into historical times. Ancient traditions were preserved in newly constructed sanctuaries. Sometimes a symbolic remnant of the earliest shrine, like a rocky outcrop or altar, was cherished in the *adyton* of the new cult centre. Or again votives and offerings show that a cult had been moved to its new location for no apparent reason. This happened in the case of Artemis Orthia's worship whose relatively late precinct at

Sparta early in the Iron Age suggested to archaeologists that a new cult had been instituted there.

However, beside the undoubted survival of divinities and their basic ritual and beside genuinely fresh foundations, which were inspired by reverence for the heroes of the Mycenaean past, there were other cult figures and objects in archaic Greece with few or no echoes from the Bronze Age. Astonishingly many of these, too, had been part of ancient traditions that even predated the Bronze Age. Phallus and mask, which were important to many historic Greek religious practices, also certain festivals of goddesses like Demeter and Artemis had been part of Neolithic cult. Such and related features now re-emerged and returned to prominence in archaic Greek religion. Attic tragedy, comedy, the most significant aspects of Dionysiac cult could not have developed without them. They were known to Minoans and Mycenaeans but apparently considered unimportant or irrelevant manifestations of rustic worship in their theocratic, palace-oriented society. In many respects it appears as if Aegean Bronze Age culture in the west represented a kind of self-contained episode which contributed to the development of official religion in the *polis* but left untouched other brilliant areas of Greek intellectual achievement. The impression of unity is cultural and not necessarily political. It is the palace-centred 'urbanised' culture of both Minoans and Mycenaeans which seems intrusive and in contrast with the earlier and immediately subsequent non-urban centred communities. Earlier religious figures of the Stone Age like Athena and possibly Hermes and Demeter found their way into Bronze Age cult, but they were transformed to serve the new society. Nilsson's goddess of the palace was not Athena's first manifestation. She was a community goddess before she became the guardian of the palace and its king. Odysseus' close relationship with her in Homer may have retained a memory of Athena's Minoan/Mycenaean function but ultimately was the result of a most felicitous poetic invention[1]. What is so remarkable in this history in which multiple strands from Neolithic Europe, the Aegean, the Minoan and Mycenaean cultures combined

---

[1] Schachermeyr also emphasizes the contrast between Athena as a palace goddess and as protector of the community. But he believes that she had originally been a kind of Anatolian/Aegean Mothergoddess, F. Schachermeyr, *Griechische Frühgeschichte*, Vienna 1984, 281, 'Athene als Schützerin der Polis'.

to contribute to Greek religion, is the survival of some basic religious values. Religious conservatism and what must have been great religious tolerance between different communities were responsible for the coalescence of all these elements into one quite harmonious system. The gods' intensely personal humanised nature, however, was new. This was an epic and ultimately Homeric characteristic which determined the religion of the *polis.*

In its outward manifestations of ritual, processions and munificence of temples much of the official cult of the *polis* was for show. The Homeric Olympians were figures of myth rather than faith and their worship contained a certain quality of the fairy tale and early on engendered cynicism among the congregation. The Homeric gods were more like men or heroes than awesome numinous powers. They were conceived to conform with the ideals of human shape and aspirations. The system worked eminently well for the Greeks although it might have been low on theological content. Several modern scholars from W. F. Otto to Jasper Griffin[2] have appealed against a too literary view of these gods who should be taken seriously as true figures of religious belief. Homer's gods were indeed serious forces of considerable moment but not by virtue of the spiritual inspiration of their cult so much as in the measure of their impact on classical religion. The Olympian gods nicely complemented the aristocratic human government of the *polis* reflecting its aims and values. But their Homeric conception also dominated many subsequent generations of poets and philosophers. Their personal character set the Greek gods apart from those of most Mediterranean, including Italian, cultures. Thus Greek religion pursued its own idiosyncratic ways which eventually led to its decline.

In the context of older traditions, which have been the main subject of this book, a wider perspective across the Aegean can fill in gaps of knowledge from one area to the next because of the remarkable conformity in religious practices over long periods of prehistory. Where poverty and political turmoil have erased much in Greece common traditions in other parts of the Aegean may illuminate some of the darkness. Neither Crete nor many of the islands could have been as cut off from the mainland as is sometimes supposed. Cyprus,

---

[2] W. F. Otto, *Die Götter Griechenlands*[4], Frankfurt 1956; J. Griffin, *Homer on Life and Death*, Oxford 1980. *Cf.* J. de Romilly, *Homère*, Paris 1985.

however, remains one of the most rewarding models of how tradition in the Aegean/Greek world endured and grew in a continuous line from prehistoric to archaic times and beyond. The Karpas Peninsula points to the east and geographically Cyprus belongs to Asia. Throughout its history it was exposed to and absorbed oriental influence. By tradition, however, the island also favoured western ways ever since Mycenaean settlers arrived at the end of the Bronze Age. Until the very end of the classical age the Cypriots tenaciously preserved the language of the past together with the ancient cults and customs. Their country became a microcosm of Aegean culture: there was a lively trade in gods and cults from east to west and back again. Archaic sanctuaries in city or country faithfully reproduced Bronze Age traditions of which countless votives and offerings bear eloquent testimony. The change in type and emphasis of dedications over generations of worshippers reflects the influence of contemporary politics on the cult.

Cyprus was the home of Aphrodite *Kyprogenes*. Her roots had been eastern but she travelled to the west before Homer's time because the Mycenaeans brought her with them to Paphos where they worshipped her as *Wanassa* or Queen in her Bronze Age sanctuary in the city. Her close partner and second major deity of Cyprus was Apollo. Both shared numerous cults and myths and both prospered through the Cypriots' deep attachment to tradition. The centre of Apollo's worship on the island from archaic times was Kourion whose remains again betray an astonishing recall of past religious practices. What occurred at Kourion over the centuries until Roman times mirrored the history of innumerable rustic and more elaborate sanctuaries in Cyprus and even across the Aegean as far as Greece at least. New forms of dedications and the inscriptions at Kourion show a gradual evolution of cult which never fully broke with the past. Although Cypriot links with Greece at no time were totally severed after the Mycenaean age, they grew particularly strong at certain moments in the island's history, such as the 6th century B.C. for example and especially the 5th under the pro-Athenian administration fo Evagoras I. This meant a renewed religious impetus from the west. Apollo in his final classical guise then enjoyed a second coming as lord of dance and music. But there was no sense of contradiction between new and old both of which arose from the same tradition. Late in the 4th century B.C. Nikokles of Paphos built a cave-like sanctuary to Apollo Hylates. The precinct is most impressive. The cult was evidently popular and much frequented although in substance it harkened back to the Bronze Age. The two manifestations of the god had come together without stress. Rarely has the sanctity of tradition in the Aegean world received a finer monument.

Abbreviations

Many commonly accepted abbreviations are not given here

AA	*Archäologischer Anzeiger*
AAA	*Archaiologika Analekta ex Athenon*
AAlt	*Anzeiger für die Altertumswissenschaft*
ACE	*Auckland Classical Essays presented to E. M. Blaiklock*, B. F. Harris ed., Auckland 1970.
AE	*Archaiologike Ephemeris*
AfO	*Archiv für Orientforschung*
AJA	*American Journal of Archaeology*
AM	*Mitteilungen des deutschen Archäologischen Instituts, Athenische Abteilung*
Ant Class	*Antiquité Classique (Belg.)*
AR	*Journal of Hellenic Studies Archaeological Reports*
BdA	*Bolletino d'Arte*
BCH	*Bulletin de Correspondence Hellénique*
BICS	*Bulletin of the Institute of Classical Studies of the University of London*
CAH³	*Cambridge Ancient History*, revised edition.
CNRS	*Centre National de la Recherche Scientifique (Colloques internationaux)*
CRAI	*Comptes rendus de l'Academie des Inscriptions et Belles Lettres*
Cultes	O. Masson, *Cultes Indigènes, Cultes Grecques et Cultes Orientaux à Chypre* (Elements Orientaux dans la Religion Grecque Ancienne, Travaux du Centre d'Études Supérieures Spécialisé d'Histoire des Religions de Strasbourg). Paris 1960.
Cults	C. Bennett, *The Cults of the Ancient Greek Cypriotes*, thesis Un. Microf. Int. Ann. Arbor 1980.
Cyprus 82	*Acts of the International Congress of Cypriot Studies, 20–25th April 1982.*
Cyprus & Crete	*Acts Intern. Archaeol. Sympos. 'The Relations between Cyprus and Crete, ca. 2000–500 B. C. (1978)'*, Nicosia 1979.
East Med	*Acts International Archaeological Symposium, 'The Mycenaeans in the Eastern Mediterranean'*, Nicosia 1973.
Ergon	*to Ergon tes Archaiologikes Hetaireias*
Gr & It	*Greece and Italy in the Classical World (Acts XI International Con-*

	gress of Archaeology 1978). (N. Coldstream & M. Colledge eds.), London 1979.
ICS	O. Masson, *Les Inscriptions Chypriotes Syllabiques*, Paris 1961.
IKourion	T. B. Mitford, *The Inscriptions of Kourion*, Philadelphia 1971.
JÖI	*Jahreshefte des österreichischen archäologischen Instituts*
KC	*Kretika Chronika*
Kourion	*An Archaeological Guide to the Ancient Kourion Area and the Akrotiri Peninsula*, H. W. Swiny (ed.), Nicosia 1982.
La Sot	*La Soteriologia dei Cult Orientali nell'Impero Romano, Atti Coll. Intern. Rome 1979*, Leiden 1982.
Olympia	*Neue Forschungen in griechischen Heiligtümern (Symposium Olypia, 1974).*
OpAth	*Acta Instituti Atheniensis Regni Sueciae: Opuscula Atheniensia*
PBA	*Proceedings British Academy*
PdP	*La Parola Del Passato*
RAC	*Reallexikon für Antike und Christentum*
Renaissance	*The Greek Renaissance of the Eighth Century B. C.: Tradition and Innovation* (Proceedings of the 2nd International Symposium at the Swedish Institute in Athens, 1–5 June 1981), Stockholm 1983.
RDAC	*Report of the Department of Antiquities, Cyprus*
Rivista	*Rivista Storica dell' Antichità*
SCA	*Studies in Cypriote Archaeology*, J. C. Biers – D. Soren (eds.), U.C.L.A. 1981.
SCABA	*Sanctuaries and Cults in the Aegean Bronze Age* (Proceedings of the 1st International Symposium, Swedish Institute in Athens, 12–13th May 1980), Stockholm 1981.
SCE	*Swedish Cyprus Expedition*
SIMA	*Studies in Mediterranean Archaeology*, Göteborg 1980.
SMEA	Studi Micenei ed Egeo Anatolici
Studs Schach	Greece and the Eastern Mediterranean in Ancient History and Prehistory (Studies presented to F. Schachermeyr), K. H. Kinzl. ed., Berlin 1977.
TAPS	R. Scranton, *The Architecture of the Sanctuary of Apollo Hylates at Kourion*, (Trans. Am. Philos. Soc. 57) 1967.
Temples	*Temples and High Places in Biblical Times, Proc. Coll. Cent. Hebrew Union College – Jewish Inst. of Religion, Jerusalem 14–16th March 1977, A. Biran (ed.), Jerusalem 1981*
Terrac	J. H. & S. H. Young, *Terracotta Figurines from Kourion in Cyprus*, Philadelphia 1955.
Thalassocracy	*The Minoan Thalassocracy. Myth and Reality* (Proceedings of the 3rd International Symposium, Swedish Institute in Athens, 31 May–5 June 1982), Stockholm 1984.

WA   *World Archaeology*
ZAW   *Zeitschrift für die alttestamentliche Wissenschaft*

Bibliography

F. R. Adrados, 'Les Institutions Religieuses Mycéniennes', *Acta Mycenae (Proceedings of the 5th International Colloquium on Mycenaean Studies, Salamanca 1970 (S. Ruiperez ed.) I, Salamanca 1972.

S. Alexiou, *The Minoan Goddess with Upraised Hands,* Herakleion 1958.

St. Alexiou, *Minoische Kultur,* Germ. trans. Göttingen 1976.

P. Amandry, *La mantique apollinienne à Délphes, essai sur le functionnement de l'oracle* (Bibl. des ecoles francaises d'Athènes et de Rome), fasc. 170 (1950).

R. Amiran, 'Some Observations on Chalcolithic and Early Bronze Age Sanctuaries and Religion', *Temples.*

M. Arwe, 'A Cypriote Cubical Stamp Seal', *SCA.*

R. L. N. Barber, 'The Status of Phylakopi in Creto-Cycladic Relations', *Thalassocracy.*

R. D. Barnett, 'Bringing the God into the Temple', *Temples.*

L. Baumbach, 'The Mycenaean Contribution to the Study of Greek Religion in the Bronze Age', *SMEA* (1979).

J. L. Benson, 'Bamboula at Kourion: The Stratification of the Settlement', Parts 1 & 2, *RDAC* 1969 & 1970.

J. L. Benson, *Bamboula at Kourion: The Necropolis and Finds,* Univ. Mus. Philadelphia, 1972.

J. L. Benson, 'The Necropolis of Kaloriziki', *SIMA* 36 (1973).

C. Bérard, *Anodoi. Essai sur l'Imagerie des Passages Chthoniens,* Rome 1974.

P. Betancourt, S. Immerwahr, S. Hiller on R. Laffineur 'Mycenaeans at Thera: Further Evidence?', *Thalassocracy.*

H. Biesantz, *Kretisch-mykenische Siegelbilder,* Marburg 1954.

J. Bintliff, (ed.) *Mycenaean Geography (Proc. Cambr. Collqu., Sept. 1976),* Cambridge 1977.

J. Bintliff, *Natural environment and human settlement in prehistoric Greece,* Oxford 1977.

K. Bittel, 'Hittite Temples and High Places', *Temples.*

K. Bittel, 'The Great Temple of Hattusha – Bogazköy', *AJA* 80 (1976).

C. W. Blegen, *Prosymna. The Helladic Settlement preceding the Argive Heraeum,* 1937.

J. Boardman, *Athenian Black Figure Vases,* London 1974.

J. Boardman, *Athenian Red Figure Vases. The Archaic Period,* London 1975.

J. Boardman, *Greek Sculpture: The Archaic Period,* London 1978.

J. Bouzek, 'Syrian and Anatolian Figurines in Europe', *Proc. Prehist. Soc.* 38 (1972).

K. Branigan, 'The earliest Minoan Scripts – the Prepalatial background', *Kadmos* 8 (1969).

K. Branigan, *The Tombs of Mesara*, London 1970.

A. Brelich, *Gli eroi Greci,* Rome 1958.

H. Browne, 'A Bronze Belt from the Sanctuary of Apollo at Kourion', *SCA.*

Martin Buber, *Gottesfinsterniss,* Zurich 1953.

H. G. Buchholz, 'Beobachtungen zum prähistorischen Bronzeguss in Zypern und der Ägäis', *Cyprus & Crete.*

H. G. Buchholz – V. Karageorghis, *Altägäis und Altkypros,* Tübingen 1971.

D. Buitron – D. Soren, 'Excavations in the Sanctuary of Apollo Hylates at Kourion', *SCA.*

W. Burkert, *Homo Necans. Interpretationen Altgriechischer Opferriten,* Berlin 1972.

W. Burkert, 'Apellai und Apollon', *RM* 118 (1975).

W. Burkert, 'Rešep-Figuren, Apollon von Amyklai und die 'Erfindung' des Opfers auf Zypern', *Grazer Beiträge* 4 (1975).

W. Burkert, *Griechische Religion der archaischen und klassischen Epoche,* Stuttgart 1977.

W. Burkert, *Structure and History in Greek Mythology and Ritual* (Sather Class, Lect. 47), Berkeley 1979.

G. Cadogan, 'Pyrgos, Crete, 1970–77', *AR* 1977/78.

G. Cadogan, 'Cyprus & Crete ca. 2000–1400 B.C.', *Cyprus & Crete.*

J. R. Carpenter, 'Episkopi-Phaneromeni', *Kourion.*

J. R. Carpenter, 'Excavations at Phaneronomeni', *SCA.*

R. Carpenter, *Greek Sculpture. A Critical Review,* Chicago 1960.

J. L. Caskey, 'The Bronze Age Temple at Ayia Irini in Keos and its later History', *Gr & It.*

H. W. Catling, *Cypriote Bronzework in the Mycenaean World,* Oxford 1964.

H. W. Catling, 'Cyprus in the Neolithic and Bronze Age Periods', *CAH²,* Cambridge 1966.

A. Caubet – J. C. Courtois, 'masques chypriotes en terre cuite d'Enkomi', *RDAC* 1982.

J. Chadwick – L. Baumbach, 'The Mycenaean Greek Vocabulary', *Glotta* 41 (1963).

J. Chadwick, *Documents in Mycenaean Greek²,* Cambridge 1973.

J. Chadwick, *The Mycenaean World,* Cambridge 1976.

F. Chapouthier, *La Notion du Divin depuis Homère jusqu'à Platon, Fond. Hardt* I, Geneva 1952.

J. F. Cherry, 'The Emergence of the State in the Prehistoric Aegean', *Proc. Cambr. Phil. Soc.* 210, NS 30 (1984).

I. Chirassi, *Elementi di culture precereali nei miti e riti Greci,* Rome 1968.

A. K. Choremis, 'M. H. altar on Nissakouli', *AAA* 2 (1969).

G. A. Christopoulos – J. C. Bastias (eds.), *Prehistory and Protohistory,* Athens 1974.

J. N. Coldstream & G. L. Huxley, 'The Minoans of Kythera', *Thalassocracy.*

J. N. Coldstream, *Geometric Greece*, London 1977.

C. Colpe, 'Gottessohn', *RAC* 89 (1981).

D. Conrad, 'Der Gott Reschef', *ZAW* 83 (1971).

A. B. Cook, *Zeus. A Study in Ancient Religion*, Cambridge 1914–40.

F. A. Cooper, 'Arkadian Epikouroi and the date of the temple at Bassae', *Gr & It.*

A. Morpurgo Davies, 'Terminology of Power and Terminology of Work in Greek and Linear B', *Coll Myc.*

J. L. Davis, 'Cultural Transaction and the Minoan Thalassocracy at Ayia Irini', *Thalassocracy.*

R. M. Dawkins, 'The Sanctuary of Artemis Orthia', *JHS* Suppl. 5 (1929).

V. Desborough, *The Last Mycenaeans and their Successors*, Oxford 1964.

V. Desborough, *The Greek Dark Ages*, New York 1972.

L. Deubner, *Attische Feste*, repr. Berlin 1956.

O. T. P. K. Dickinson, *The Origins of Mycenaean Civilization*, *(SIMA)*, Göteborg 1977.

B. C. Dietrich, *The Origins of Greek Religion*, Berlin 1974.

B. C. Dietrich, 'The Dorian Hyacinthia. A Survival from the Bronze Age', *Kadmos* 14 (1975).

B. C. Dietrich, 'Reflections on the Origins of Oracular Apollo', *BICS* 25 (1978).

B. C. Dietrich, 'Some Evidence from Cyprus of Apolline Cult in the Brone Age', *RM* N.F. 121 (1978).

P. Dikaios, *Enkomi. Excavations 1948–58*, vols. I–III, Mainz 1961 & 1971.

P. Dikaios, *Sotira*, Philadelphia 1961.

P. Dikaios, 'The Bronze Statue of a Horned God from Enkomi', *AA* (1962).

P. Dikaios, 'The Stone Age of Cyprus', *SCE* IV, IA, Lund 1962.

H. Dörrie, 'Gottesvorstellung', *RAC* fasc. 89 (1981).

H. Drerup, 'Griechische Architektur zur Zeit Homers', *AA* (1964).

H. Drerup, *Griechische Baukunst in geometrischer Zeit*, (Arch Hom), Göttingen 1969.

T. J. Dunbabin, *The Greeks and their Eastern Neighbours*, London 1957.

M. Eliade, *Traité d'Histoire des Religions*, Paris 1949.

A. Evans, *The Palace of Minos at Knossos*, I–IV, London 1921–36.

J. D. Evans, *Malta*, London 1959.

L. R. Farnell, *Cults of the Greek States*, 5 vols., Oxford 1896–1909.

P. Faure, 'Cultes Populaires dans la Crète Antique', *BCH* 96 (1972).

P. Faure, 'Chronique des Cavernes Cretoises (1927–77)', *BCH* 102 (1978).

K. Fittschen, *Untersuchungen zum Beginn der Sagendarstellungen bei den Griechen*, Berlin 1969.

J. Fontenrose, *The Delphic Oracle*, Berkeley 1978.

R. J. Forbes, *Bergbau-Steinbruchtätigkeit-Hüttenwesen*, *(Arch Hom)*, Göttingen 1967.

H. Frankfort, *Ancient Egyptian Religion*, Harper Torch Books 1961.

E. French, 'Cult Places at Mycenae', *SCABA.*

E. French, 'The Development of Mycenaean Terracotta Figurines', *BSA* LXVI (1971).

P. Friedrich, *The Meaning of Aphrodite*, Chicago 1978.

M. Gérard-Rousseau, *Les Mentions Religieuses dans les Tablettes Myceniennes*, Rome 1968.

G. C. Gesell, *The Archaeological Evidence for the Minoan House Cult and its survival in Iron Age Crete*, thesis Chapel Hill 1972.

M. Gimbutas, *The Gods and Goddesses of Old Europe*, London 1974.

M. Gimbutas, 'The Mask in Old Europe from 6500–3500 B.C.', *Archaeology* 27 (1974).

S. Glover, 'The Cult of Apollo At Kourion', *Kourion.*

F. Graf, 'Das Götterbild aus dem Taurerland', *Antike Welt* 4 (1979).

J. Griffin, *Homer on Life and Death*, Oxford 1980.

G. Gruben, *Die Tempel der Griechen*[3], Munich 1980.

F. Gschnitzer, 'Vocabulaire et Institutions: La Continuité Historique du deuxième au premier millenaire', *Coll Myc.*

R. Hägg, 'On the nature of the Minoan influence in early Mcenaean Messenia', *OpAth* 14 (1982).

R. Hägg, 'Degrees and Character of the Minoan Influence on the Mainland', *Thalassocracy.*

E. Hallager, *The Mycenaean Palace at Knossos*, Stockholm 1977.

N. G. L. Hammond, *A History of Greece*[2], Oxford 1967.

J. Harrison, *Prolegomena to the Study of Greek Religion*, rept. New York 1955.

L. Hellbing, *Alasia Problems (SIMA 57)*, Göteborg 1979.

R. Herbig, *Pan, der griechische Bocksgott*, Frankfurt 1949.

C. J. Herington, *Athena Parthenos and Athena Polias*, 1955.

A. Hermary, 'Statuette d'un "Prêtre" Masqué', *BCH* 103 (1979).

H. Herter, 'Hermes', *RM* 119 (1976).

H. Herter, 'Phallos', *Kl P* vol. 4 (1979).

Z. Herzog, 'Israelite Sanctuaries at Arad and Beer-Sheba', *Temples.*

A. Heubeck, *Aus der Welt der frühgriechischen Lineartafeln*, Göttingen 1966.

G. Hill, *A History of Cyprus* I, Cambridge 1940.

S. Hiller – O. Panagl, *Die frühgriechischen Texte aus mykenischer Zeit*, Darmstadt 1976.

S. Hiller, 'Mykenische Archäologie', *SMEA* (1979).

H. Hoffmann, *Early Greek Armorers*, Mainz 1972.

R. Holte, 'Gottessymbol und soziale Struktur', *RSF.*

M. S. F. Hood, 'Tholos tombs of the Aegean', *Antiquity* 34 (1960).

M. S. F. Hood, *The Minoans*, London 1971.

M. S. F. Hood, *The Arts in Prehistoric Greece* (Pelican History of Art), 1978.

M. S. F. Hood, 'Minoan Town-Shrines?', *Studs Schach.*

S. H. Hooke, *Babylonian and Assyrian Religion*, repr. Oxford 1962.

J. T. Hooker, *Mycenaean Greece*, London 1976.

A. Hultgard, 'Man as Symbol of God', *RSF.*

J. Hurwitt, 'The Dendra Octopus Cup', *AJA* 83 (1979).

Sp. Iakovides, 'Thera and Mycenaean Greece', *AJA* 83 (1979).

S. A. Immerwahr, 'Mycenaeans at Thera', *Studs Schach.*

F. Jacoby, *Die Fragmente der griechischen Historiker,* Berlin/Leiden 1923–58.

W. Jäger, *The Theology of the Early Greek Philosophers,* Oxford 1947.

H. Jeanmaire, *Dionysos. Histoire du Culte de Bacchus,* Paris 1951.

L. H. Jeffery, *The Local Scripts of Archaic Greece,* Oxford 1961.

Jessen, 'Hylates', *P-W.*

L. Kahil, 'La Deésse Artemis: Mythologie et Iconographie', *Gr & It.*

A. Kanta, *The Late Minoan III Period in Crete. A Survey of Sites, Pottery and their Distribution, (SIMA),* Göteborg 1980.

J. Karageorghis, *La Grande Deésse de Chypre et son Culte,* Lyon 1977.

V. Karageorghis, 'The Mycenaean Origin of the Cypriote Culture', *XII Congr. Intern. des Science Histor. Rapports* (1965) IV & V.

V. Karageorghis, *The Ancient Civilization of Cyprus,* London 1969.

V. Karageorghis, 'Kition, Mycenaean and Phoenician' *(Mortimer Wheeler Archaeological Lecture, British Academy 1973) PBA* 1973.

V. Karageorghis, 'Chroniques des Fouilles et Découvertes Archéologiques à Chypre', *BCH* 96 to 99 (1972 to 1975).

V. Karageorghis, *Kition: Mycenaean and Phoenician Discoveries in Cyprus,* London 1976.

V. Karageorghis, 'The goddes with uplifted arms in Cyprus', *Scripta Minora 1977–78, in hon. E. Gjerstad (Kungl. Hum. Vetenskaps Lund),* Lund 1977.

V. Karageorghis, *Two Cypriote Sanctuaries of the End of the Cypro-Archaic Period,* Rome 1977.

V. Karageorghis – M.G. Guzzo-Amadasi, *Fouilles de Kition III. Les Inscriptions Pheniciennes,* 1977.

V. Karageorghis, *Cyprus. From the Stone Age to the Romans,* London 1982.

V. Karageorghis, 'The Sacred Area of Kition', *Temples.*

V. Karageorghis, 'Some Reflections on the Relations between Cyprus and Crete during the Late Minoan IIIB Period', *Cyprus & Crete.*

A. Karetsou, 'The Peak Sanctuary of Mt. Juktas', *SCABA.*

G. Karo, *Greek Personality in Archaic Sculpture, Martin Class. Lect. XI,* Harvard 1948.

Chr. Karusos, *Zur Geschichte der spätarchaisch-attischen Plastik und der Grabstatue,* Stuttgart 1961.

V. E. G. Kenna, *Cretan Seals,* Oxford 1960.

K. Kerenyi, *Eleusis. Archetypal Image of Mother and Doughter,* London 1967.

K. Kerenyi, *Antike Religion,* Munich and Vienna 1971.

K. Kerenyi, *The Religions of the Greeks and Romans,* trans. C. Holme, London 1962.

K. Kerenyi, *Zeus und Hera,* trans. C. Holme, London 1975.

K. Kilian, 'Zeugnisse Mykenischer Kultausübung in Tiryns', *SCABA.*

G. S. Kirk, *The Songs of Homer,* Cambridge 1962.

N. M. Kontoleon, *Les ecoles de l'art grec antique, Coll. de France*, Paris 1970.

G. S. Korres, 'The Relations between Crete and Messenia', *Thalassocracy*.

W. Kullmann, *Das Wirken der Götter in der Ilias*, Berlin 1956.

E. Kunze, *Berichte über die Ausgrabungen in Olympia VII. Frühjahr 1956 bis 1958*, Berlin 1961.

V. Lambrinoudakis, 'Remains of the Mycenaean Period in the Sanctuary of Apollo Maleatas', *SCABA*.

G. Landtman, 'The Origins of Images as Objects of Cult', *AfR* (1926).

M. K. Langdon, *A Sanctuary of Zeus on Mount Hymettos (Hesperia Suppl. XVI)*, Princeton 1976.

K. Latte, *Römische Religionsgeschichte*, Munich 1960.

Ch. Le Roy, 'La Naissance d'Apollon et les Palmiers Déliens', *Études Déliennes, BCH* Suppl. I (1973).

J. C. van Leuven, 'The mainland tradition of sanctuaries in prehistoric Greece', *WA* 10 (1978).

H. Lewy, *Die Semitischen Fremdwörter im Griechischen*, Berlin 1895.

F. G. Maier, 'The Paphian Shrine of Aphrodite and Crete', *Cyprus & Crete*.

A. Mallwitz, *Olympia und seine Bauten*, Darmstadt 1972.

N. Marinatos, 'Minoan Threskeiocracy on Thera', *Thalassocracy*.

N. Marinatos, 'The West House at Akrotiri as a Cult Center', *AM* 98 (1983).

Sp. Marinatos – M. Hirmer, *Kreta, Thera und das Mykenische Hellas*[3], Munich 1976.

O. Masson, *Les Inscriptions Chypriotes Syllabiques*, Paris 1961.

O. Masson, 'Remarques sur les Cultes Cypriotes à l'Europe du Bronze Récent', *East Med.*

O. Masson, *Cultes Indigènes, Cultes Grecs et Cultes Orientaux à Chypre* (Élements Orientaux dans la Religion Grecque Ancienne, travaux du centre d'études supérieures spécialisé d'histoire des religions de Strasbourg), Paris 1960.

F. Matz, *Crete and Early Greece*, London 1962.

A. Mazar, 'The Philistine Sanctuary at Tell Qasile', *Temples*.

P. Mazon, *Introduction à l'Iliade*, Paris 1942.

R. Meiggs, *The Athenian Empire*, 1972, Appendix.

J. Mellaart, *The Neolithic of the Near East*, London 1965.

J. Mellaart, *Earliest Civilizations of the Near East*, London 1965.

K. Meuli, *Handwörterbuch des deutschen Aberglaubens* 5, 1932/33.

J. D. Mikalson, *The Sacred and Civil Calendar of the Athenian Year*, Princeton 1975.

J. Milojčic, *Samos I: die prähistorische Siedlung unter dem Heraion*, 1961.

T. B. Mitford, *The Inscriptions of Kourion*, Philadelphia 1971.

J. Mlynarzyk, 'The Paphian Shrine of Apollo Hylates', *RDAC* 1980.

U. v. W. Möllendorff, *Der Glaube der Hellenen*[3], repr. Darmstadt 1959.

S. Morenz, *Ägyptische Religion*, Stuttgart 1960.

O. Murray, 'The Symposium as Social Organisation', *SCABA*.

G. E. Mylonas, *Eleusis and the Eleusinian Mysteries*, 3rd print, Princeton 1974.

G. E. Mylonas, 'The Cult Centre of Mycenae', *PBA* 67 (1981).

J. L. Myres, *Handbook of the Cesnola Collection of Antiquities from Cyprus*, Metropolitan Museum of Art, New York 1914.

M. P. Nilsson, *The Mycenaean Origin of Greek Mythology*, Berkeley 1932.

M. P. Nilsson, *Minoan/Mycenaean Religion and ist Survival in Greek Religion²*, Lund 1950.

M. P. Nilsson, *Griechische Feste von religiöser Bedeutung mit Ausschluß der Attischen*, Leipzig 1960.

M. P. Nilsson, *Die Entstehung und Bedeutung des griechischen Kalendars²*, Lund 1962.

M. P. Nilsson, *Geschichte der griechischen Religion³*, Munich 1967.

A. D. Nock, 'The Cult of Heroes', *Harvard Theological Review* 37 (1944).

M. Ohnefalsch-Richter, *Kypros. The Bible and Homer*, London 1893.

P. Oliva, *The Birth of Greek Civilization*, London 1981.

A. L. Oppenheim, *Ancient Mesopotamia*, Chicago 1964.

W. F. Otto, *Dionysus, Mythos und Kultus²*, Frankfurt 1948.

W. F. Otto, *Die Götter Griechenlands⁴*, Frankfurt 1956.

L. R. Palmer, *The Interpretation of Mycenaean Greek Texts*, Oxford 1963.

L. R. Palmer, *Mycenaeans and Minoans²*, London 1965.

Jeanette Papadopoulos, *Xoana e Sphyrelata*, Rome 1980.

H. W. Parker, *Festivals of the Athenians*, London 1977.

S. T. Parker, 'Cimon's Expedition to Cyprus', *AJP* 97 (1976).

J. G. Parr, *Man, Metals and Modern Magic*, 1958.

E. Pax, 'Epiphanie', *RAC* 5 (962).

O. Pelon, 'Sur deux tholoi de Messenie', *BCH* 98 (1974).

E. J. Peltenburg, 'The Sotira Culture: Regional Diversity and Cultural Unity in Late Neolithic Cyprus', *Levant* X (1978).

J. D. S. Pendlebury, *The Archaeology of Crete*, London 1939.

F. Pfister, 'Ephiphanie', *P–W* Suppl. IV (1924).

P. Philips, *The Prehistory of Europe*, London 1980.

C. Picard, 'Midea à Salamis de Chypre', *GAK*, Athens 1953.

A. Pickard-Cambridge, *The Dramatic Festivals of Athens²*, Oxford 1968.

I. Pini, *Beiträge zur Minoischen Gräberkunde*, Wiesbaden 1968.

I. Pini, 'Minoische Siegel außerhalb Kretas', *Thalassocracy*.

Ed. des Places, *Syngeneia*, Paris 1964.

J. du Plat Taylor, *Myrtou-Pigadhes*, Oxford 1957.

F. de Polignac, *La Naissance de la Cité Grecque*, Paris 1984.

W. K. Pritchett, *The Greek State at War*, Berkeley 1979.

J. K. Promponas, *The Athenian Festival Thronoelkteria and its Survival into Historical Times*, Athens 1974.

G. Pugliese-Carratelli, 'Afrodite Cretese', *SMEA* 20 (1979).

G. Rachet, *Dictionnaire de l'Archeologie*, Paris 1983.

G. Radke, *Die Götter Altitaliens*, Münster 1965.

C. Renfrew, 'Questions of Minoan and Mycenaean Cult', *SCABA*.

C. Renfrew, 'The Mycenaean Sanctuary at Phylakopi', *Antiquity* 52 (1978).

N. J. Richardson, *The Homeric Hymn to Demeter*, Oxford 1974.

G. Richter, *Kouroi²*, New York 1970.

H. Ringgren, 'The Religion of Ancient Syria', *Historia Religionum*, Leiden 1969.

H. Ringgren, 'The Symbolism of Mesopotamian Cult Images', *RSF.*

G. Rizza – V.S.M. Scrinari, *Il Santuario sull' Acropoli di Gortina*, Rome 1968.

M. E. Robbins, *Indo-European Female Figures*, thesis, Los Angeles 1978.

F. Robert, *La Religion Grecque*, Paris 1981.

Dietrich Roloff, *Gottähnlichkeit, Vergöttlichung und Erhöhung zum seligen Leben*, Berlin 1970.

A. Rowe, *The Topography and History of Beth Shan*, Philadelphia 1930.

R. A. van Royen – B.H. Isaac, *The Arrival of the Greeks, The Evidence of The Settlements*, Amsterdam 1979.

B. Rutkowski, *Cult Places in the Aegean World*, Warsaw 1972.

B. Rutkowski, *Frühgriechische Kultdarstellungen*, Berlin 1981.

B. Rutkowski, 'Religious Architecture in Cyprus and Crete in the Late Bronze Age', *Cyprus & Crete.*

J. B. Rutter, 'Stone Vases and Minoan Ware: A Facet of Minoan Influence on Middle Laconia', *AJA* 83 (1979).

J. B. Rutter & C.W. Zerner, 'Early Helladic-Minoan Contacts', *Thalassocracy.*

G. Säflund, 'Cretan and Theran Questions', *SCABA*.

G. Säflund, 'Sacrificial Banquets in the "Palace of Nestor"', *OpAth* 13 (1980).

J. A. Sakellarakis, *Herakleion Museum* (Guide), 1979.

A. Sakellariou, *Mycenaean Glyptic*, Athens 1966.

A. Sakellariou, 'A propos de la chronologie des gemmes mycéniennes', *Die Kretisch-mykenische Glyptik und ihre gegenwärtige Probleme*, Boppard 1974.

A. E. Samuel, *Greek and Roman Chronology*, 1972.

N. K. Sanders, *The Sea Peoples*, 1978.

J. Sarkady, 'Die Jonischen Feste und die Jonische Urgeschichte', *ACD* 1 (1965).

J. Sarkady, 'Outlines of the Development of Greek Society in the Period between the 12th and 8th Centuries B.C.', *A Ant* 23 (1975).

F. Schachermeyr, *Griechische Geschichte*, 1960.

F. Schachermeyr, *Die Ägäische Frühzeit*, vol. 1 *(Die vormykenischen Perioden des griechischen Festlandes und der Kykladen)*, Vienna 1976.

F. Schachermeyr, *Die Ägäische Frühzeit*, vol. 2 *(Die Mykenische Zeit und die Gesittung von Thera)*, Vienna 1976.

F. Schachermeyr, *Die Ägäische Frühzeit* vol. 5 *(Die Levante im Zeitalter der Wanderungen vom 13 bis zum 11 Jahrhundert v. Chr.)*, Vienna 1982.

F. Schachermeyr, *Griechische Frühgeschichte*, Vienna 1984.

K. Schefold, *Myth and Legend in Greek Art*, London 1966.

H. Schliemann, *Mykenae*, new ed. Darmstadt 1963.

B. Schmaltz, *Das Kabirenheiligtum bei Theben* V (1974).

L. A. Schneider, *Zur sozialen Bedeutung der archaischen Korenstatuen, Hamburger Beitr. z. Arch. II,* Hamburg 1975.

R. Scranton, *The Architecture of the Sanctuary of Apollo Hylates at Kourion, TAPS.*

H. Seeden, *The Standing Armed Figurines in the Levant* (Inst. f. Vorgeschichte, Univ. Frankfurt a. Main, Prähistorische Bronzefunde I, 1), Munich 1980.

E. Simon, *Die Götter der Griechen²*, Munich 1980.

E. Sjöquist, 'Die Kultgeschichte eines Cyprischen Temenos', *AfR* 30 (1933).

B. Snell, 'Der Welt der Götter bei Hesiod', *Entr. Fond. Hardt* I (1952).

A. M. Snodgrass, *The Dark Age of Greece,* Edinburgh 1971.

A. M. Snodgrass, *Archaic Greece,* London 1980.

S. Solders, 'Der ursprüngliche Apollo', *AfR* 32 (1935).

D. Soren, 'Earthquake: The Last Days of Kourion', *SCA.*

C. G. Starr, *The Economic and Social Growth of Early Greece 800–500 B. C.,* Oxford 1977.

L. A. Stella, *Tradizione Micenea e Poesia dell'Iliade,* Urbino/Rome 1978.

G. Stephenson (ed.), *Der Religionswandel unserer Zeit im Spiegel der Religionswissenschaft,* Wissensch. Buchgesellschft., Darmstadt 1976.

S. Swiny, 'Standing Stones: Perforated Monoliths', *Kourion.*

O. Szemerenyi, 'Homerica et Mycenaica', *SMEA* (1979).

W. Taylour, 'New Aspects on Mycenaean Religion', *AP,* Athens 1972.

D. H. Trump, *The Prehistory of the Mediterranean,* London 1980.

E. Tyree, *Cretan Cults and Festivals,* London 1962.

P. J. Ucko, *Anthropomorphic Figurines of Predynastic Egypt and Neolithic Crete,* 1978.

Ch. Uhsadel-Gülke, *Knochen und Kessel,* Maisheim 1972 (*Beitr. z. klass. Philol.* no 43).

H. Usener, *Götternamen,* Bonn 1896.

E. Vermeule, *Götterkult (Arch Hom),* Göttingen 1974.

E. Vermeule, *The Art of the Shaft Graves* (Lectures in memory of Louise Taft Semple, Third Series), Cincinnati 1975.

P. Warren, *Myrtos,* Oxford 1972.

W. J. Wedlake, *The Excavation of the Shrine of Apollo at Nettleton, Wilts., 1956–1971,* London 1982.

S. S. Weinberg, 'Kourion – Bamboula: The Late Bronze Age Architecture', *AJA* 56 (1972).

S. S. Weinberg, 'Exploring the Early Bronze Age in Cyprus', *Archaeology* 9 (1956).

S. S. Weinberg, 'The Stone Age in The Aegean', *CAH³,* Cambridge 1970.

L. Weniger, 'Theophanien, altgriechische Götteradvente', *AfR* 22 (1924).

M. L. West, *Theogony,* Oxford 1966.

M. L. West, *Immortal Helen,* Inaugural Lecutre, London 1975.

M. L. West, *Hesiod's Works & Days,* Oxford 1978.

D. Whittingham, 'The Small Basilica: "At Meydan"', *Kourion.*

D. Whittingham, 'Kourion: the Roman Stadium', *Kourion.*

S. Wide, *Lakonische Kulte*, repr. Darmstadt 1973.

J. Wiesner, *Olympos*, Darmstadt 1960.

F. Willemsen, *Frühe Griechische Kultbilder*, diss. Munich 1939.

R. F. Willetts, *Cretan Cults and Festivals*, London 1962.

G. Wissowa, *Religion und Kults der Römer*, repr. of 2nd ed., Munich 1971.

D. E. W. Wormell, *The Delphic Oracle*, Oxford 1956.

C. G. Yavis, *Greek Altars. Origin and Topology. Including the Minoan/Mycenaean Offertory Apparatus*, St. Louis Univ. Studs. 1949.

M. Yon, *Salamine de Chypre V. Un dépôt de sculptures archaiques*, Paris 1974.

M. Yon, 'Du Taureau à l'Aigle', *CNRS*, Paris 1981.

J. H. & S. H. Young, *Terracotta Figurines from Kourion in Cyprus*, Philadelphia 1955.

L. Ziehen, 'Palladion', *P–W* (1949).

Index

Names

Achaeans 124, 175
Achilles 96, 97, 98
Actium 25, 154, 176
Aditi 110
Aegean 7, 9, 106, 110, 139, 149, 180, 183
– architecture 136
– culture 182
Aegys 163
Aelian 148, 150
Aeneas 96
Aeolians 51
Aeschylus 115
Agad 136
Agamemnon 45, 124
Agapenor 13, 125, 159, 160 n.25
Agyiates 171
Ahura Mazda 90
Aidos 89
Aius 88
Ajax 95, 97
Akraiphia 156
Alasia 162, 163
Alasiotas 162
Alepotrypon Cave 24
Alexander 176
Al Mina 159
Amamassos 158
Amargetti 157
Amarna 162
Amathus 65, 80, 147
Amnisos 30 u. 190, 108
Amphictyons 156 u. 262
Amun 88
Amyclae 25, 43, 44, 49, 59, 80, 106, 107f.,
    160, 169, 174
Amyklaios 80, 170

Anactorion 25
Anatolia 173
Anemospilia 140
Anthesteria 51
Apeilon 161
Apellon 161
Apesokari 23, 31
Aphaea 48, 56, 117
Aphrodite 8, 13, 15f., 24, 32, 45, 48, 65,
    68, 70f., 77, 80–86, 109, 116, 120,
    136, 141, 146f., 153, 154, 159, 160, 167
    n.341, 172, 175, 179
– armed 110
– bearded 71
– birth 81 n.254
– bisexual 71, 81, 86
– Cypriot 16, 80, 146
– Golgia 16, 80, 163
– Kypris 80
– Kyprogenes 182
– mysteries 175 n.397
– nude 47
– oriental 71, 81
– Paphia 11, 16, 24, 80, 125, 160 n.295,
    163
– Urania 81 n.260
Aphroditos 71
Apollo 25, 28, 44 n.17, 48, 57, 59, 60, 93,
    96 n.62, 99, 102, 107, 109, 115, 116,
    125, 126, 127, 128, 129, 136, 137,
    146f., 148, 150, 152f., 154–176,
    177,
    178, 179, 182
– Agyates 162
– Agyieus 109 n.141, 111, 169–174
– Aktios 25, 154

– Alasiotas 161
– Alexikakos 156, 164, 166 n.334, 169
– Amyklaios 111, 123, 133 n.76, 160f.,
    162, 167, 170, 173
– Amyklos 160, 162, 167
– and cave 156 n.263
– and lyre 152f.
– and oracle 156, 157f.
– Apotropaios 156, 169
– armed 107, 110, 173
– Aulaites 157 n.265
– birth of 155 n.248
– chthonic 175
– Daphnephoros 155, 156
– Daukhnapherios 156, 162
– Epikourios 108, 166, 169
– festivals 51
– Gruneios 157
– healer 152, 156
– Heleitas 151, 162
– Hyacinthus 25, 44
– Hylates 126, 128 n.45, 129, 153, 157,
    158, 160, 162, 175, 183
– Hymn 101
– in the Marsh 161, 163
– Kaisar 129, 153, 169, 179
– Karinos 173
– Karnasios 157
– Karneios 154, 155 n.248
– Keraiates 163
– Kereatas 163f.
– Kyprios 162 n.308
– Lakeutes 153, n.227
– Lenaios 153
– Maleatas 28, 44, 60 n.108, 139
– Mantiklos 167
– Melathios 157 n.266
– Mikal 160 n.297
– Myrikaios 155 n.248
– Myrtates 155 n.248, 162
– Myrtoos 155 n.248
– Nomios 165
– of The Grove 163
– Pagasaios 157
– Pagasites 154 n. 239, 157
– Platanistios 155 n.248

– Polykteanos 153
– Proopsios 28
– Propylaios 170
– Prostaterios 170, 173
– protector 173
– Ptoios 156, 157, 158
– purifyer 152, 156, 170
– Pythios 153, 155, 162, 175
– Smintheus 170
– Telphousios 157
– Thyraios 170
– youthful 78 n.230
Aporodita 81
Arcadia 160, 169, 170
Arcadians 51, 58
Ares 86, 89, 98 n.72, 120
Argives 124
Argolid 58
Argos 24, 60, 81, 93
Ariadne 80, 117
Arkalokhori 29, 30 n.190
Arkhanes 12, 23, 140 n.131
Artemis 34, 46, 48, 51, 58, 60, 66, 67, 70,
    75, 78, 110, 112, 113, 154, 179
– festivals 51, 58, 69, 70, 180
– Kedreatis 83
– Leucophryene 96 n.62
– Lygodesma 113
– Orthia 39, 46f., 70, 113, 114, 117, 118,
    179
– Taurian 113
Asclepius 28, 96 n.62, 177
Ashtar 71
Astarte 13, 15f., 65, 70f., 137, 138
Astort 81 n.253
Athena 47, 48, 55, 58, 60, 79, 93, 95, 96,
    97 n.62, n.65, 98, 99, 101, 104, 109,
    116, 117, 118, 120, 135, 136, 162
    n.315, 180
– armed 47, 79 n.241, 101, 102, 110,
    119
– Chalkinaos 55
– Chalkioikos 55
– image 104 n.112
– Itonia 55
– Minoa 55

– Neith 79 n.234
– Polias 47, 113
– Pronaia 48
– Telchinia 85 n.293
– Tritogeneia 79
Athens 24, 27, 58, 59, 60, 79, 81, 95, 103,
    105, 109
Athienou 85
Attica 25, 119, 155, 173
Augustus 25, 128, 154, 176
Aulis 34, 60
Axos 84
Ayia Irini, Cyprus 54, 66f., 71, 84 n.286,
    131, 135, 142, 144f., 148, 150, 151,
    152, 167, 169, 179
Ayia Irini, Keos 7, 18, 32, 39, 44, 45, 48,
    53, 56, 64 n.134, 67, 75
Ayia Triada 53
Ayios Iakovos 134, 139, 151, 152
Ayios Stephanos 3, 4

Baal 137, 164 n.326
Babylon 41
Bamboula 121 f.
Bassae 108, 166
Bes 133, 168 n.353
Beth Shan 9, 166, 170
Bogazköy 171
Brauron 34, 60
Britomartis 117
Byblos 9

Camirus 83
Cassandra 115
Çatal Hüyük 9, 35, 63 n.132, 107, 112
Ceres 88
Charis 89
Chios 154, 156
Chous 88
Chytroi 152, 157, 158, 175
Cimon 116
Cnidus 37, 38
Corinth 59, 146
Crete 3, 7, 10, 38, 43, 80, 181
Cyprus 9f., 12, 14f., 38, 43, 44, 49, 54,
    64, 80, 84, 116, 121, 126, 138f.,

    148, 150, 158, 159, 162, 165, 168, 174,
    179, 181, 182
Cyrus 41

Daedalus 106
Dali 142
Daphnae 156
Daphne 154
Daukhnaphorios 156, 162
Delos 42, 48, 53, 60, 80, 109, 146, 155,
    156
Delphi 39, 42, 46, 59, 60, 73, 101, 155,
    156, 159, 165, 177
Demeter 35, 36f., 57, 58, 66, 69, 70, 73,
    75, 78, 83, 88, 101, 112, 118, 119,
    123
– Baubo 175 n.397
– Eleusinia 70
– festivals 51, 69, 78, 180
– Kidaria 83 n.280
– Mysteries 119, 175 n.397
– Thesmia 70
Demodocus 159
Despoina 37 n.229, 66, 78
Dia 117
Diarrhizos 147
Didyma 146, 155
Diktynna 117
Diomede 96, 97, 113
Dionysus 32, 48, 57, 68f., 72, 74–77, 78,
    83, 101, 108, 112, 117, 119, 179,
    180
– bearded 73 n.198
– 73, 77
– Enorchos 74 n.205
– ithyphallic 74 n.205
– mask 74
– Orthos 74 n.205
– Perikionios 68, 72, 75, 108
– Phallen 73
– Thyonicas 74 n.205
Dios 50
diwija 117
Dodona 59
Dorians 51, 61
Dreros 53, 168, 179

Drimios 49, 117
Drimou 157, 158, 175

Echetlaeus 95
Egypt 87 f., 122, 159
Eileithyia 107
El 90 n.18, 164 n.326
Eleos 89
Eleusis 36, 38, 43, 45, 119, 177
Emporio 60
Enkomi 11 f., 15, 23, 65, 84, 106, 135,
    138, 140 f., 150, 164, 165, 167, 172
Enyalios 113 n.169
Epidaurus 27, 139, 140, 177
Epirus 156
Erechtheus 58
Eretria 155
Eris 89, 97
Evagoras I 159, 182

Fortetsa 84
Fournou Korifi 26
Franchthi Cave 24
Frangissa 161, 168

Gazi 109 n.143
Ge 48
Geneta 89
Genius 88
Gezer 138, 166
Golgoi 16, 116
Gortyn 24, 27, 44, 45, 46 f., 48, 60, 79, 82,
    119, 146 n.168
Gournia 18
Grace 89
Gruneion 154, 155 n.245
Hala Sultan Tekke 172, 173
Halae 34
Hazor 138
Hebe 89
Hecate 77 n.228
Hector 99
Heleitas 161
Helen 45, 93, 95
Helenus 99
Helios 114

Helos 161
Hephaestus 86, 89, 106, 120, 167 n.341
Hera 24, 42, 43, 60, 91 n.32, 101, 105,
    109, 110, 114, 117, 120
– Heleia 161 n.304
– Tonaia 113
Hermaeus 159
Hermaphroditos 82
Hermes 32, 48, 68, 72, 73–77, 78, 80–83,
    96, 97 n.64, 102, 111, 117, 118, 120,
    179, 180
– and rebirth 76
– Kedrites 83
– Ledrites 83
– Nomios 77
– of Ledrai 83 n.277
– Orthannes 74 n.205
– Perpheraeus 73
– phallic 81 f., 111
– Psychopompus 76
– youthful 78 n.230, 83
Hermione 69
Hesiod 37, 89, 91, 92 f., 95, 116
Hestia 114
Homer 24, 42, 45, 49, 86, 89, 91, 92 f., 94,
    96, 97 n.71, 98–102, 104, 106, 114,
    115, 116, 120, 124, 159, 180 f., 182
– Hymns 100
Honos 89
Hunger 89
Hyacinthus 59, 174
Hylates 133, 154, 157, 158, 175, 177, 179
Hyle 158

Idaean Cane 30 n.190, 82
Idalion 135, 136, 150, 160, 170
Iktinos 108, 169
Ionians 51, 58, 61, 119
Iphigenia 37 n.229
Iris 96
Ishtar 71
Isopata 6
Ithaca 46

Jericho 67

Kalapodi 44, 67
Kaloriziki 122, 124, 150
Kamilari 69, 71, 143
Karneios 163
Karpas 182
Karphi 8, 26, 109 n.143
Kastri 3
Kato Symi 14 n.92, 23, 32f., 39, 44, 48,
    54, 69, 80, 82f., 106, 119, 179
Kato Zakro 10
Keos 106, 138
Kera 114
Kerea 164
Kereatas 163f.
Kinyradae 125, 160
Kinyras 124f., 153, 159, 160 n.295, 164
    n.326
Kir 122
Kition 9, 13, 14f., 23, 44, 48, 65, 81
    n.253, 84, 85, 130, 135, 136, 137,
    138, 140f., 149, 161, 170, 171,
    172
Kitsos Cave 24
Klaros 146
Knossos 8, 10, 31, 39, 48, 50, 56, 58, 79,
    106, 117, 140
Kommissariato 137
Kommos 19 n.118, 133 n.76
Kore 36 n.223, 73, 78, 123
Kos 17
Kotchati 151
Kouklia 147, 172 n.377
Koureus 124
Kourians 123
Kourion
– city 123, 126 n.33, 169, 176
    n.398
– sanctuary 116, 121–134, 135, 137, 138,
    139, 142, 144, 145, 146f., 148, 149,
    150, 152, 153, 154, 155, 156, 158, 165,
    168f., 171, 172, 174f., 176, 177,
    178, 179, 182
Kouris 122
Kumasa 69
Kythera 6
Kythrea 171

Lachish 136, 166
Laconia 147, 160
Laconians 124
Lamia 29
Laodice 160 n.295
Laodocus 98
Lapatos 50
Lefkandi 67
Lefkoniko 156
Lerna 3
Leto 155
Leucas 148, 156
Limniti 167
Lindos 60
Lousoi 60
Lycosoura 36, 66

Magnesia 156
Manasa 117
Marathon 45
Marduk 87
Marion 157
Marmaria 177
Mavriki 60
Megara 173
Megiddo 136, 166
Melos 6
Menelaus 45
Menidi 45
Meniko 137
Mentor 98
Mesara 23
Methone 4
Mikal 160f., 170, 173
Miletus 59, 119
Min 88
Minoans 1, 8, 9, 12, 34, 42, 76, 86, 180
– see also religion, cult, goddess
Mt. Anchesmos 28
Mt. Hymettus 25, 28f.
Mt. Ida 99, 100
Mt. Jouktas 13, 23, 27, 54, 140
Mt. Kynortion 27, 28, 44, 54, 60 n.108,
    139, 140
Mt. Parnes 28
Mt. Ptoon 60

Mycenae 3, 6, 13, 19, 34, 35, 36, 45, 53,
  64 n.134, 92, 106, 139, 140, 143,
  166, 173
– Shaft Graves 3, 4, 5f., 10f., 64 n.134
Mycenaeans 1, 4, 8, 9, 10, 39, 42, 76, 86,
  122, 135, 139, 146, 159, 160, 163,
  172, 180, 182
– see also religion, cult, goddess, art
Mycale 59
Myrtos 18, 53
– Lady of 18
Myrtou Pigadhes 13, 14, 172

Nausicaa 97 n.71
Naxos 156
Nergal 164 n.326
Nero 128
Nestor 56
Nettleton 133 n.76, 178
Nikokles 157, 158, 160, 182

Odysseus 46, 96, 98, 99, 113, 180
Oichalia 154
Olympia 43, 53, 59, 60, 103, 109, 110,
  165
Olympus 99
Opanon Melanthios 157
Orestes 93, 113
Orchomenos 50
Our Lady 114

Pagasae 154
Pain 89
Paion 80 n.248
Pakijane 50
Palestine 135, 136, 138, 166
Pan 29, 72, 83
Paphia 160
Paphos 11, 13, 15, 24, 44, 48, 80, 116,
  125, 140, 152, 157, 158, 159, 175,
  177, 182
– New 147, 157, 160, 175
– Old 136, 138, 147, 160, 172, 175, 182
Parca 88
Paros 156
Patrae 154, 165

Patsos Cave 30 n.190, 166
Pausanias 28f., 105, 125, 163, 164, 165
Pediaeus River 168
Peisistratus 36, 95, 98, 177
Peitho 81
Penelope 95
Perachora 42
Persephone 37 n.227
Perseus 125, 126
Perseutes 125
Phaistos 6, 84, 106
Phanae 60
Phaneromeni 30 n.190, 121, 122
Pheidias 104
Pheme 89
Pheneus 69
Pherae 60
Phoenicians 9, 23, 124, 135, 136, 137, 138,
  161
Phrygia 75, 154
Phylakopi 7, 18, 20f., 34, 36, 53, 69, 71,
  141–146, 166, 169
– East Shrine 141, 142, 145
– figurines 84 n.286, 166
– Lady of 21, 143, 144
– West Shrine 34, 35, 141, 142, 143
Pipituna 117
Pissouri 147
Platanus 23
Politiko 168
Pollentia 89
Polycrates 174
Poseidon 97, 98, 100, 101, 112, 117, 118,
  167
posidaeja 117
Potamia 152
Prayers 89
Priam 96
Priapus 75 n.209
Priene 37
Psithyros 81
Psychro Cave 29, 30 n.190, 33 n.207, 83
Ptoios 158
Pyla 150 n.198, 163
Pylos 6, 48, 54, 56, 58, 117
Pyrgos 25, 26, 69, 82 n.265

Pythia 156
Pythion 146 n.168
Python 154

Qasile 136, 138f.

Ramses III 122
Reshef 160f., 164f., 166, 170, 173
Rhea 85
Rhodes 17
Romans 129
Ryzenia 27

Salamis 125, 152, 159
Samos 43, 47, 60, 105, 113, 114
Sappho 80
Sarakinos Cave 24
Sesklo 68
Silen 72
Skephros 174
Skill 89
Skoteino Cave 30 n.190
Slavokambos 33
Smyrna 59, 75
Soloi 152
Sotira Kaminoudhia 121
Sotira Teppes 121
Sparta 39, 47, 49, 59, 60, 180
Spes 89
Strabo 148
Syria 135, 136, 166

Tamassos 65, 70, 86, 158, 161, 162, 167, 168
Tarsus 159
Tegea 59, 160, 174
Telamon 95
Tell Farah 136
Tembros 158
Tempo 155
Teucer 125
Theano 104
Thebes 8, 34, 59, 155, 167

Theophrastus 82
Thera 6, 109 n.142
Therapne 45
Thermon 57, 60
Theseus 58, 66, 93, 95
Thessaly 166
Thetis 98
Thornax 107
Tilphossion 154
Timna 138
Tiryns 6, 13, 15, 21f., 23, 53, 93, 106, 139, 166
Toil 89
Trajan 129, 153
Troad 85
Troy 9, 13, 93, 104, 113, 154
Tsoutsouras Cave 30 n.190

Ugarit 166

Valentia 89
Vathypetro 10
Victoria 89
Virtus 89
Vouni 136
Vounous 64, 134, 138, 149, 151

Yahwe 90
Yerokarka 122

Zeus 25, 28, 42, 48, 49, 77 n.230, 90, 99, 100, 102, 103, 104, 115, 117, 120, 167
– Anchesmios 28
– Apemios 29
– born and died 29, 35
– festival 50
– Hyetios 28
– Hymettios 28
– Hypistos 29
– Ombrios 28, 29
– Parnethios 28
– Weather god 29

Subjects

Achilleion 62 n.118, 68
adyton 34, 157, 179
aegis 98, 102
agalma 102
agyia 171
Aiora 74, n.204
altar 4, 13, 14, 19, 20f., 23, 32, 36, 45, 46,
    52, 54, 89, 108, 132, 134, 135, 136,
    139, 140, 141, 142, 145, 148, 159, 174,
    175, 179
– ash 53
– circular 20, 127, 131, 132, 133, 134, 139,
    172, 176
– fire 54 n.75
– 19, 21
– horse-shoe 139
– internal 53
– Mycenaean 27, 172
– open air 27, 28, 44 n.17
– oval 19
– precinct 131
– semi circular 132, 133
Altis 53
anaktoron 35, 38
anax 117
– see also Wanax
androgynism 82 n.264
animal votives 44 n.17
anodos 67, 70, 83, 84, 108
Anthesteria 68, 73, 77, 108 n.136
anthropomorphism 93, 94, 104f., 167
– see also gods, statue, deity
Apaturia 51
Apellai 51, 170 n.362
Apolloniou 53
apotropaeic 73, 109, 163
apulunas 170 n.362
arms
– votive 166
art 92
– Anatolian 63
– archaic 72
– Greek 74

– Minoan 2, 5, 7, 8, 66, 117
– Mycenaean 2, 3, 5, 66, 117
– Neolithic 64
Artemisia 51, 58
atonement 148

baetyl 8, 20, 141, 145, 147, 169, 170, 171,
    172f.
banquet 53, 55, 100
baths 154
bear 64
– bear-woman 65
beetles 26
bird 64, 98, 149
– woman 65
birth 35, 36, 108, 112, 155
Boedromia 51
bothros 138, 149, 177
bryllichistai 70
bucrania 149
bull 21, 22, 23, 40, 43, 65, 73, 77, 82, 132,
    138, 140 n.131, 142, 144f., 149,
    150, 151, 165
– head 112
– horns 112
– man 65
– mask 64, 112, 138, 151
– votive 35, 142, 148, 149

calendar
– Greek 50f.
– Ionic/Attic 58 n.96
cattle 61, 77
cave 17, 18, 24, 29, 34, 36, 38, 83, 156
    n.263, 157, 183
– Academus 46
– Amnisos 107
– burial in 30 n.190
– Dictaean 43, 48
– Idaean 99
– Inatos 107
– oracle 158, 175, 177
– Polis 46

– shelter 33
cella 12, 53, 131, 134, 135, 139, 140, 141, 142, 165
Centaur 67, 72, 112, 144, 145
chalkinaos 55
chapel 135
chariot 50, 129, 132, 137, 149, 150, 168, 174
children 174
Choes 68, 73, 74 n.204
Christian Church 41
Chthonia 69
Chytrae 74 n.204
Citadel House 19, 34, 56
cloak 108
cock 149
column 151, 169, 173
comedy 180
copper 86, 138, 165
– ingot 82, 84, 86, 165
Corybants 85, 106
Couretes 37 n.229, 85
court, open 22f., 32, 131, 134, 135, 136, 139, 141, 142
cult 1, 13, 41, 46, 182
– Aegean 107, 142, 182
– apotropaeic 148
– archaic 120, 126, 175
– birth 30 n.190
– buildings 32, 139
– bull 65
– cave 18, 24, 27, 29, 30 n.190, 31, 33, 35, 36, 72, 78, 82, 86, 108, 179, 180
– chthonic 62, 67, 69f.
– continuity 30 n.190, 32, 42–5, 48, 50, 56, 119, 144, 148
– Cycladic 7, 142, 144
– Cypriot 146, 148, 151
– domestic 18, 33, 80
– eastern 21, 114
– European 114
– fertility 30 n.190, 62, 81, 137, 148f.
– funerary 16
– Greek 61
– Helladic 7
– hero 45, 46, 91–3, 177 n.5

– image 13, 23, 102, 105, 112
– implements 2, 13, 23, 27, 30 n.190, 119
– localised 51, 93
– Minoan 7, 8, 13f., 17f., 21, 24, 56, 59, 61, 119, 142, 179
– Mycenaean 7, 8, 13f., 17f., 21, 24, 35, 36, 48, 56, 59, 61, 119, 140, 142, 160
– mystery 67, 70, 78, 83, 123
– Neolithic 70, 72, 109, 180
– open air 10, 30 n.190, 32, 53, 148
– peak 10, 13, 24f., 26, 30 n.190, 32, 33, 44, 80, 82, 86, 140, 179
– Roman 175
– room 140, 141
– scene 5
– Semitic 108
– site 2, 5, 13, 118, 179
– subterranean 34
– symbol 23, 143
– tree 131, 155
– tribal 51
– vegetation 155
curse 129, 136
Cycladic
– art 6
– shrines 38
– votives 141
cymbals 152

Dactyls 85
Daedala 109
daemon 22, 95, 113
dance 70, 152, 173, 174, 176, 182
Daphnephoria 155
death 82, 161
deer 148, 150
defixiones 129
deity
– aniconic 145
– anthropomorphic 145
– chthonic 34
– community 110
– multiple 12
– nature 26, 137
– prehistoric 118

– theriomorphic 145
– see also god, goddess
Delion 156 n.260
Dendrites 68, 83 n.277
divine
– administration 138
– Child 72, 75, 77, 78
– function 115
– image 107
– Mother 49
– names 114–116, 117f., 158, 179
– power 98, 99, 101, 104, 108f., 110f.,
    113, 120, 141, 142, 145, 181
– iconography 104
– warrior 165
dog 149
double axe 4, 21 n.131, 27, 30 n.190, 140,
    142
drama
– Greek 72f.
drum 152

East Building 127
East Complex 127, 128, 129
Enuma Elish 91 n.30
epic 91f., 93f., 100, 104f., 116, 118, 120,
    181
– Creation 88 n.2, 91
epikouroi 166 n.334
epiphany 83, 84, 94–101, 104, 109, 168,
    175
Erechtheum 104
ethnos 61 n.110

festivals 50f., 58f.
– Dorian 59
– Ionic 58
– women 57
figurine
– see also idol
– armed 110, 165
– bearded 71
– bisexual 32, 40, 61, 69, 71, 82, 110, 143,
    144
– bull 38, 137
– cave 107

– classical 149
– cylindrical 143
– horse 137
– iron 166
– ithyphallic 62, 68f.
– male 32, 40, 137, 138, 143, 144
– masked 68f., 71f.
– Minoan 80
– on ingot 84, 165
– 'phi' 44 n.17
– 'psi' 143
– rider 137
– sexless 143, 144
fire 35, 36
frescoes 2, 6 n.32, 19, 34

games 176
garden 130, 151, 157, 177
gates 171 n.371
– of the Nymphs 173
genos 61
Geraistia 59 n.97
goat 64, 77, 133
– man 65
god 1, 22, 39, 49, 91, 92, 93, 98, 174
– Aegean 159
– anthropomorphic 87, 90, 93–107, 110,
    151
– apotropaeic 41, 62f., 161, 167
– Christian 94
– chthonic 83
– city 93, 110, 129
– community 28, 41, 49, 107, 117, 120,
    132, 137, 138, 145, 150, 153, 165,
    168f., 173, 175
– Cypriot 159 n.279
– Egyptian 88
– fertility 157
– Greek 88, 181
– Hittite 166
– Homeric 90, 96, 98–102, 181, 182
– Horned 11, 135, 163f., 165, 167
– iconography of 87, 101
– Indo-European 115
– Ingot 84f., 86, 165, 167
– invocatory 115, 118

- Italian 88, 181
- moon 88
- of city gates 171 n.371
- patron 86
- personal 87, 115, 118 f., 181
- protecting 161
- Roman 88
- shepherd 163
- Sky-god 115
- Smiting 21, 145, 166
- Sumerian 88
- Warrior 84, 106 f., 145 f., 150, 165–9, 170, 173
goddess 10, 15, 20, 23, 34, 36, 43, 106, 141, 160
- and bull 82
- birth 29
- chthonic 37
- city 47, 60, 79
- community 15 f., 60, 180
- Dove 4, 8
- Eastern 8
- fertility, nature 15, 86, 155
- figurine – see idol
- Great goddess 5, 15, 85, 111, 180 n.1
- Kean 109 n.143
- male associate 36, 82, 86
- Minoan 8, 119
- nude 8
- on ingot 165 n.332, 167 n.341
- palace 55, 79, 180
- Shauskaya 9 n.51
- sitting 8
- Snake 10
- with animals 47, 64
- with upraised arms 10, 15 f., 20 f., 22, 24, 26, 35, 84 n.286, 139, 144
Goetes 84 n.290
gorgon 82
Gorgoneion 62
griffin 8, 133
grove 126, 133, 146, 150, 151, 154 f., 156, 157, 158, 175, 176

hagnos 50
Harpies 29

head 64, 65, 73, 143
- animal 71, 165
- Chatsworth 168
- masked 68
hearth 19, 20, 52
helmet 146, 164, 165, 167, 168, 173
hemitheoi 92
Heraia 55
Heraion 53
herm 67, 68, 74–6 n.307, 81, 82 n.264, 111
- grave 77 n.225
herma 76
hero 91–93, 95, 96, 97, 103, 113, 114, 125, 181
hestiatorion 53
hiereus 50
hierophant 35
hieros 50
horns 164 f.
- of consecration 4, 10, 12, 13, 19, 21 n.131, 26, 30 n.190, 82, 139, 142, 172
horse 66, 112, 137, 165
horseman 132, 137, 149, 150, 151
House of Tsountas 14, 20, 139
Hyacinthia 25, 59, 169, 173 f.
Hyakinthides 59 n.102
hyle 154

icon 114
- iconography 118, 161
idol 15, 16, 20, 22
- aniconic 147
- bell 108
- board 109
- cylindrical 109 n.143
- goddess 34
- Greek 113
- in tombs 16
- Minoan 144
- 'phi' 27, 44 n.17, 108
- 'psi' 15, 21, 22, 108, 143
- stalagmite 24
- 'tau' 108
- see also figurine, goddess, image

Iliad 92, 93, 95, 96, 97, 98, 100, 104f., 161
image, aniconic 8, 68, 75, 105, 107f., 109
    n.141, 172
initiation 86, 175 n.397
intervention
– divine 97
ithyphallic 67, 68, 72, 74, 82, 88
– herm 76, 111

Karneia 59 n.97, 164
Kephallen 73 n.201
keratinos bomos 155
kernos 30 n.190
kidaris 70 n.172
king 49, 117, 180
kingship 99
kinnot 153
kinyra 153
knife, sacrificial 134
kore 103
kouros 102f. n.101, 167
Kyprogenes 80

Lady 119
lamp 149
laurel 155, 156
Lenaea 68, 73, 108 n.136
liknon 68, 73
Linear B 49, 50, 58 n.96, 76, 80, 117f.,
    179
Little Palace 107
lombai 70
Lord 117, 160, 163
Lygos 113 n.169
lyre 152, 153, 174

Machanitis 81
magic 85, 106
mask 46f., 61, 63–74, 77, 78, 108, 109
    n.142, 112, 143, 149, 150, 151, 180
– animal 63, 64, 72f.
– apotropaeic 70
– bull 68, 151
– death 64 n.134
– goat 68
– god 72

– Gorgon 82
– human 72, 138
– miniature 65
– wooden 73
mecara 37
megaron 19, 36, 37, 52, 55, 57, 66
– Megaron A 57
– Megaron B 36 n.219, 57
– shrine 34, 35, 37
Metageitnia 51
metallurgy 84f.
Minotaur 66, 67, 112, 144
Mistress 116
months
– names of 50
music 152
mysteries 35, 36, 72f., 86, 119, 160, 175
    n.397
myth 66, 85, 93, 112f., 120, 125, 181,
    182
– aetiological 173
– cosmogonic 87
– epic 103, 112, 114
– foundation 100
– Greek 59, 88, 117

naiskos 136
naos 54
Nymphs 29

obelos 147 n.178
Odyssey 93, 95, 96, 159
offerings 130, 132, 134
– aniconic 105
– bowls 33
– burnt 4, 14, 54
– tables 32, 142
– votive 149
oikos 53, 55
– Delian Oikos 53
Olympians 42, 87, 94, 96, 97, 100, 101,
    114f., 117, 118, 120, 159, 179, 181
omphalos 141, 169
oracle 154, 155 n.248, 156, 158
– cave 158, 175, 177
– chthonic 177

– Klarian 158
ox 165

paean 174
palace 9 n.50, 10, 26, 31, 36, 55, 56, 107,
   139, 180
palaistra 129 n.52
Palladion 110, 113
palm 155, 177 n.3
Panathenaea 104
Panionion 59
paredros 40
Parthenon 104
peaks 24 f.
Pelopion 43
peplos 104 f., 109, 159
peribolos 127, 128, 129, 130, 133, 134,
   140, 146 n.168, 154, 156, 170 n.362
perioche 91, 94, 100, 114
personification 89, 98, 115
phallus 57, 61, 62 f., 68 f., 70 f., 72 f.,
   74–77, 78, 107, 111, 137, 180
pharmakos 148, 157
phratry 61
phyle 61
pig 57, 61, 66, 78
pillar 8, 10, 12, 68, 72, 107 f., 108, 111,
   169, 170, 171, 172 f., 178
– crypt 33 n.207
pit 128, 130, 131, 177, 178
plague 161
Plutonium 36 n.223, 177
polis 61 n.110, 93, 95, 118, 120, 146, 180
Poseidea 51, 55, 58
Potnia 55, 116, 119
priest 96, 128, 134, 148, 151, 160
– masked 138
procession 151, 174, 175 n.397, 181
purification 155, 156 f.

Queen 116, 182

ram 66, 164, 165
rebirth 57, 63, 70, 72, 75 f., 77, 86,
   119
refuge 156, 158

religion
– archaic 60, 180
– classical 181
– common 114
– eastern 10
– Greek 1, 4, 17, 40, 56, 89, 180, 181
– Minoan 1, 7, 9, 10, 13, 15, 17, 38, 39,
   64, 66, 76, 117
– Mycenaean 1, 3, 7, 9, 10, 13, 15, 17, 38,
   39, 66, 76, 117, 159, 172
– Neolithic 56 f.
– Phoenician 172
– polis 181
– Roman 41
renewal 35, 70, 72, 82, 99, 119
rhyton 4, 10, 21, 22, 30 n.190
rider see horseman
Rigveda 110
ring-dance 152
ritual 119, 181
– chthonic 30 n.190, 67, 70, 108, 177
– dance 176
– purificatory 156, 173 f.
– vegetation 150
– whipping 114
rock 33, 34, 36, 70, 179
– chamber 34, 35

sacrifice 20, 96, 134, 177
– animal 139
– blood 50
– burnt 33, 52, 54
– human 148
– victim 61
sanctuary 23, 42, 43, 102, 135, 136, 161,
   178, 179
– archaic 136, 138, 144, 145, 146, 148,
   165, 182
– Bronze Age 54, 182
– cave 107, 183
– classical 146
– Cycladic 38
– Cypriot 134, 136, 137, 142, 144, 150,
   168, 174, 177
– domestic 26, 38
– Hittite 136

– Kourion 121–134
– Minoan 19, 140
– multiroom 32
– Mycenaean 19, 34
– Open air 18, 54, 139, 140
– palace 107
– peak 23, 26, 38, 107, 140
– Pediaeus 168
– rural 134, 135, 141, 142, 146, 148, 150, 151, 174, 182
satyrs 68, 72
scarab 132, 133
script, syllabic 137
sculpture
– Greek 105, 167
seal 5 f., 131
semi-iconic 68, 72, 74, 75, 167
Shaft Graves see Mycenae
sheep 61, 77, 133
shield 82, 165
shrine
– palace 10
– separate 53
– tripartite 4, 10–13, 18
– see also sanctuary
Siege Rhyton 6
Skira 58 n.94
skulls 63
snake 144, 149, 154
spear 165
Sphinx 8
spring 151, 154 f., 158, 175
stadium 123, 129, 169
stag 112
stalagmite 24, 31, 33, 107, 108
stamp seal 133, 168 n.353
statue 68, 74, 85, 102 f., 104 f., 112 f., 123, 147
– Egyptian 105
– anthropomorphic 105, 107 f.
– stalagmitic 107
– warrior 168
stele 156, 171, 172
stone
– conical 141, 147, 173
– sacred 131 f., 142, 169, 171, 172 f. n.377

syncretism 60, 78, 86, 138
synoecism 60

tables of offering 27
tauromorphic 75
Telchines 85, 106
Telesterion 35, 36
temenos 13, 21, 26, 28, 38, 49, 52, 121, 126, 127, 128, 129, 130, 131, 132, 135, 140, 142, 146 n.168, 147, 148, 149, 151, 154, 156, 157, 158, 174
temple 7, 13, 14, 19, 22, 23, 27, 34, 36, 42, 44 n.17, 52, 54, 60, 66, 93, 100, 102 f., 104, 118, 136, 138 f., 147, 177, 178, 181
– archaic 52, 59, 65
– Canaanite 136
– circular 133 n.76, 176–8
– city 135
– classical 108, 128, 169
– Doric 57
– Greek 55, 135
– Ionic 57
– liwan 135
– Mycenaean 9, 11, 19, 36, 38, 54, 106, 171, 172
– Paphian 141 f.
– Philistine 136, 138
– Roman 128, 131
– separate 18, 52
– tripartite 12, 135, 140
– Ugaritic 136
Thargelia 51
theatre 176 n.398
theodaisia 100
theomorphic 90
theos 179
theoxenia 100
theriomorphic 22, 37, 101, 145
Thesmophoria 38, 51 n.63, 57, 58, 61
tholos 3, 45, 130, 131, 151, 176–78
Throne Room 55
thymos 99
tomb 22, 31, 45, 62, 150, 157
– hero 92
– Mycenaean 45

– prehistoric 127
Tonaea 114 n.172
Tradition see Minoan, Mycenaean Religion
tragedy 180
Treasury of Atreus 173
tree 8, 68, 83, 108, 109, 130f., 133, 146, 151, 155 n.245, 156 n.263, 168 n.353, 177
tribe 61 n.110
tripartite
– see cella, shrine, temple
tripod 82, 84, 159, 165
triton 79
tympanon 152

votives 27
– Mycenaean 27

Wanassa 16, 48, 80, 116, 160, 182
Wanax 160
warrior 106 n.125, 133, 145, 149, 150, 164, 165, 167, 168
well 151
West Enclosure 130, 131
woodland 154

xoanon 73, 81 n.259, 105, 114

Zoroastrianism 90

Modern Authors

Adrados, F. R. 71 n.181
Alexiou, St. 16, 82 n.270
Amandry, P. 156 n.253
Arwe, M. 133 n.78

Baumbach, L. 43 n.6
Benson, J. L. 121 n.2
Bérard, C. 83 n.280
Bintliff, J. 27 n.170
Bittel, K. 136 n.100
Blegen, C. W. 60 n.107
Boardman, J. 100 n.86
Bouzek, J. 166 n.336
Branigan, K. 3 n.11, 23 n.141, 30 n.190
Browne, H. 133 n.77
Buber, M. 94
Buchholz, H. G. 84 n.285
Buitron, D. 127
Burkert, W. 14, 43 n.6, 59
Bury, J. R. 89

Cadogan, G. 26 n.162
Caskey, J. L. 44 n.16
Catling, H. W. 64 n.137, 84 n.285
Chadwick, J. 54 n.80, 117 n.192

Chirassi, I. 84 n.281
Coldstream, J. N. 3 n.10, 23 n.145, 41 n.1, 42 n.2, 5, 43, 146 n.167
Cook, A. B. 28 n.180
Cook, J. M. 45 n.23

Daux, G. 83 n.277
Deroy, L. 59 n.98
Desborough, V. 36 n.219, 43 n.6, 14
des Places, Ed. 90 n.16
Deubner, L. 68 n.165, 108 n.136
Dickens, G. 66 n.150
Dickinson O. T. P. K. 2 n.4, 3 n.11, 4 n.15
Dikaios, P. 121 n.1, 136 n.98, 164
Dörrie, H. 89 n.13
Drerup, H. 52, 53
Dunbabin, T. J. 143 n.155

Eitrem, S. 163 n.321
Eliade, M. 83 n.276
Evans, A. 10 n.53, 54, 83 n.275
Evans, J. D. 71 n.182

Faure, P. 24 n.147, 30 n.190
Felsch, R. C. S. 44 n.18, 67 n.158

Fittschen, K. 103 n.103
Fontenrose, J. 73 n.201
French, E. 143 n.151
Friedrich, P. 80 n.247

Gallet de Santerre, H. 53 n.71
Gérard-Rousseau, 51 n.59, 76 n.219
Gimbutas, M. 62 n.117, 111
Gjerstad, E. 131 n.61, 135, 136
Glover, S. 129 n.51
Graf, F. 113 n.165
Griffin, J. 181
Grimal, P. 79 n.238
Gruben, G. 52 n.68
Gschnitzer, F. 42 n.6, 49 n.48

Hadjiioannou, K. 159 n.284
Hägg, R. 4 n.15
Hammond, N. G. L. 41 n.1
Harrison, J. 69 n.166
Hermary, A. 65 n.148
Herter, H. 62, 74, 75
Heubeck, A. 76 n.219
Hill, G. 148, 153
Hiller, S. 39 n.241, 49, 54 n.80, 117
Hood, M. S. F. 3 n.11, 16, 18 n.114, 53
    n.72, 105 n.117
Hoffmann, H. 84 n.283
Hooke, S. H. 113 n.161
Hooker, J. T. 3 n.6 n.11, 4 n.15
Hurwitt, J. 2 n.3
Huxley G. L. 3 n.10

Immerwahr, S. A. 2 n.3

Jacobsson, I. 172 n.378
Jäger, W. 93 n.49
Jeanmaire, H. 72 n.194

Kahil, L. 34 n.211
Kanty, A. 39 n.239
Karageorghis, J. 14, 15, 16, 65 n.142, 136,
    137, 172
Karageorghis, V. 15, 16, 62 n.115
Kerenyi, K. 56 n.88
Kilian, K. 139 n.127

Kirk, G. S. 101 n.92
Kullmann, W. 95 n.59

Laffineur, R. 2 n.3
Lambrinudakis, V. 27 n.170, 139 n.126
Langdon, M. K. 25 n.157
Lembessis, A. 44 n.20, 81 n.259
Leuven, J. C. van 18 n.115, 23, 53 n.72
Levi, D. 14, 30 n.190, 33
Long, C. R. 30 n.190
Love, I. C. 82 n.272

Maier, F. G. 136, 147 n.176
Mallwitz, A. 111 n.150
Marinatos, N. 2 n.3
Marinatos, Sp. 4 n.13, 33 n.204
Masson, O. 81 n.254
Matz, F. 10 n.55
Mazar, A. 139 n.122
Mazon, P. 91 n.29
McFadden, G. 123 n.14, 147, 149
Mellaart, J. 63 n.132
Mikalson, J. D. 51 n.60
Milojčic, J. 60 n.107
Mitford, T. B. 116 n.186, 157
Mlynarzak, J. 157 n.270
Morpurgo Davies, A. 49 n.43, n.48
Murray, O. 56 n.89
Mylonas, G. E. 35 n.215, 139 n.124
Myres, J. L. 65 n.145

Nicholls, R. V. 16, 64 n.134
Nicolau, K. 24 n.146
Nilsson, M. P. 1, 18, 36 n.223, 51 n.60,
    59, 75, 79, 148, 180
Nock, A. D. 91 n.31

Ohnefalsch-Richter, M. 168
Otto, W. F. 75 n.213, 181

Palmer, L. R. 54 n.80, 115 n.181
Panagl, O. 39 n.241, 49
Parker, H. W. 57 n.93
Peatfield, A. A. D. 26 n.160
Peltenburg, E. J. 121 n.1
Pendlebury, J. D. S. 26 n.163

Pfister, F. 91 n.27
Picard, Ch. 73 n.202, 164 n.327
Pini, I. 30 n.190
Pötscher, W. 72 n.192
Promponas, J. K. 51 n.59
Pugliese-Carratelli, G. 80 n.246

Radke, G 88 n.5
Renfrew, C. 2 n.2, 20, 21 n.131, 53 n.72, 141 n.132
Richardson, N. J. 101 n.88
Ringgren, H. 90 n.23
Rizza, G. 44 n.19
Rolley, C. 167 n.343
Roloff, D. 91 n.28
Roux, G. 53 n.716, 146 n.168
Rutkowski, B. 10, 17, 33 n.207, 53 n.72, 105 n.113, 140 n.130
Rutter, J. B. 3 n.9, n.11

Säflund, G. 55 n.85
Sakellarakis, G. 3 n.11, 140 n.131
Sarkady, J. 51 n.62
Schachermeyr, F. 3 n.5, n.8, 9 n.50, 20
Schachter, A. 155 n.250
Schaeffer, C. F. A. 164 n.325
Schefold, K. 74 n.208
Schliemann, H. 11
Schwyzer, E. 50 n.57
Scranton, R. 132
Scrinari, V. S. M. 44 n.19
Simon, E. 101 n.93
Sjöquist, E. 131
Snell, B. 93 n.41

Snodgrass, A. M. 41 n.1, 42 n.3, 4, 43, 45
Soren, D. 127
Speiser, E. A. 91 n.30
Starr, C. G. 103 n.102
Stella, L. 43 n.6
Studniczka, F. 36 n.225
Swiny, S. 132 n.69, 172 n.377
Szemerenyi, O. 79 n.233, 117 n.188

Taylour, W. 19, 20, 34 n.210, 53 n.72, 109 n.143, 143
Travlos, I. 34 n.211
Tyree, E. 30 n.190
Tzavella-Evjen, H. 177 n.1

Ucko, P. J. 110 n.147
Uhsadel-Gülke, Ch. 83 n.273
Usener, H. 115

Vermeule, E. 5 n.19, 43 n.6, 93 n.46

Warren, P. 9 n.50, 18 n.114, 53 n.72
Wedlake, W. J. 133 n.76, 178 n.7
Weinberg, S. S. 3 n.7, 121 n.2
West, M. L. 89 n.12
Whittingham, D. 123 n.9
Wide, S. 163 n.321
Wiesner, J. 76 n.221
Wilamowitz-M., U. v. 74 n.205
Willetts, R. F. 79 n.239
Wrede, W. 72 n.194

Yalouris, N. 169 n.361
Young, J. H. u. S. H. 149

B. C. DIETRICH
The Origins of Greek Religion
Large-octavo. VIII, 345 pages. 1973. Cloth DM 160,–
ISBN 3110039826

EDRIC ALLEN BUTTERWORTH
Some Traces of the Pre-Olympian World in Greek Literature and Myth
Large-octav. X, 196 pages, 17 plates. 1966. Cloth DM 59,–
ISBN 3110050102

EDRIC ALLEN BUTTERWORTH
The Tree at the Navel of the Earth
Large-octavo. XII, 239 pages, 31 plates. 1970. Cloth DM 80,–
ISBN 3110063492

The Law Code of Gortyn
Edited with Introduction, Translation and Commentary
by Ronald F. Willetts
Folio. VIII, 90 pages, 13 plates and 1 Facsimile. 1967.
Cloth DM 150,– ISBN 3110051761

TERENCE B. MITFORD
The Nymphaeum of Kafizin
The Inscribed Pottery
Folio. XXIV, 286 pages, 1 colored frontispiece, 1 illustration, 8 figures,
3 tables and 2 maps. 1980. Cloth DM 270,– ISBN 3110066637

Prices are subject to change

Walter de Gruyter Berlin · New York

BEIHEFTE ZUR ZEITSCHRIFT FÜR DIE ALTTESTAMENTLICHE WISSENSCHAFT

Prophecy

Essays presented to Georg Fohrer on his sixty-fifth birthday
6. September 1980. Edited by J. A. Emerton
Large-octavo, VIII, 202 pages. Frontispiece. 1980. Cloth DM 92,–
ISBN 3 11 007761 2 (Volume 150)

GERALD SHEPPARD
Wisdom as a Hermeneutical Construct

A Study in the Sapientializing of the Old Testament
Large octavo. XII, 178 pages. 1980. Cloth DM 78,–
ISBN 3 11 007504 0 (Volume 151)

J. A. LOADER
Polar Structures in the Book of Qohelet

Edited by Georg Fohrer
Large-octavo. XII, 138 pages. 1979. Cloth DM 69.50,–
ISBN 3 11 007636 5 (Volume 152)

PHILIP J. NEL
The Structure and Ethos of the Wisdom Admonitions in Proverbs

Large-octavo. XII, 142 pages. 1982. Cloth DM 74,–
ISBN 3 11 008750 2 (Volume 158)

WILLEM S. PRINSLOO
The Theology of the Book of Joel

Large-octavo. VIII, 136 pages. 1985. Cloth DM 74,–
ISBN 3 11 010301 X (Volume 163)

Prices are subject to change

Walter de Gruyter Berlin · New York